PREFACE

In 1945, Merkos L'Inyonei Chinuch introduced *Shaloh*, a pamphlet series for Jewish children. *Shaloh* was indeed a unique publication, appearing in a time when wholesome, Torah-true reading material for youths was difficult, if not impossible, to come by. *Shaloh* filled this vital need, and the 24 issues appearing that year were warmly and enthusiastically received. The series resumed in 1961, and another 24 issues were released.

Shaloh was designed for children to read either on their own or with the aid of parents or teachers. Each issue contains four features: 1) a story with a moral related to good behavior and character training; 2) Biblical history in serial form; 3) a story, the subject of which is a precept or a custom; and 4) a story in cartoon form.

Shaloh was later released in book form, in two volumes (Vol. I, 1-24; Vol. II, 25-48). However, at that time, a detailed *Table of Contents* was compiled only for Volume II. In this new, digitally enlarged edition, all the issues appear in one volume. The original *Table of Contents* for Volume II remains before Issue 25, while a new *Table of Contents* for Volume I (Issues 1-24) follows this preface.

For those who fondly remember these booklets, and for those who have yet to get to know them, we present this new edition.

Merkos L'Inyonei Chinuch

28 Sivan 5765

TABLE OF CONTENTS

Published & Copyright 1945 by
MERKOS L'INYONEI CHINUCH, INC.
770 EASTERN PARKWAY
Brooklyn 13; N. Y.
HYacinth 3-9250

No. 1

ב״ה

MODEH ANI

Inquisitive little Esther was thinking. Her mother waited for the question that was sure to come.

"Mother," began Esther, "every single morning, ever since I can remember, I do the same thing. The minute I get up I say a prayer 'Modeh Ani' . . . Why do we say it, mommy? What does it mean?"

Esther's mother smiled as she answered: "Even though you don't admit it, studying and playing all day long makes you tired. You fall asleep the moment your head touches the pillow, don't you, now?"

Esther nodded, "You're right, mother. But then in the morning I'm not tired any more. I'm full of energy, and anxious to learn and play again. But what has that to do with 'Modeh Ani?' "

"Everything, dear. You see, when we say 'Modeh Ani' in the morning, we thank G-d for the wonderful thing that happens to us every day. We go to sleep exhausted from our day's work, and we awake entirely refreshed and happy, ready to work again. We know that it is G-d who puts this new energy and strength into our souls, and we are very grateful to Him."

"I wish I'd known that before, so I could say it with all my heart. Tell me, mommy, please, what's the exact meaning of the Hebrew words of 'Modeh Ani'?"

I thank Thee, O living and eternal King, who hast mercifully restored my soul within me; great is Thy faithfulness."

"You know, mother, now that I know what it's all about, I'll never once forget to say 'Modeh Ani' when I get up!"

Do YOU know *Modeh Ani* by heart?
Do YOU remember to say it every morning?

THE CREATION OF THE WORLD

Everyone knows that it was G-d who created our great world with its mighty oceans, tall mountains, and huge continents filled with different kinds of plant, beast and bird. Now we shall learn in what order G-d made all this in just six days.

In the beginning, G-d made the heavens and the earth. The first day, when everything was bare and black, G-d created LIGHT and He separated the light from the darkness.

On the second day, the Almighty formed the Heavens.

When the third day dawned, G-d said: "Let the waters of the earth be gathered together in certain places which will be called Seas and Oceans. Then the earth, the dry land, shall appear." And as He commanded so it was. The many waterways of the world, and all the good earth, were now clearly visible. That very same day, at G-d's bidding, there began to sprout from the earth every kind of plant and tree. The tiniest weeds, the loveliest flowers, the most majestic trees, all were created on the third day.

Now that the earth was no longer bare, G-d turned to the heavens again. On the fourth day, He made the heavenly bodies: the SUN, the MOON, and the STARS. They would provide light for the earth day and night.

On the fifth day the fish, and all other creatures that live in water, were created. G-d also made, on the fifth day, all our winged friends, the birds.

Now the sixth day of Creation came. First, G-d created everything that lives and moves on earth. And what a variety there was! Insects and reptiles, and all sorts of animals. Flies and grasshoppers, snakes and worms, horses and dogs, elephants and lions, and a million other living creatures.

Last and most important, G-d created MAN. Man was different from everything else on earth. After the Almighty made Man's body from earth, G-d breathed into Man's body a holy soul.

Then G-d made a woman, a wife for Adam, as the first man was called. The woman was created to be a helpmate to man in his own life and the life of the whole world. Adam called his wife Eve, which in Hebrew means 'the mother of all living things.'

G-d blessed Adam and Eve thus: "May you multiply and rule over everything in this world."

At the end of the sixth day, the world, and everything in it, was completed. G-d blessed the seventh day, and declared it a rest day, for by that day He had finished the creation of the world and rested thereon. The very name of the seventh day, Sabbath, means, in Hebrew, rest.

* * *

When we obey the laws of the Sabbath rest, we show that we realize that G-d, and only He, made our world. Therefore, the commandment to observe the Sabbath is one of the greatest and most important of all our laws.

* * *

As we read the story of the Creation, we see that first G-d made everything else in the world, and when all was ready, He created the Man.

When we invite an important guest to our home, we put everything in order first. The house is spick and span.

We put soft chairs, bright lights, and pretty pictures in the guest's room. We plan delicious meals for him. When he finally arrives, he finds everything arranged for his comfort. How grateful he is!

G-d treats Man and Woman as most honored guests on the earth and everything was arranged for their comfort. G-d Himself considers Man important and worthy of care. Let us show our thankfulness to G-d for His kindness. Let us try, by our actions, to show that we appreciate the beautiful world He gave us. Let us, by our conduct always try to be worthy of G-d's love and care! Let us be grateful guests on earth!

* * *

Do you remember what G-d created on the first day? The third? The sixth?

HONOR YOUR FATHER
AND YOUR MOTHER

The two little boys were so deeply engrossed in their story-book, they almost didn't hear Meyer's mother enter the room. But Meyer jumped up immediately and helped her set the tray down.

"Mother, you must be tired. Aren't there any errands for me to do?"

"Thank you, son, you can play now. I'd like you to go to the store for me though, in half an hour."

Meyer returned to his seat when his mother left.

"Have some milk and cookies, David. Isn't my mother good? I think she's the best mother a fellow ever had, always thinking of how to make me healthy and happy. But I guess everybody feels that way about his parents."

David stared, "Is that why you offered to run errands? Do you really like to go to the store?"

"Not particularly. But I'd be an ungrateful thing if I didn't help my parents in every way I could. They've given me all I have—a fine home and a good education. Besides, I want to show them I love them."

David blushed. He was thinking of his own conduct. "Do you always obey them?" he asked.

Meyer snorted. "Only babies and dopes disobey their parents. When my parents tell me something, I know it's for my own benefit. You want to see something—wait—"

He ran to his bookcase, took out a book, and opened it in front of David.

"This is what I've learned," he pointed. "It's one of the ten Commandments—'Honor thy father and thy mother!' Would you like to know how a child should really behave!"

"How?"

"He should treat his father and mother as if they were a king and queen, and he was a member of their court."

"Just like in that story we were just reading!" exclaimed David.

"Yes. He would stand up when the king or queen entered the room, never sit in their personal seats or interrupt them. A good courtier would always speak respectfully to their majesties, and be ready to do their bidding. And it would break his heart to cause them any worry or trouble. He would be so proud to be able to serve them."

David listened in open-mouthed wonder. Suddenly he jumped up—"I'm giving my mother needless worry right now. I didn't tell her I'd go to your house. She must be wondering what happened to me!"

And when David was already by the door, he added resolutely:

"From this minute on—'Honor your father and mother' is my motto! So long, Meyer, I'm going home to help the best queen in the world."

NOTE:

Keep this booklet. It is the first of a series. Many more are coming—all interesting and exciting.

Joe (Pee Wee) Meyer was a baseball star before he was inducted into the army. His last game was his greatest triumph.

(To be continued)

[PRINTED IN U·S·A]

Published & Copyright 1945 by
MERKOS L'INYONEI CHINUCH, INC.
770 EASTERN PARKWAY
Brooklyn 13, N. Y.
HYacinth 3-9250

No. 2

ב״ה

WASHING THE HANDS
IN THE MORNING

Hannah and Joseph, dressed in their very best clothes, kept looking excitedly out of the window. Their beloved Aunt Leah was coming on a visit.

The bell rang, and they ran to the door. Aunt Leah kissed and hugged them, and exclaimed, "My, how you've grown! And what pretty clothes you're wearing!"

After she'd had a long chat with their parents, Aunt Leah turned to the children. "Well, you know I am a teacher," she said, "so let's see what my favorite niece and nephew have learned lately."

"Guess what we've learned to do in the morning?" Joseph said mysteriously.

« 1 »

"Now what could it be?" Aunt Leah smiled, making believe she didn't know.

"Let *me* tell," begged Hannah. "We've learned to wash our hands in a special way as soon as we get up in the morning!"

"And just what is that special way?"

"When we go to sleep, Daddy puts a basin and a pitcher of water right near our beds. As soon as we wake up, we take the pitcher in our right hand then pass it over to the left hand, clench our right hand into a loose fist, and pour water on it from the pitcher up to our wrist . . ."

"Then we take the pitcher in our right hand and pour water over our left fist," interrupted Joseph as Hannah paused for breath, "and then again on our right hand. We do that three times on each hand, six times in all."

"Good for you, children. But is that all?"

"Oh no!" Joseph replied.

"We also have to say a special prayer to G-d. We read it on page two of the Manual of Blessings that Mommy bought us," said Hannah proudly.

"Did you ever ask your teacher the meaning of washing the hands in that particular way?" asked Aunt Leah.

"I did!" Hannah declared, "and this is what she said: 'By doing things just the way G-d commanded us to do, we show that we love Him. It's like being eager to do what Dad tells you to! When we do what G-d requires of us, and say the prayer or blessing, we show that we understand that there is a *higher authority*—G-d, King of the Universe—who created the world and has given us laws and instructions how to live happily on it!"

"That's splendid!", Aunt Leah exclaimed enthusiastically. "I am sure, if you start the day by saying *Modeh Ani* and washing your hands in that special way, you can never do anything wrong during the rest of the day!"

"Of course, Aunt Leah, we later wash ourselves the regular way, with soap and hot water, but first we always wash the way Mommy showed us," Joseph said.

"Well, I think having such a clever niece and nephew calls for a celebration," said Aunt Leah. "Let's all have some ice-cream sodas!"

And off the happy family went.

* * *

Do YOU wash your hands the Jewish way every morning?

Do YOU know the proper prayer to say afterward?

THE GARDEN OF EDEN

G-d chose the most beautiful part of the earth, called Eden, and there He planted a garden. On the trees of this lovely garden grew the most luscious and delicious fruits.

In the center of the garden, G-d planted two special

« 3 »

trees. One tree was called the Tree of Life. If one ate the fruit of this tree, one lived forever. The second tree was called the Tree of Knowledge. If someone ate of its fruit, he would become exceedingly clever and cunning.

G-d put the first two people on earth, Adam and Eve, in this beautiful Garden of Eden to live there and guard it. And G-d said to them: "You may eat the fruit of all the trees in the garden—but not of the Tree of Knowledge, lest you die!"

G-d did not want them to eat of that tree because He knew that they would use their cunning to do harm to themselves as well as to others.

Adam and Eve would have lived very happily in the garden, but for the Serpent. The Serpent, which was the cleverest and the most cunning of all the animals, came to Eve. He talked to her slyly and persuaded her to eat the fruit of the Tree of Knowledge. Eve could not resist the temptation and she ate the tasty fruit that G-d had forbidden her to eat. What's more, she gave some to Adam, and he also ate the fruit. G-d then called to Adam, and asked him, "Why did you eat of the forbidden fruit?"

Adam gave his excuse—Eve had given him the fruit to eat. Eve said it was all the fault of the snake that persuaded her to do it.

Thereupon G-d punished the Serpent, Eve and Adam. To the Serpent G-d said that from that day on, it would only be able to move by crawling on its stomach, and an everlasting hate would exist between snakes and human beings.

Eve's punishment was that she would bear and raise her children with pain and trouble.

And to Adam G-d said: "Because you did not obey My commandment, you will have to work and toil with all your strength to make the earth produce for you, until you die and return to the earth from which you were created."

As a further punishment, Adam and Eve were chased out of the Garden of Eden. No longer could they stay in the beautiful garden, and live in leisure on the fruit of the lovely trees. Now they had to work on the soil to obtain their food.

* * *

How kind G-d had been to Adam and Eve! He had made a lovely garden for them. He had given them every opportunity to live happily and contentedly. But they disobeyed G-d's one commandment, and by doing so, brought great trouble upon themselves. Instead of living peacefully in the garden, they now had to toil and suffer forever after. What a lesson this is for us! If we obey G-d's commandments, we can be happy and contented, as G-d wants us to be. But woe to us if we disobey G-d's laws! Then we bring great trouble upon ourselves and others. Let us beware of the "snake" within us, and not let ourselves be misled by his sly temptations!

THE GREAT DAY

As soon as he heard his parents' voices, Aaron jumped out of his bed. He'd been up for several hours already, too excited to sleep. This was the Great Day they had been planning since his fourth birthday last week. Would it be as interesting as he imagined?

"Good Shabbos, sonnie! Have you washed your hands and said your morning prayers?" father asked when he entered Aaron's bedroom, mother following.

"Yes, daddy, I did." Then Aaron asked. "Is it time? Can I get dressed now?"

"You may," his mother replied, "Come, we'll get ready."

Out came the new blue suit with the matching hat, saved for that day. Soon, all dressed and shining, they were on their way.

As Aaron walked between his parents, half-jumping for joy, he thought of his father's warnings about his conduct. Oh, he'd make sure that his behaviour were perfect! He wanted to go every Saturday.

At last they were in front of the synagogue. Today, for the first time, Aaron would be allowed to sit throughout the services. He was a little frightened. He knew the synagogue was a holy place where G-d listened as the Jews prayed to Him.

His mother smiled encouragingly as she went up to the balcony. The synagogue was full of men, most of them standing wrapped in prayer shawls. They took their seats, and his father handed him a prayer book. Aaron felt so proud and grown-up, praying to G-d with all the men. He hoped his behaviour was grown-up, too!

Aaron never missed to answer a single "Amen." He watched with fascination when the holy Ark was opened, and a scroll was taken from there. He was very happy when his father lifted him up to kiss the Torah.

Then he sat very still as the Torah was read. He scowled at two other boys who were conversing behind him. Weren't they ashamed to show such disrespect for the holy words of the Torah that G-d had given to the Jews?

It was over too soon. The portion of the Torah had been read, the prayers finished. Now he would have to leave the beautiful *shul*.

"Did I behave correctly, daddy? May I go next week too?"

"You certainly may, my son. I was very proud of you!"

"I never ran around, and I only spoke when I had to, and then only in a whisper, didn't I, daddy? And I tried to follow the prayers, too. I loved it, daddy. It was very wonderful and interesting."

"You showed you understood how holy a place a synagogue is—where Jews thank G-d for His kindness, and pray to deserve it in the future. Keep on loving and respecting our prayers, and prayer-house, and you may come every week with me!"

Dave Roth, another lad in uniform, never misses his prayers. Pee Wee (Joe) respects him for that, and teaches a lesson to someone who doesn't.

(To be continued)

[PRINTED IN U·S·A]

Published & Copyright 1945 by
MERKOS L'INYONEI CHINUCH, INC
770 EASTERN PARKWAY
Brooklyn 13, N. Y.
HYacinth 3-9250

No. 3

ב"ה

SHEMA YISROEL

"Tell me a story and I'll go to sleep," begged Miriam of her father when he came to put out the light in her room.

"Well, do you know what the prayer 'Shema Yisroel' you say at night means?"

"No, daddy, what does it mean? Do tell me!"

Miriam made herself snug and comfortable and prepared to listen to her father.

"This prayer is written in the Holy Bible," he began. "From the earliest times, Jews everywhere have always said Shema Yisroel. It has given them courage and made them feel happy, even in moments of their greatest trouble."

"But what does it mean, daddy dear?"

"*Shema Yisroel* — *Hear*, O *Israel*—This prayer is said by and for *all Jews*. In every country, in every corner of the earth, in good times and bad, whenever and wherever Jews have lived, this prayer has been on their lips . . . Hear, O Israel—All of Israel, young and old, great and small, rich and poor."

"Even I say it, papa, don't I?"

"That's right, Miriam, and you know the next words: 'G-d our G-d, G-d is One'. Thousands of years ago, all the people of the earth did not know that there was one G-d who created the world. They had many gods and idols whom they imagined to be as wicked as they themselves. At that time the first Jew appeared and told the world there was but One G-d, who created the whole universe, who watches over the human beings, rewards the good, and punishes the wicked, for He loves justice, righteousness and mercy . . . "

"I know, daddy. I learned in school about Abraham, the first Jew who knew that there is only one G-d, and that He has no helpers."

"Yes, my dear. It was then that G-d made a covenant with Abraham that his children—that is we, the Jewish people—would be chosen to carry the torch of G-d's word throughout the world. We, the Jewish people, remained faithful to our sacred task. Nothing could shake our faith. Everywhere and at all times we proclaimed—'G-d our G-d, G-d is One', and with these words upon their lips many of our brethren bravely faced death. Night and morning, every Jew repeats this prayer to show he does believe in G-d, and is ready to die for G-d's holy word."

"Oh, daddy, I dian t know 'Shema Yisroel' was so important. I'll never forget to say it before I go to sleep."

Miriam closed her eyes and recited the Shema very solemnly. Then she opened her sparkling eyes and flung her arms about her father, kissing him "Good night."

* * *

Do YOU know the Shema by heart?

Do YOU say it every morning and every night?

CAIN AND ABEL

Adam and Eve, the first people on Earth, had two sons—Cain and Abel. Abel became a shepherd and Cain chose farming for his vocation.

One day, both decided to offer gifts to G-d. They wanted to express their thanks to Him for giving them abundant produce. Cain brought, as his offering, some of the fruits and vegetables he had grown on his land. Abel chose carefully the fattest and best sheep in his flock as his gift to G-d.

G-d accepted Abel's fine gifts. A fire came down and burned the offering. But Cain's offering was not accepted by G-d, and remained where he had put it. For G-d looked into their hearts and saw that Cain was not sincere.

Cain felt hurt and disgraced. He became jealous of his brother and began to hate him. G-d told Cain he could better himself, but he didn't. Instead he killed his brother Abel.

G-d who sees all and knows all, called Cain and said to him: "Where is your brother Abel?"

"Am I my brother's keeper?" replied Cain arrogantly.

Then G-d said: "What have you done? Your brother's blood is crying out to Me from the earth! Because you did this terrible thing, you will be punished all your life. For the rest of your days you will be a wanderer all over the earth. You will not know peace and happiness any more, as long as you live!"

Cain was sorry he had committed such a crime and he promised G-d he would never sin again. But being sorry could not bring his brother back to life. Cain spent his life roving all over the face of the earth. Never did he enjoy the happiness of peace of mind. We can be sure he realized what a terrible thing he had done.

* * *

At the very beginning of the world's history, everything was peaceful and quiet. There was plenty of room and food for Adam and his family. They could enjoy the benefits of nature without fear. What reason could there be for trouble? But even here jealousy reared its ugly head. Because he was jealous, one man killed his brother, his own flesh and blood. How dreadful a thing jealousy is! Let us never permit it to enter our lives. It is too dangerous. It poisons our mind. It brings anger and quarrels. We see that it can make a person commit the most horrible crime. How much happier we will all be if we never, never let ourselves be jealous of anyone else.

* * *

Do YOU know who killed a quarter of the world's population?

Why did Cain say "Am I my brother's keeper?"

NOAH AND THE FLOOD

Nine generations after Adam and Eve, there lived a man whose name was Noah. He had three sons—Shem, Ham, and Japheth. Noah and his family were good, honest, and religious people.

But all the other people who lived in those days were very wicked—sinful to G-d, and mean to each other. G-d decided to destroy them all. He would save only Noah and his family.

Thereupon, G-d commanded Noah to build a large ark where he and his whole family would be sheltered. G-d also told him to bring into the Ark of every kind of living creature. Noah did as he was told, even though the people laughed at him when they saw him building the Ark. "G-d could never destroy us," they said.

Sixteen-hundred and fifty-six years after G-d had created the world, G-d did bring the Flood. For forty days and forty nights there raged a mighty storm. All the fountains of the earth poured forth their waters, which grew steadily stronger and more violent. The waters covered all the trees and even the higher mountains. All the people and all the living things on earth died. But Noah and his family together with the creatures that were with him in the Ark, were safe from the terrible rain, for the Ark safely floated on the waters like a huge ship.

(To be continued)

BROCHOS

Sammy took a juicy red apple from the fruit-bowl and bit into it.

"Uh-uh," his mother said, "you forgot something!"

"I'm wearing a hat, mom. I know a Jewish boy isn't allowed to eat without one."

"No, Sammy, you forgot something else, something. you just learned."

"Now I remember! I forgot to say a *brochah*. Can I still make one?"

"Yes, you can always say the brochah when you remember, while eating, you hadn't said it."

Sammy said the blessing, took another bite of apple and said, "See mother, I know it by heart."

"Good for you. But do you also know *why* we make the brochah?"

"Surely. A brochah is a prayer of thanks. We're saying 'Thank You' to G-d for giving us food."

"That's right, darling. Think how much of our food comes from the earth. Our fruits and vegetables grow on the earth. The wheat and corn from which we make bread and cakes and cereals come from the earth. Olives and cottonseed and soy bean from which we get oils and fats, sugar beet or cane from which we make sugar, all are grown from the earth. All animals and birds depend on the earth for food.

"And it is G-d who made this wonderful earth and everything on it. It is G-d who makes all things grow by sending rains and bright sunshine in the proper seasons. If G-d didn't take care of the earth, we wouldn't have any food—and we couldn't live. So you see, all the food we eat is really G-d's gift to us, because everything belongs to Him."

"And I almost forgot to thank Him!", exclaimed Sammy. "It's almost like stealing when you eat G-d's food and don't thank Him for it, isn't it?"

"Do you want to know how to make sure you'll never forget to show G-d how grateful you are for what He has so graciously given you?" asked his mother. "Do you want to be sure you're saying the right prayer when you eat?"

"How can I be sure, mother?"

"Take this little book. It's called 'Manual of Blessings and Prayers.'* You know we say a different prayer for different foods: there's a prayer for bread, one for fruit, another for cake, and so on. Everyone of these prayers, and many others too, are in this book. It will fit in your pocket. Carry it with you always, and you'll always know what prayer to say on every occasion."

"Thank you, mother," said Sammy, "for this nice gift. It will remind me to thank G-d for His gifts!"

---

* Published by the Merkos L'Inyonei Chinuch, Inc.

Pee Wee (Joe) becomes an ardent pupil of his best friend.
On his birthday he gets an unusual gift from Dave.

(To be continued)

Published & Copyright 1945 by
MERKOS L'INYONEI CHINUCH, INC.
770 EASTERN PARKWAY
Brooklyn 13, N. Y.
HYacinth 3-9250

No. 4

ב"ה

FRIENDSHIP

Jacob Shapiro looked surprised as he walked out of his house. There was his youngest brother David fighting with another little boy. He went over and pulled them apart.

"Now what is this all about?" he asked as he firmly held David with one hand, and Israel, the neighbor boy, with his other. "You should be ashamed of yourselves!"

"David pushed me because I won the game of marbles," Israel said angrily.

"That's a lie." David shouted back. "You stepped on my toe when you went to pick up the marbles. And anyway, I'm a better player."

« 1 »

"Boys, listen!" Jacob quieted them. "Do you know the club I belong to?"

"Oh yes!" they both exclaimed. Jacob, with several older boys in the neighborhood, belonged to a very special group. These boys were the finest anywhere, and every little boy in the section had one ambition; some day to belong to such a club.

"I'm going to join when I'm 15," Israel said.

"Not the way you're behaving now," Jacob shook his head, "because, do you know what our password is?"

David jumped, "What is it, Jacob? You never wanted to tell me!"

"I'll tell you now. It's Love Your Neighbor As Yourself. Every boy that joins must make a solemn promise: from that day on, he'd act like a gentleman and always respect his friends and all other people."

"Can't he join otherwise, Jacob?"

"No, he cannot. We want to grow up to be good, helpful citizens. Fighting and quarreling with friends shows you don't know how to live among other people. If two of us disagree, we try to understand each other. We talk things over and remain friends. But a boy who fights and can't keep friends when he is young, will grow up to be a bully whom no one likes.

"We only accept fellows who can live up to our motto.

If they practice what it teaches, than we know they are worthy of joining us."

"I guess those older boys know what they're talking about. Let's forget our silly quarrel and shake hands, David." Israel held out his hand.

"Right," David answered. "Let's love and respect each other from now on—and make all our other friends feel that way, too."

 ## NOAH AND THE FLOOD
(*Continued*)

After five months, G-d sent a soft wind over the earth. Slowly the waters ebbed away. The peaks of the mountains were soon visible. Noah's Ark came to rest on the top of Mt. Ararat.

When he saw that the waters were receding, Noah opened the window of his Ark and sent out a raven. He wanted to know how far the waters had gone down. The raven flew this way and that, but soon returned to the Ark.

Noah waited seven days, and then he sent a dove out of the Ark. But the dove, too, returned quickly. She could find no place to rest—water still covered the ground.

Again Noah waited seven days, and again the dove was let out through the window. This time the dove returned in the evening. **In her mouth was a leaf** from an olive tree. That meant that the waters were almost gone, and green leaves were already growing on the trees.

Noah waited one more week, and sent out the dove once more. This time she did not return at all. Noah removed the roof of the Ark and looked out. The earth was now completely dry! At G-d's command, Noah with his family and the animals, left the Ark.

Noah wanted to show how grateful he was to G-d for saving him. He built an altar and brought a sacrifice to G-d.

Then G-d blessed Noah and his family, and all the creatures that came out of the Ark. He said: "May you all multiply on the earth and live happily now. I will never destroy the earth with a flood again. The rainbow in the sky will always be a sign to you of this promise."

*   *   *

When G-d told Noah to build the Ark, He ordered him to build it very slowly, taking a long time. All the people would naturally ask Noah what he was doing. "Tell them," G-d said, "that I am going to bring a flood to destroy the earth because all the people are bad. But if they are sorry, and resolve never to repeat their sins, I will forgive them."

Alas! The people didn't believe Noah, and they continued their wicked conduct.

We should learn from their mistakes. No matter

what our conduct has been in the past, we see that G-d is always ready to forgive us if we only improve. We should take advantage of the chance G-d gives us, and begin to be better from now on.

*　　*　　*

Who had the greatest Zoo on earth?

Do you think of the Flood when you see a rainbow in the sky?

Do you know the blessing we make on seeing a rainbow?

MEAL-TIME

At five-thirty Sarah came in breathless. "That was a swell ball-game. Ruth is still playing. I'll get washed and get ready for supper now."

At six, Sarah was seated at the dinner table with her parents and Uncle Nathan. But no sister Ruth.

Finally, in walked Ruth.

"You've been keeping us waiting," said her mother.

"Oh, I was busy playing. O. K., then, let's eat now."

"First go and get washed, Ruth," her father ordered.

"I'm hungry. My hands aren't so dirty, anyway," Ruth said as she went sulkily away.

Soon she was back. Jumping down into her seat, she grabbed a slice of bread, reached across the table for the butter, and began eating. She didn't seem to notice that no one else was eating yet.

« 5 »

Sarah quietly said, "Can I help you serve, mother?"

"Yes, dear. Come and help me bring in the fish."

"Excuse me," Sarah said, as she left the table to go to the kitchen.

The first course on the table, Sarah waited till the grownups began eating. Only then did she take up her fork and knife.

Meanwhile, Ruth, her mouth full of food, kept chattering all the time.

"Ruth, haven't I told you many times to swallow your food before you speak!" said her mother sternly.

Ruth stopped talking. Without a word, she left her seat. Soon she returned with a comic book.

"Might as well read while I'm waiting for the next course," she remarked, sitting lopsided in her seat.

"Ruth, please pass the salt," asked Sarah quietly.

"I'm reading—reach for it yourself."

"Sarah is right," her father said, " you know it isn't polite to dive across the table!"

Ruth shrugged her shoulders and passed the salt.

She turned up her nose at the second course.

"You know I don't like vegetables, mother. I won't eat these. Anyway, I have no time. I promised my friends I'd play another game at six-thirty. Give me my dessert and I'll go."

"You'll have to wait your turn, my dear," her mother said. "I wish you'd sit still. You seem to be sitting on pins and needles!"

But no amount of coaxing could make her sit still. When the milk and dessert was served, she gulped them down impatiently, then away she dashed from the table, leaving her comic-book there.

Uncle Nathan just sat and watched. He turned to see what Sarah was doing. Eating quietly, she finished the meal with everyone. She then took out of her pocket a little prayer book and read grace after meals.

"Mother, may I go out and play after we wash the dishes?", she asked.

"Yes, dear, I'll wash and you'll dry them, and we'll be ready in a jiffy!"

That evening Uncle Nathan called everyone into the living room.

"I have a surprise for you," he said. "I've decided to send one of the girls to camp this summer at my expense."

Sarah and Ruth caught their breath.

Uncle Nathan continued, "My visit decided which one I'd send. It will be Sarah. I know you're disappointed, Ruth, but I was disappointed in your conduct at the table today."

That night, one little girl dreamed of the good times in camp, another little girl made a firm resolution to learn better table manners right away.

PEE WEE — 4

Before going "over there," Dave and Joe exchange visits on their furlough. Joe gets his stripes a few days before D-day. On that fateful day . . . *(To be continued)*

PRINTED IN U.S.A

Published & Copyright 1945 by
MERKOS L'INYONEI CHINUCH, INC.
770 EASTERN PARKWAY
Brooklyn 13, N. Y.
HYacinth 3-9250

No. 5

ב"ה

SABBATH PLEASURE

"Mother, something smells delicious!" exclaimed David as soon as he entered the house.

"That's the *challah* (Sabbath loaves) and cake I baked for Shabbos. It's only right to make good things with which to enjoy our rest day. Now, David, put away your books while I get you some milk and cookies, and then you'll get to work."

"Okay, ma, I'm ready. This Friday, its my turn to tidy up the porch and the back yard, isn't it?" Though David said it cheerfully enough, mother detected a sour note in his voice.

"Yes, son, it's your turn, and make a good job! We want the house to look its best in honor of Shabbos. Besides, you should feel proud to be doing it; do you realize

« 1 »

that some of our greatest sages made it their business to join in the household preparations for the holy day by doing what they could—chopping wood and the like?"

The afternoon passed quickly as David did his work, then bathed and dressed in his handsome brown Shabbos suit complete with long pants and grown-up hat. By that time the house was sparkling clean—the table set with a pearly white tablecloth, two golden brown *challahs*, a shining silver candelabra, and the family's best china and silverware.

"David, let's look at you," his mother called. "You look fine, my dear. You may go to the synagogue with father now. I must go and light the Sabbath candles."

As he watched his mother light the candles and say a prayer over them, David thought that Shabbos was certainly the best day of the week. Everyone seemed different. They seemed to have dropped from their shoulders all the cares and worries of the week; his father was free from his business worries, his mother from her housekeeping cares, and he himself was free from all thought of homework and schooltests and the like.

There seemed to be a different spirit in the house on Saturday. The members of the family were so much closer to each other on that day. Mother was so rested and amiable; father laughed and was in good spirits. He told the most interesting Bible stories at the table, and listened to David review his Bible lessons of the week, explaining everything very clearly and patiently.

And, of course, the good things to eat every Saturday! The *gefilte fish* and delicious chicken, the cake and fruit, and—well just about everything that's good.

"Yes," David smiled to himself as he joined his father. "I'm certainly lucky to enjoy our wonderful Shabbos every week."

THE TOWER OF BABEL

The Flood was now but a memory. Soon there were many thousands of people living and working together. Now in the time before the great Flood everyone had lived for himself and was not at all interested in what happened to his neighbors. People were selfish and cruel, and this finally led to the destruction of the entire world by the Flood.

Noah's children had well listened to the wise words of advice their ancestor gave them every time they gathered about him. They did not want to make the same mistake as their forefathers before the Flood. Therefore they came together, held a long council and decided to form one single community in which everyone had to take a share. They did so, and their community thrived wonderfully. Sharing joy and happiness like brothers, they felt strong and unconquerable.

One day a shepherd returned from a long trip and brought wonderful news. A few of his sheep had run away and he had gone far beyond the mountain to look for them.

There he had discovered a valley stretching far out in the country called Shinear. Sparkling wells and rivers dotted and crossed the plains, and the soil was black and fertile. They could all live there together as one great family, tilling the soil and reaping the harvest, while their cattle and sheep would peacefully graze on the green pastures. A group of aldermen followed the shepherd's trail and found that he had spoken the truth. The sound of horns called all the men together. They broke up their tents and wandered into the plain of Shinear.

The community prospered. Every year the population increased in numbers until the tents became crowded. Some of the wise men urged the people to seek new pastures, new plains and valleys, where they could build cities. But most of the people were afraid to break up their community and venture out into strange and unknown regions.

One of the elders then said that if they all remained living together so crowded, they would all perish should there be another Flood like in the days of Noah. Therefore, if they would build a tower tall enough to reach into the heavens, nothing could happen to them.

"But we need not fear a flood," a wise man said, "for did not G-d promise our ancestor Noah that never again would He destroy the earth by a flood?"

As if to confirm his words, a rainbow suddenly appeared in the sky, and the people fell on their faces and worshipped the Almighty G-d.

For a few days there was a great deal of agitation in the valley of Shinear. Most people were in favor of erecting a huge tower that would reach into the very heavens. This tower would be a landmark that would be seen for miles and miles around. If anyone ventured out too far, he would see the Tower and know how to get back. In times of danger, they could all seek the safety of the Tower. And finally, the Tower would be the symbol of their unity and strength for all times to come!

Before long, almost all the people were won over to the idea of the Tower. Immediately they set out to build the edifice that was to reach from earth to heaven.

And as the Tower began to take shape, rising higher and higher above the valley, the people became prouder and prouder. They were no longer afraid of Almighty G-d, for soon their Tower would reach the heavens, and they could match their strength with that of G-d.

Then G-d looked at the building growing up in Shinear, and He looked into the hearts of the children of man building it. He saw that their hearts were full of conceit and foolishness. G-d saw that it would do them no good to let them go on like this. He would, therefore, divide them into groups strong enough to live and work together, but not so strong that they could think they were supermen.

And so, one morning, as the people resumed their work, they met confusion everywhere. They could no longer understand each other perfectly. Everything went wrong. If someone asked for mortar, he would be given bricks. If he asked for bricks he would be brought water. People lost their tempers and began throwing bricks and splashing water upon each other. The entire organization which had been running so smoothly before, now fell apart. The construction of the Tower had to be given up!

What caused all this confusion?

(To be continued)

 ## REBECCA LEARNS TO TELL
THE TRUTH

Rebecca was a nice little girl, but she had one fault. Very often, for no reason at all, she would tell a lie. People always used to talk to her about it. "But Rebecca," they used to say, "Don't you know that it's wrong to tell a lie? You can be sure that nothing good will come of it." Rebecca did not care. She would simply shrug her shoulders, and keep on telling as many lies as before.

One morning, Rebecca was in the kitchen with her mother. "Mother, may I go out today?" she asked, "I want to go to Sylvia's house."

"Very well," her mother said, "but make sure that you don't go anywhere else. It looks as though there's a storm coming up, and I want to know where I can find you if I want to bring you home."

"I won't," Rebecca said reassuringly, and walked out of the house.

Sylvia's house was across the street, but as soon as she left the house Rebecca turned right, and walked down the street. Since they lived near the end of town, she soon reached the road, and strolled along gaily, singing as she went.

In a little while, just as her mother had feared, it began to rain. The lightning and thunder frightened her terribly, and in a few minutes her clothes were soaked by the rain. Rebecca turned back and began to run. With the rain came heavy darkness, and she stumbled many times as she hurried back home. Then she lost her way.

Meanwhile, back in town, Rebecca's parents were frantic with fear. Her mother had gone to Sylvia's house to bring Rebecca home, and when she found that Rebecca had not been there that day, she ran home quickly to tell father. Together they went from one house to another trying to find Rebecca, but it was no use; Rebecca seemed to have disappeared completely. With heavy hearts they walked homewards, unable to speak because of the great sorrow that had seized them. Just as they reached the house they noticed a small, bruised figure limping towards them. Rebecca had finally found her way home. She was soaked to the skin, frightened and weeping.

A few minutes later Rebecca was safe and dry in her warm bed, and she felt all cozy and sleepy. She was in the middle of telling her mother what had happened to her, but her eyelids were so heavy that she could not continue. Slowly her head fell back on the pillow and her eyes closed. Before she fell asleep she mumbled a few words. "Mother," she said, "I won't tell any more lies."

"D" can mean anything on "D-Day," it might mean Death. Joe was among the first to land. Has situation well in hand, and gets a bullet badly in his shoulder. While Joe awaits first-aid, Dave takes over. (*To be continued*).

שעורי למור הדת

SHALOH

Published & Copyright 1945 by
MERKOS L'INYONEI CHINUCH, INC.
770 EASTERN PARKWAY
Brooklyn 13, N. Y.
HYacinth 3-9250

No. 6

ב"ה

WASHING THE HANDS BEFORE A MEAL

At noontime all the students of the Yeshivah gathered in the lunchroom. Rabbi Levine, their beloved principal, raised both hands and smiled. Instantly the noise and laughter ceased.

"My boys," he began, "new students and old, I welcome you back to school. I hope you have benefitted from your vacation, and are looking forward to a successful and happy year's work. Now let us see what you remember of your lessons of last year. Before we start our meal, what must we do?"

Rabbi Levine smiled as he saw hands shoot up eagerly all over the room. He pointel to a red-headed boy in the fourth grade.

« 1 »

The boy jumped **up and said, "Before** we may eat, we must wash our hands."

"Correct," nodded the principal. "Now, that boy in the blue sweater, tell us how we wash our hands before we eat."

"Well, first we make sure our hands are perfectly clean and dry, and we take off any rings we're wearing . . ."

"Good for you to remember that."

"Then we go to the sink, take a smooth clean glass or cup in our right hand, fill it with water, put it in our left hand, and holding our right hand in a loose fist—like this," he clenched his fist lightly, "we pour water over our right hand twice in succession, up till our wrist."

"Go on," said the rabbi, obviously pleased.

"Then you put the cup in your right hand and pour water from it twice over your left fist."

"Enough for you; very well said. And can anyone tell us more? All right, you in the glasses."

The tall boy got up. "After our hands are washed, we rub them against each other and say a *B'rochah* (blessing) —a prayer on washing the hands. It's the same one we say when we wash our hands in the morning. Then we dry them. We must not speak or say anything until we make the blessing for bread and eat a piece of it. We must not talk from the time we start to pour water on our hands till after we swallow a bite of bread. If anything touches our hands while they're wet, we must dry them and wash them all over again, but we don't have to say the prayer twice."

"Must we do this before every meal?"

"Before every meal, no matter how big or how small—even a sandwich—whenever we eat *bread* we must wash this way first."

"Correct; an excellent answer. And now, dear students, let us remember why we wash this way.

"Thus, when he washes his hands before eating a meal, before we eat bread is a law of our Holy Torah, and our first duty is to obey all the laws of our Torah.

"Secondly, we are always sure to eat our meals in absolute cleanliness.

"Thirdly, and this also is very important: washing our hands before we eat reminds us to eat like Jews. A Jew does not rush like a hungry animal to stuff himself up at the table. No! A Jew first washes his hands, and by doing so he remembers that he is going to partake of food which G-d provided. So he eats not only to satisfy his hunger, but also to get strength to be able to study and fulfill all G-d's commandments.

"Thus, when he washes his hands before eating a meal, a Jew is happy in the knowledge that he had taken one more step on the way to becoming good and learned as his Creator wants him to be."

THE TOWER OF BABEL

(CONTINUED)

G-d had confused the language of the people. People began to talk various tongues and dialects. Only small groups were able to converse and communicate with each other, while the rest looked bewildered and puzzled.

The people soon realized that G-d was more powerful than they. There was nothing they could do except to give up their ambition which they had begun with such proud hopes. Many families broke up their tents and wandered out of Shinear. Some went far, some stayed near. New communities sprang up, new cities and states. But for a long time the people spoke of their once proud venture in Shinear, which was now called *Babel*, meaning *confusion*.

THE STORY OF ABRAHAM
The Shining Star

In the city of Ur Kasdim (Ur of the Chaldees) there lived a man of noble birth whose name was Terah. He was a very close friend of King Nimrod. One of Terah's great ancestors, nine generations before, was the righteous and pious Noah. Terah was proud of his noble family, but he did not believe in one and only G-d, as his great ancestor of old. Like all the other people around him, Terah worshipped the stars, the sun, and the moon, and animals. He even made his living out of selling images carved out of stone, or wood, or precious metals.

Terah had three sons of whom the eldest was Abram. The other two were Nahor and Haran. Abram's life was full of adventure.

When Abraham was born, he was called Abram then, Terah, his proud father, made a gerat feast to which he invited all the kings, ministers, and advisers.

All day long, the feast lasted merrily, and when the sun set and the first stars appeared, the guests decided they had had enough. Walking home under a sky studded with many stars, they suddenly saw a very bright star appear in the east, growing brighter and brighter. As they were admiring its beauty, the star suddenly darted from east to west, and then to the north and south, swallowing up the other stars on its course.

King Nimrod's astrologers immediately became frightened. They said that the strange sight can mean only one thing—that Terah's newly born son would grow and outshine all the other children of the earth.

"We must tell King Nimrod of the danger," they added gravely.

At the advice of the astrologers, Nimrod sent for Terah and offered to buy his newly born child. "I will fill your house with gold and silver. Will you sell your child to me?"

"My King!" Terah said. "I just had another strange offer. A friend of mine came to me and said, 'Terah, old man, will you sell me the stallion the King had given you as a present? I will fill your stable with oats and hay in price of the horse. Shall I sell it to him?"

"Have you lost your mind?" the king exclaimed angrily. "Who will eat the oats and hay if you give away the horse?"

"And who will inherit my gold and silver if I sell my son?" Terah said in reply.

At this, King Nimrod became very angry. Terah thought at once that not only his son's but his own life too, was in danger, and so he hastened to add, "Your

Majesty, my son as well as I belong to you, take him for nothing."

"No, I will buy him as I said," Nimrod insisted.

"Very good, your Majesty," Terah said, "but grant us three days so that my wife and I might rejoice with our son before we part with him."

(To be continued)

 THE UNWRITTEN ASSIGNMENT

David and Saul were on their way to school. Suddenly David began searching through his pockets, a frightened look on his face. "Say, Saul," he asked, "do you have an extra pencil to lend me? I left mine home, and Mr. Feinstein will be awfully angry if I don't have one."

"Yes, I have an extra pencil," he answered, " but I don't think that I am going to lend it to you. Why should I do you a favor?"

"Please," David pleaded, "just this once. You'll never be sorry if you do."

"No," Saul told him, and would not listen to another word.

The two boys entered the school and walked into the classroom, where Mr. Feinstein was already putting the day's work on the board. Everybody was writing except David, since he could not disturb the class to ask someone for a pencil. Therefore, as soon as Mr. Feinstein finished writing on the board, he raised his hand.

"Yes, David. What is it?"

David, blushing with shame, told Mr. Feinstein that he could not do his work because he had no pencil. The teacher noticed his discomfort and said, "That's all right David, I know this is the first time that it happened. Just sit quietly for the rest of the lesson and read, but don't let it happen again."

A few minutes later Mr. Feinstein told the class that he would have to leave for a while, and he put some work on the board to be ready when he returned. Since the teacher had given them permission to work together, Saul immediately ran over to David to have him do his work for him. Before David even had a chance to say anything he was already gone, joining his friends in the back, who were working very hard at making as much noise as possible.

Before long Mr. Feinstein was back, and he told the class to have their papers ready. Saul ran over to David to get his paper, but David only had a blank page in front of him. When Saul saw that, he became very angry, and told David that it was a very mean trick to do a thing like that.

David waited quietly until Saul had finished, and then he said, "It's your own fault. This should teach you a lesson that from now on when somebody asks you for help you should give it to him. The only reason that I did not help you with your work was that you did not lend me a pencil this morning, and you forgot to leave your pencil before you ran out. So, I had nothing to write with."

Being K.O.'ed in the first round hurts Joe more than a bullet. Re-inforcements arrive on schedule, however. While, back home, Joe is being decorated for valor, his buddies gain a further objective.

(TO BE CONTINUED)

Published & Copyright 1945 by
MERKOS L'INYONEI CHINUCH, INC.
770 EASTERN PARKWAY
Brooklyn 13, N. Y.
PResident 4-0507 - 1866

No. 7

ב"ה

THE BIRTHDAY GIFTS

Joseph got up bright and early one morning. It **was** his third birthday, and he could hardly wait to get ready for breakfast. His parents had already hinted that they had some gifts for him, but when he asked about the gifts **they** told him to wait and see. Now he would finally discover what they were going to give him.

When he sat down to the breakfast table there were two packages at his place, and his mother and father both **had** a broad smile on their faces. Although his curiosity was almost impossible to control, he did not even touch the packages, until his father said: "Happy birthday, Joseph. We have decided that you have been a good boy this **year,** and we have each bought you a little gift. See if you **like** them."

« 1 »

With trembling hands and a pounding heart Joseph opened the first package. It was from his mother: a beautiful shirt and tie. "I must wear this on Shabbos," was his first thought, and he began unwrapping the second package. He took off the string and opened the box, and there was the most beautiful *arba kanfoth* (four-cornered garment with *tzitzis*) that he had ever seen.

He unfolded it tenderly, and looked at it with admiration. He felt the smooth, shiny cloth, and the finely woven threads, and he could not find the words to express his happiness. "Do you know what they are?" asked his father with a smile.

"Of course," Joseph replied. They're *tzitzis*. All my best friends wear them. But I don't really know why."

"In that case," his father said, "I will explain it to you. Do you remember the time we went by bus to visit your aunt in Pennsylvania?"

"Oh sure," Joseph said. "It was a beautiful ride."

"Well, along the road you must have seen all those different warning signs. Some warned about trains, some about street crossings, and some about sharp curves. *Tzitzis* are supposed to do the same thing. Whenever you are about to do something wrong, the *tzitzis* are supposed to be the warning signal; they are supposed to tell you, 'Beware! There is danger ahead! Think before you take another step.' Therefore, if you will always think of the *tzitzis*, it will help you to be good all the time.

"And another thing," father continued. "Remember when your brother Al came home on furlough, first thing you asked him was about his so-called "insignia", his "wings" and **decorations. You** wanted to know what **they** meant? Remember, he told you that they showed his **rank,** his special duties, and so on. Well, the *tzitzis* are also **like** that; they remind us of our special duties as Jews; we **are** also like soldiers, serving our dear G-d and our fellow human beings."

"Oh! Now I know!" cried Joseph, "I'll always be proud to wear the *tzitizis.*"

THE STORY OF ABRAHAM
(CONTINUED)

When Terah told his wife Amathlai of the king's request, she was overcome with grief. "We must find some way to save our son," she said, and then a happy thought came to her. She remembered that one of her maid servants gave birth to a son at the very same time Abram was born. She took the maid's baby, wrapped him up in silk and lace, and when the king's messengers came, she handed him over to them. In the meantime, they hid little Abram in a cave.

When Abram reached his third birthday, he walked out of the cave for the first time. It was night, and a beautiful moon and stars smiled at him from the sky. Little Abram exclaimed, "Oh, how beautiful they are! The moon must surely be G-d, and the stars—the servants, I will worship them." All night he watched the sky until the moon and the stars grew dimmer and dimmer. Finally, they disappeared, and Abram was very disappointed.

Presently, out came a blazing ball of fire, growing stronger and hotter, until Abram could not look at it at all.

"The stars could not be gods," Abram thought. "This ball of fire, the Sun, must be a god, I will worship the Sun."

The sun, too, began to go down and finally sank behind the peaks of the mountains. Darkness fell, and the sun was no more.

Abraham knew the sun could be no G-d either. He thought hard and began to reason it out, young though he was: "If the sun and the moon and the stars are not gods, there must be One who created them, and created the earth too, and all the beautiful flowers, and birds and animals; I will worship G-d, the Creator of the whole world."

ABRAM AND THE IDOLS

Abram's father, Terah, had a large collection of idols in his store. An idol is merely a figure carved in wood, like a cigar-store Indian, or made of gold or silver. In those days, the people used to worship these idols, believing that they could do good or evil. Everyone in the kingdom, from King Nimrod down, used to have one or more of these idols in his home. And Terah had a profitable business, because he used to make and sell these idols to the people.

One day, Terah had to go away, and he said to Abram: "You are quite a man now, and I can leave you to take care of my business. I am going away. I am leaving you in charge of the idols while I am gone." Then Terah went away.

The first customer to come into the store was an old man. The man said to Abram: "Sell me that new idol over there."

Abram then asked the man: "How old are you, sir?"

The man replied: "I am sixty years old."

"What?" asked the amazed **Abram**, "Can it be that a man of sixty will bow down to an idol which is only one day old?"

The man grew ashamed of himself and went away. Then came an old woman, also to buy an idol.

"Give me the largest idol you have," she said, "and I will worship it and love it."

"Listen, dear woman," said Abram, "neither the largest nor the smallest will help you one bit."

But the woman continued: "Yesterday, I left the house for a few minutes, and some thieves came and stole my idols."

Abram laughed and said: "If your idols were not capable of saving themselves from the thieves, how are they going to protect you?"

The woman saw Abram was right. "To whom shall I pray?" she asked.

"Pray to the Creator of the heaven and the earth, in whose hand is the life of every man," Abram told her.

Abram then went on to tell her of the ways of G-d, of His goodness and graciousness. The woman listened to all that he told her, thanked Abram very much for opening her eyes and for showing her the right way to worship G-d.

A short time later, a woman came to Abram and brought a gift, which she wanted to place before the idols. As soon as she was gone, Abram took a big axe and smashed all the idols in his father's shop, except the largest one. Into the hands of this largest idol he placed the axe, and in front of it, the gift which the woman had brought.

When Terah returned and saw that all his precious

idols were destroyed, he scolded **Abram severely**. But Abram merely replied: "A woman came here and brought a present **for** the idols. I put the offering in front of the idols. Soon they began to fight with each other over it. Then the big idol took that large axe and broke all the little idols into pieces."

Terah became angry. "What foolishness is this?" he asked. "These idols have no sense at all. They have eyes but they can't see; ears, but they can't hear; and mouths, but they can't eat or speak. They cannot even move!"

"You are quite right,' answered Abram. "Why then do you pray to them?"

Terah had no answer.

(TO BE CONTINUED)

 ## THE TWO KEEPERS

Little Simon came into the living room throwing a 'Hello' to his dad and mum, and sat down to read his favorite *Shaloh booklet.* He had been playing ball with his friends and he was full of dust and grime. But he did not bother to wash and change, for he didn't think it mattered very much, and he wanted to relax.

"Simon!" his father said. "How many times have I told you to be sure to have your hands and clothes clean when you come back from play. Really, I think you are now old enough to know the importance of cleanliness."

"But really what does it matter, dad?"

"Very well," answered Simon's father, "then listen to

this little story. I want you to answer a question at the end."

"A story? That's fine. Let me hear it."

The father began. "Once there was a king who had two very precious diamonds. He always kept them in a box made of ivory, trimmed with gold. One day he called two of his noblemen and gave each one of them one of these diamonds to guard, promising them a reward for their service.

"Several months later the king again summoned the two noblemen, and asked them to return the jewels. When the first one returned it, the king was very angry. The beautiful ivory box was full of cracks and stains, and the gold was dull and tarnished. Since the king had promised a reward he tossed him a piece of gold, and sent him away. The other nobleman came a few minutes later. The box he had was as perfect as when he first received it, and the gold shone as brilliantly as ever. The king gave this nobleman a whole bag of gold for his service. and gave him much honor.

"That is the story, and now I want you to tell me whether the king did the right thing."

"Of course," Simon answered, surprised that his father should ask such an easy question.

"It is the same way with us. G-d gives us a precious jewel, the soul, and he enclosed it in a container of amazing workmanship, the body. Don't you think that the one who keeps himself neat and clean should be rewarded for it?"

Simon was silent for a while, and then he said: "You know, Dad, I guess you're right after all."

On a dangerous patrol, Dave and buddies pause for refreshments. Never eating before washing his hands, Dave ventures out in search of water. While reciting blessing, Nazi tank guns wipe out ambushed patrol. Stealthily creeping back, Dave avenges his buddies by a well-aimed hand grenade. (*To be continued*)

Published & Copyright 1945 by
MERKOS L'INYONEI CHINUCH, INC.
770 EASTERN PARKWAY
Brooklyn 13, N. Y.
PResident 4-0507 - 1866

No. 8

ב"ה

CHANUKAH LIGHTS AND SHADOWS

Sammy lay awake in his bed, his eyes fixed on the wall in front of him. He could not sleep; the excitement of the evening was too much for him. He kept thinking of his father lighting the first Chanukah candle and he kept hearing the lovely tune. The door of his bedroom was open and the Chanukah lamp in the adjoining room was throwing shadows on the bedroom wall. The shadows jumped on the wall forming strange and fantastic shapes and figures. Sammy looked at the shadows very closely and then he began to see things.

First he saw the march of the cruel Greek legions advancing towards Jerusalem. He saw them storm into the grounds of the Holy Temple, breaking and smashing every-

« 1 »

thing they could lay their hands on. They put out the light of the sacred *Menorah;* then they rushed into the store-rooms where the sacred oil was stored away in containers, each sealed with the seal of the High-priest. They broke the seals and spilled the oil. But wait! One little container slipped away. It rolled and rolled, and a wicked soldier began chasing it.

Sammy closed his eyes; he prayed that the little container escape and disappear so that it should not fall into the unclean hands of the wicked soldier. When Sammy opened his eyes again, he saw that the shadows on the wall had become even darker and gloomier than before. No, they were not shadows at all. There was wicked Antiochus, and in front of him Hannah and her seven sons. Sammy saw how the wicked Antiochus put all the boys to death one after another for refusing to bow to him. Now it is the turn of the younger one, a boy of his own age.

Again Sammy closed his eyes, he could not look any more.

Slowly Sammy opened his eyes. Now the shadows on the wall were dancing merrily. Judas Maccabeeas was leading his victorious Hasmoneans, driving the enemies away. Now the Hasmoneans are in the Holy Temple. They get busy cleaning and tidying up the Holy place. The Temple is crowded with happy Jews; they are all waiting for the *Menoroh* to be lit again. But alas! There is no oil. They look everywhere, but throw their hands up in despair.

Sammy wanted to shout, "But there is some clean and pure oil somewhere! I saw a little container escape."

As if they could read his thoughts, the shadows go into a hustle, and soon a little container rolls out of its hiding place.

Now the shadows have almost disappeared. For there is so much light, ever so much light. Sammy wondered how a little bit of pure olive oil could give so much light. The light grew bigger and better until it was almost dazzling to the eye. Sammy closed his eyes and heard very sweet music ... The Priests and Levites were chanting psalms in the Holy Temple, thanking G-d for the wonderful miracle. It was really his father in the next room, but Sammy was drowsy and falling asleep. He was very very happy.

 ## THE STORY OF ABRAHAM (*continued*)
ABRAM THROWN INTO THE FURNACE

When King Nimrod heard that Abram destroyed all his father's idols, he called him to the palace.

"Bring forth a fire, and bow to it," commanded the king.

"Why should I bow to the fire, when the water is stronger; it can put out the fire!"

"All right then, bow to the water."

"But why the water?" asked Abram, "when the clouds are stronger than the water; they can keep back the waters from falling."

Again the king agreed: "All right, bow to the clouds."

"Not the clouds," said Abram. "How can I, when the winds which drive the clouds in the sky, are stronger still?"

In this way, Abram continued to defy the king and kept refusing to bow to anything. The king could stand it no longer, and called for his advisers.

"What shall we do with this man who refused to bow when I commanded and who broke the idols?"

"Let us," advised the counsellors, "make a fierce fire in the furnace, and throw Abram into it." The king ordered this done.

On the appointed day, all the advisers, judges, men, women, and children, came to witness the burning of Abram in the furnace. The servants of the king tied Abram hand and foot and carried him to the furnace.

At this moment, the angel Gabriel pleaded with G-d in heaven.

"Let me go down to earth and save Abram from the furnace."

G-d was willing and said: "There is none like Abram on the whole earth."

Gabriel went down to the furnace just as Abram was thrown into it, and made a few changes in the huge fire. He turned all the flames to large trees, and on the branches grew fruit of all wonderful kinds. For three days and nights, Abrah walked about in this magic "garden," and sang songs of praise to G-d.

When Abram was thrown into the furnace, the servants

of the King said to Terah: "See what became of your son. We heard you boasting that he would inherit this earth, and that also the next world would be his. See the result."

Terah rushed over to the furnace. When he got there, he found the king and all his advisers, staring with wide eyes into the furnace. When Terah saw the wonderous miracle, he jumped for joy.

The king was terrified at the sight of Abram being alive, and he said to Abram, "You may now come out of the furnace. I will do you no harm."

Abram came out into the light of day and presented himself before the king. The king asked him:

"Tell me, Abram, how was the fierce fire extinguished, and how did the flames become such a paradise as I've never witnessed before?"

"That," said Abram, "is the work of G-d, the Creator of heaven and earth. He protected me and guarded me from death. He is the G-d to whom I pray."

Upon hearing this, the king arose and bowed to Abram. But Abram only remarked:

"Do not bow to me. Bow to the Creator of the world, because he alone holds in His hand the power of life and death. Serve Him with all your heart and He will keep you from all harm."

That day, King Nimrod and all his followers presented to Abram much gold and silver, and sent him on his way. And as he left the palace, more than three hundred people followed him, and vowed to serve him in all his needs.

AT WAR

Aaron declared war. His enemy was a sneaky Jap hiding inside of him waiting to pounce on him when Aaron expected it least. This enemy was his bad Temptation, and he had decided to lick it. When he was going to Hebrew School, a little voice inside of him—his enemy —would say, "Hey! Take your time. What's your rush? It's nothing if you come a few minutes late." Aaron knew it was that Tempter again, and he would begin running at once, and get there before anybody else. If it would say, "Why do you have to say a blessing every time you eat?" he would say the blessing with greater care than ever. Then came one of the toughest battles of this continuous war.

Once a year, on a Sunday morning, all the kids in the neighborhood were taken on a free boat ride. The round trip took almost a whole day, and everyone was given ice cream and soda aboard the ship's deck. Aaron had never gone before because he was too young; this was the first year that he had the chance. But if he went, it would mean that he would have to miss the class in Hebrew School. The little voice inside of him was now bothering him something awful.

It was not as though he would be the only one to be absent if he went. He knew of at least ten other boys from Hebrew School who were going on the trip. Maybe it would not be so bad if he lost this battle with his enemy. After all, he had been doing pretty well until that time. Would this one time make such a big difference? He was at the point of surrendering already, but at the last moment —in fact, the very morning of the boat ride—he decided against it. He knew that one defeat would lead to another, and that if he gave his enemy the slightest chance to strengthen his forces, he would have a much tougher fight on his hands. He went to Hebrew School on that Sunday morning.

When he entered his classroom nobody was there yet, and when the time for the class to begin came, only he and the teacher were there. They waited together in silence for a few minutes, and then the teacher spoke. "It seems," he said to Aaron, "that my students think a boat ride is more important than coming to class. I am glad that I have at least one student who understands the importance of learning. I will see to it, Aaron, that you get a special prize for showing so much spirit. And now, since it is very unusual to have one student in a class, I will give you permission to go to the boat ride after all. If you hurry you can still make it."

Aaron thanked his teacher and ran to the pier where the boat was docked. In his mind he chalked up another victory over that little voice inside. It had not been an easy fight, but it sure paid to win it!

David's feat get big headlines, while Joe, once champion ball player, returns to civil life. Is soon joined by Dave, now also a vet. The two friends know that both were saved by the merit of a *mitzvah*. [END]

Published & Copyright 1945 by
MERKOS L'INYONEI CHINUCH, INC.
770 EASTERN PARKWAY
Brooklyn 13, N. Y.
PResident 4-0507 - 1866

No. 9

ב"ה

ROSH HASHANAH OF THE TREES

When Obadiah left Hebrew School one day, he had a white paper bag firmly clutched in his hand. It contained a delightful assortment of figs, dates, carobs, almonds and other fruits and nuts. As he wandered aimlessly through the streets, stopping every once in a while to take another fruit out of the bag, he turned over in his mind the many things that had been told to him that day by his teacher.

Today is the New Year For Trees! Just think! The fate of the trees is decided on *Chamishah-a'sar B'shevat* just as the fate of men is decided on *Rosh Hashanah.* Today G-d will decide which trees would grow strong, and

« 1 »

which ones would wither; which trees would give fruit, and which ones would be destroyed. If a tree had fulfilled its duties this year, it had a chance to live in the next. Otherwise, it was doomed to sickness or death. Perhaps that explains why the apple tree back of Mr. Goldberg's house had fallen down during a storm? Many times he had found worms in the fruit of that tree. . . .

Presently he had finished the contents of the bag, and so he was able to devote his attention to his surroundings. He discovered that he was now on the parkway, which was lined with trees on both sides. Many times he had walked along this parkway — at least twice or three times a day, and never before had he taken any notice of the trees. He had taken them for granted like the letter boxes and fire alarms on the street corners. Today, however, he took a lively interest in the trees. Poor things, they looked bare and sad. One might have thought they were dead, except that now and again they swayed in the wind, as though they were praying, like the worshippers in the synagogue on *Rosh Hashanah*. It was *Rosh Hashanah* for the trees, and who knows, perhaps they were really praying?

Suddenly his thoughts took a leap to a distant land where it was sunny and warm, where the evergreen olive grew, and the tall date palm and the fig tree. He was thinking of the Holy Land of Israel. How he longed to be there to walk on the sacred soil where the holy Prophets had walked and where the brave Hasmoneans had fought for freedom to worship G-d and observe His commands!

* * *

A broken twig fell in his way, and his thoughts returned to his immediate surroundings. Isn't it wonderful, thought Obadiah, how these seemingly lifeless trees come back to life in the spring? Already the roots must be working to supply the tree with its vital food for recovery.

The roots! How important it is for the tree to have many healthy roots! Didn't the teacher say that Jewish children, boys and girls attending a good Talmud Torah or Yeshiva and getting a good Hebrew education, are the life-giving roots of our people Israel? Each Jewish child, whether boy or girl, receiving a good Jewish education is an additional healthy root, so vital to that huge tree that is our people Israel. How could the tree live without roots? How could the Jewish people exist without *all* Jewish children receiving a good Jewish education?

"Obadiah, you are a lucky boy! You are a healthy root! Keep on being healthy!" Obadiah thought to himself.

THE STORY OF ABRAHAM
(*Continued*)
ABRAM GOES TO CANAAN

Abram grew older and married Sarai, his beautiful niece. One day he was out in the fields thinking in what

« 3 »

way he could best serve G-d, when he heard G-d's voice ordering him to leave his father's house, his city and native country, and wander out to a distant land. There Abram was to make his new home, and there, G-d promised him, he should become a great and famous chieftain, and the father of a new and holy nation, a nation that would be dedicated to the service of G-d and a blessing to mankind.

Now anyone but Abram would have hesitated to take up the wanderer's staff at the ripe age of 75 years to start life anew, especially if he was not short of anything in his native land. But Abram's faith in G-d was boundless. He packed up everything he could take along, took his wife and his nephew Lot, and off they went, as G-d had bidden them, to a strange land with strange people and strange customs — the land of Canaan.

Upon arrival in Canaan G-d spoke to Abram again. He told him to stay in that land, promising him that his descendants would inherit the entire country. Abram was very grateful, and built an altar upon which he offered sacrifices to G-d.

For some time Abram and his family had been living in their new home. They worked and were blessed with much success. They soon owned many cattle and many servants. But a famine came to the country, and again Abram had to break up his tents and wander down to Egypt where, he was told, there was food in plenty.

Knowing the Egyptians as a people of bad morals, Abram tried to hide his wife Sarai. She was discovered, however, and despite Abram's protests was taken to King Pharaoh's palace. That night Pharaoh had a dream in which G-d warned him that he and his people would die if Sarai were not returned to her husband immediately. In the morning Pharaoh sent for Abram, and scolded him for not disclosing that Sarai was his wife. Abram explained that the Egyptian soliders would surely have killed him in order to take his wife away, for she was very beautiful. Pharaoh then sent him and Sarai away, after he had given them many presents, cattle and servants, to compensate for the anxiety he had caused them.

Abram returned to Canaan richer than he had left it. He had everything in plenty. He entrusted his servant Eliezer of Dameshek with the management of his entire household, while he and his wife Sarai spent their time in spreading the true belief in G-d among the heathens, teaching them the right way to conduct their lives.

Lot, too, had become rich and had many servants tending his herds. But his men had not been so carefully instructed by their master to keep away from other people's property. Abram's honest servants frequently chided Lot's shepherds. When Abram heard of the strife between his shepherds and Lot's, he decided that Lot and he had better separate. He gave Lot the choice of selecting any pastures he liked, and the latter took the land around Sodom, where the soil was fertile and ideal for cattle raising.   (To be continued)

IN THE BUS

David sat beside his mother looking out of the bus window. He had enjoyed visiting his Aunt Deborah, but it was difficult to sit like a little gentleman for such a long ride. Just then the bus stopped near the park, and every head turned at the sound of a roaring crowd. The roaring crowd turned out to be just six boys. David recognized four of them as his classmates. Jostling and pushing everyone in their way, they stampeded into the bus. Two of them paid the fare, shouting rude remarks to the driver at the same time.

One cried, "Hey bud, let us on for free," while the other shouted, "Look at that guy's funny nose!"

Meanwhile, the others were scrambling for seats, pushing and jostling and stepping on everybody's toes. A sweet little old lady carrying a shopping basket tried to sit on an empty seat beside one of the boys.

"Say, you can't sit here," he said in an angry tone. "This seat is taken for my friend."

As the bus started again, it was impossible for anyone to carry on a conversation. At the top of their lungs the boys were jabbering. They would stop their loud voices only when changing seats up and down the bus, making it difficult for anyone to reach the exit.

The angry glances and stares of the other passengers didn't bother the boys. Finally one man got up and said, "Boys, won't you please lower your voices! Other people are here too, you know!"

"Is that so?" snarled the oldest of the lot. "It's a free country, I paid my fare, and I can do what I want."

David writhed in his seat. He blushed with shame as he realized that many a time he had ridden on a bus or train with friends and behaved just as badly. How could I — he wondered — have been so loud and noisy and insulting? Never again, he vowed, no never!

Suddenly a boy noticed him. "H'iya, Davey — Come with us and have some fun!" he called.

"I'm sorry boys," David replied, "Don't you realize you are annoying the other people in the bus? They can't stand your rude behavior."

As they looked at David open-mouthed and embarrassed, his mother smiled and said, "Son, I'm proud of you. But I hope you remember always to practise what you just told those boys."

BIBLE QUIZ

1   Who died, but was not born? — *Adam and Eve.*

2.   Who killed a quarter of the world's population? — *Cain, when he killed his brother Abel.*

3.   How many people survived the Flood? — *Nine: Noah, his three sons, their wives and O8*

4.   Where was the first skyscraper built? — *In Babylon (The Tower).*

(To be continued)

Published & Copyright 1945 by
MERKOS L'INYONEI CHINUCH, INC.
770 EASTERN PARKWAY
Brooklyn 13, N. Y.

PResident 4-0507 - 1866

No. **10**

SABBATH REST

Friday evening, after the delicious meal, Jacob approached his grandfather who was sitting, as usual, before an open *Chumash*.

"May I ask you something, Grandpa?"

"Certainly, Jacob; sit down here and ask anything that's on your mind."

"Grandpa, I am never sure what a Jew may or may not do on Shabbos. After all, Shabbos is a day of rest, so why is it forbidden to do things which do not make one tired at all? Knitting, for instance. Mother says it always makes her feel so restful when she knits, yet she told me that knitting is forbidden on Sabbath. Could

« 1 »

you tell me something more about Shabbos? What things may or may not be done, and why?"

"Delighted, my boy," Grandpa answered, and continued. "As you know, G-d created the whole universe in six days, and rested on the seventh. Then He proclaimed the seventh day of the week a holy day of rest. Was G-d really tired from His work of Creation? Of course not! But, by stopping all work of Creation before the seventh day, G-d showed man the way to live. G-d wants man to live a special life, far above the life of any other creature which He had created.

After pausing for breath, Grandpa continued: "Man is a wise and understanding being, and he must be a living memorial to the work of Creation. How does man bear witness to the fact that G-d created Heaven and Earth?

"We do it by ceasing work on the Holy Sabbath Day and by keeping it in the way G-d commanded us to keep the Holy Sabbath. Every Jewish store, business or shop closed on Shabbos loudly proclaims to the whole world that G-d created the world in six days. This is exactly what G-d wants us to do.

"For us Jews Shabbos is, therefore, more than a rest day. We need not be tired to enjoy it or keep it. For us Jews Shabbos is a day dedicated to G-d, a day completely different from the other days of the week.

"Shabbos is different in every respect, in every detail. Our clothing, food prayers, our very walk and talk, even our thoughts, all have a distinctive Shabbos mark on them. Everything connected with our daily life, our business or work, our sports and recreation, is simply banished away for twenty-four hours or a little more. On Shabbos, a Jew lives in a completely new world, a world holy and pure of spirit. That is what we mean when we speak of the *Neshamah Yeserah*, the Jew's distinctive 'Shabbos soul'."

"I am beginning to understand now, but please go on Grandpa," Jacob said. And Grandpa continued:

"This will give you some idea why the Jew is not permitted to do things on Shabbos which are quite harmless in themselves and seemingly of little significance, such as handling money, tearing paper, smoking, riding in any conveyance from a plane to a bus, going to the movies, playing ball, carrying anything out of, or into, the house, and so on. It is especially forbidden to do any *creative* work, such as writing, drawing, and, of course, knitting, sewing, mending, cooking, baking, and so on.

"I am getting out of breath Jacob, but I still have not mentioned everything."

"I know, Grandpa, I could mention a few more things. For instance, we may not light any lights. We may not strike a match, turn on the electricity, or gas."

"Yes, indeed, but there are many, many more things to learn."

"You know, Grandpa, I think that after Shabbos I will make a chart of all the things we are not allowed to do on Shabbos, which I can think of."

"A very good idea, my boy. And let me give you some advice. If ever you are in doubt about anything, don't be shy to ask your father, your teacher, your rabbi, or even me. A shy person doesn't learn much, our holy books say."

"I will always ask, Grandpa, and I am afraid I am going to give you a lot of bother. But I hear mother calling me now. Good Shabbos, Grandpa, and many thanks."

THE STORY OF ABRAHAM
(Continued)
THE JEALOUS KINGS

Abram's reputation spread far and wide. Pretty soon, everyone had heard of his greatness, wisdom, and his sincere devotion to G-d. The people throughout the land turned to Abraham for guidance on every occasion.

This made the ruling kings of that day very jealous and very angry. One day, four mighty kings got together to discuss the matter, and one of them said:

"This fellow, Abram, is getting to be too powerful around here. If this keeps up much longer, he'll become the chief ruler, and we will become his slaves. I think we should kill him."

"Yes, yes," shouted the others, "Kill him! Kill him!"

"Let's attack him right now," added another.

"'No, no, spoke the wisest among them, whose name was Chedarlaomer, the mighty king of Elam. "It does

not befit mighty kings like us to make war upon a single chieftain. But there is another way."

"Really?" they asked in unison. "Tell us quickly!"

The wise king replied: "Have you forgotten that it is well nigh thirteen years since the king of Sodom and his four allies have stopped paying us tribute, proclaiming themselves free from our dominion? It is high time we crushed the revolt!"

"Hear, hear!" shouted the others in agreement. "But what has the revolt of the five kings to do with Abram the Hebrew?"

"I am coming to that. Don't you see? If we attack Sodom and capture Lot, we would kill two birds with one stone. We would recapture our lost empire and at the same time hold Lot as bait to catch Abram. For Abram would surely rush to the rescue of his nephew and would fall into our trap!"

"Bravo, bravo!" roared the others their approval.

*   *   *

In the valley of Siddim, which later became the Dead Sea, the king of Sodom with his four allies confidently poised for battle; five kings against four. But the four won! Chedarlaomer and his allies simply routed their opponents, taking many captives on the field of battle, as well as all the inhabitants of Sodom, men, women, and children, with all their possessions and wealth. Lot was among the captives.

(To be continued)

A POOR JOKE

There were very few boys that liked Heshel. He would make shameful remarks about his friends, and he would often play mean little tricks on them, which were supposed to be "practical jokes." Whenever somebody reproached him for his behavior, he would reply, "I only meant is as a joke." No matter how many times they tried to show him that he was really being cruel, he would only laugh it off. Until one incident made him change completely.

One day Heshel and a group of other boys took a trip to one of the city parks. One of the boys, Dave, had recently moved into their neighborhood, and had been invited to come along with them. Nobody knew much about him, and since Dave did not say much, there was no opportunity to learn anything from him direct. But he seemed to be a pleasant companion, and everybody was satisfied. Heshel was the only one who plagued the life out of the newcomer.

After the boys had been in the park several hours, Heshel thought that it was time to play one of his so-called "jokes." Going over to Dave with a serious look on his face, he asked him to lend him a nickel for a few minutes Dave gave him the money without hesitation. When the money was not returned soon after, he did not worry. He felt sure that he would get it back when he asked for it.

It was getting dark, and the boys decided to go home. Dave went over to Heshel and politely reminded him about the money he had borrowed.

"What's the matter?" Heshel sneered, thinking all the while that it was a great joke. "Are you so broke that you cannot spare a nickel? Alright, let's toss it up, double or nothing!"

Dave's face turned crimson with shame. Without saying a word he walked away from the boys. When they saw how hurt he had been they turned to Heshel and clenched their fists in anger, but he only said, "What are you worrying about? It was only a little joke." Then it began to rain, and they wasted no time in argument. They ran for the bus.

The next day they did not see Dave in school. After asking his younger brother several questions, they learned the true meaning of the incident in the park the previous day. Dave's family was very poor, and his mother had only been able to give him enough money for carfare. That was why he was so embarrassed by Heshel's remark about being broke. Dave had to walk home in a heavy rain, and was drenched to the bone. During the night he developed such a high fever that he had to be taken to the hospital; it was fortunate that he had not caught pneumonia. Now he would have to be in bed for several weeks. The "joke" had turned into a tragedy.

This was the incident that made Heshel give up his bad habit.

(To be continued)

« 8 »

שעורי למוד הדת

SHALOH

Published & Copyright 1945 by
MERKOS L'INYONEI CHINUCH, INC.
770 EASTERN PARKWAY
Brooklyn 13, N. Y.
PResident 4-0507 - 1866

No. **11**

PURIM

"When Adar comes, merriment increases."

These words tell us the nature of the joyous month of Adar and its place in Jewish life. Adar brings joy and happiness. Do you want to know why? Because in Adar we have the happy festival of *Purim*. Purim is a festival of victory and triumph over a vicious and cruel enemy. On Purim we celebrate the victory of the righteous Mordecai and Esther over the cruel Amalekite (an old name for Hitlerite), Haman. It is a happy festival indeed, for unfortunately, in our present world it does not always happen that the villain is put on the gallows, or at least safely behind bars, *before* he does any harm. Not so in those days of Purim, in the Land of Persia, in the city of Shushan. There, the wicked Haman got

« **1** »

what he deserved *before* he could harm a single Jewish child.

Small wonder, therefore, that the first day of **Adar** brings a breath of joy to every Jewish home, heralding the approach of the happy festival of Purim.

Most of all, Purim brings joy to Jewish children. If you want to know why it does, let's ask Saul and Naomi, twin brother and sister, aged eleven, who live in Brownsville.

It is the night before Purim and Saul with his sister have gone to *shul* to hear the *Megillah*. So we follow them there. But we cannot ask them yet, because they are already listening very carefully to every word of the *Megillah*. Each of them has a miniature *Megillah* in a scroll form, which looks like the real thing; it has wonderful ornaments and illustrations, too. Saul and Naomi are very quiet trying not to miss a single word. Suddenly, they burst out with a thunderous stamping of their little feet, rattling those "Haman *Gragers*." This happens quite a few times during the course of the reading of the *Megillah*. Are they behaving badly? Oh no! Why even the grownups join them in this racket. Invariably the noise breaks out when "Haman" is mentioned, and the reason is obvious: They want to "boo" him, to express their indignation, yes, their hatred, for that cruel man Haman and for his counterparts in all lands and in all generations, and for all they stand for.

Now the reading of the *Megillah* is over, and Saul and Naomi return home.

Here's our chance, let's follow them and hear what they are talking about.

"I love Purim," says Naomi. "I love that sweet tune in which the *Megillah* is read, and I love stamping my feet at Haman!"

"And I love Purim for the delicious Purim cakes, the *Haman-tashen*," says Saul.

"Tell me, Saul, do you know why a *Hamantash* has three corners?" asks Naomi.

"Because if it had four corners it would require *Tzitzis*, like any four-cornered garment," Saul replies with a chuckle.

"Oh, that's an old one. Really do you know why?"

"I believe, because Haman wore a three-cornered hat like Napoleon," answers Saul more seriously.

"Well, I am going to ask someone who knows the real reason," says Naomi resolutely. "Anyway, Purim is truly a girls' festival, because Esther was the heroine of the day."

"Well, Mordecai also had something to do with it, so the boys have a good reason to celebrate, too. The truth is that Purim is a festival for both boys and girls."

"I shall not contest the point," Naomi says, "but what part did the children play in those days?"

"Don't you know that Haman had set his mind upon destroying the children first?"

"Why the children?"

"Because he saw Mordecai stopping three children going from *Cheder*. Mordecai asked them to quote something from what they had learned that morning. Each one of them quoted a passage from the Bible that greatly encouraged Mordecai to resist Haman. That is why Haman swore to destroy the children first. Besides, all bad men hate children. Then, when Haman's plan became known, Mordecai gathered the children about him and together they prayed to G-d to save the Jewish people. The children were so good, every one of them attending Cheder and loving their Hebrew studies, that G-d forgave all our people Israel for the sake of the children!"

✻   ✻   ✻

Saul and Naomi have now reached their home and so, we bid them an inaudible "Good Purim," happy that we are now a great deal wiser than before.

THE STORY OF ABRAHAM

(*Continued*)

THE VICTORS VANQUISHED

When the news reached Abram, he was deeply grieved and immediately ordered his little band to prepare for battle. Before starting out, he called them together **and** said:

"Men, we are setting out to rescue the people of Sodom and my nephew Lot, and to restore to them everything that was plundered by the victorious kings. Now, I know that you are all men of flesh and blood, and your hearts will seek to own some of the vast wealth which you will see. I am, therefore, going to give each of you plenty of gold, and silver, and precious gems as a reward for your fighting. But, promise me that you will not lay your hands on anything you see which does not belong to you."

His followers promised on oath, and after Abram had bestowed upon them much of his own riches, they grimly set out for the unequal battle.

Bravely, Abram set out with his band of valiant warriors to challenge the mighty Chedarlaomer. Abram had but a handful of men; there were only 318 of them! But there was no fear in their hearts, for they all trusted in G-d to help them. Indeed, miracles began to happen immediately they started on their march. First, every step which Abram and his band took brought them miles closer to their objective, and quite soon they overtook the wicked kings. A flood of arrows greeted Abram and his followers as soon as they were spotted. but the deadly missiles turned to sand, and harmlessly parachuted to earth. Then they threw their spears, but the spears became straws, and could do no harm to either Abram or his men.

(To be continued)

NICKNAMES

"Say, Sneaky, why don't you learn to pitch decent-ly?" jeered the fifth grade youngsters in the Hebrew school. They were so intent on their game that they didn't notice their principal standing quietly and watching them.

"Okay, give me time," the one called Sneaky answered.

"Better make it good."

Back they went to their game, shouting and arguing. Suddenly they noticed the Rabbi looking thoughtfully at them. He noticed their sudden and uncomfortable silence, so he looked up and smiled. "It's alright, boys, go on with your game."

Intent upon their studies in the classroom, the boys later forgot the incident. Suddenly a messenger handed the teacher a note. After glancing at it, he looked up and announced. "Solomon, Nathan, and Abraham. The princi-pal wishes to see you at once."

The class shuffled uneasily in their seats. These boys were three of the best students. What had they done?

When they were seated in the principal's office, he asked them quite seriously, "Why do you call Moses Glasser 'Sneaky'?"

The boys were taken aback. They had expected a lec-ture, and here they were being asked what seemed a silly question.

"Why, I don't know," Nathan answered, "we just call him that, like we call Abraham 'Red,' and they call me 'Shorty' "

Solomon thought out loud, "I believe we gave him that nickname because he's so much quieter than the rest of us."

"Are you sure it wasn't because he has a sneaky nature?"

They stared at the Rabbi. Then Abraham piped up, "But everybody knows Sneaky is the most honest boy that ever lived."

The principal smiled with relief, "I'm glad to hear that. Moses' excellent record has entitled him to an honor certificate, and I had planned to make him my personal helper. But when I heard you calling him 'Sneaky' I thought perhaps he couldn't be trusted."

"I'm glad that's straightened out," Nathan declared.

"Boys, I hope you have learned from this incident how wrong and dangerous nicknames are. Every time you use an uncomplimentary nickname, you embarrass someone. Many are the lessons you've had about how great is the sin of shaming our fellow-human beings."

The boys nodded their assent.

He continued, "You have just seen how a stupid nickname almost ruined Moses' chances for honor and reward. Now go and tell your classmates that verey boy has a good Jewish name of which he should be proud. Use those names always."

(To be continued)

« 8 »

Published & Copyright 1945 by
MERKOS L'INYONEI CHINUCH, INC.
770 EASTERN PARKWAY
Brooklyn 13, N. Y.
PResident 4-0507 - 1866

No. 12

LIONEL'S FIRST SEDER

Lionel and Michael were walking home together. Michael was talking excitedly about the *Seder* that was going to be held in his house that night. He went over every detail with great delight. He spoke of the bright room, the white table cloth, the *Seder-table* richly decorated, the *Hesev-bed* (couch for reclining), the wine and the *Matzot*, the *Four Question* which he would recite so boldly; of father's and mother's faces shining with an inner glow, the guests, the delicious meal, the *Afikomen*, the nuts to play with. . . .Oh, how wonderful it was! When he finished, his eyes shone at the very thought of sitting at the table that first night of Pesach. When he finished his thrill-

« 1 »

ing description, he turned to hear what Lionel had to say, and to his surprise his friend had tears in his eyes.

"Why, Lionel," Michael said in amazement "What have I done to make you cry?"

"Oh, it's not your fault," he answered. "It's just that I never had a real Seder. My parents died when I was very young, and since then I have been living with an aunt. That is why I feel so sad when you talk about your *Seder*."

"I'm awfully sorry," Michael said earnestly. But then more cheerfully he added: "Would you like to spend the *Seder* with us? I'll ask mother to invite you!"

"Thanks, Michael, I know that you are a true friend. But don't let it worry you; it won't be my first Pesach without a *Seder*."

The two boys continued the rest of their way home in silence, and when they reached Michael's house they parted.

As Lionel walked home, the expression on his face showed that he still felt the effect of Michael's words. How pleased he would be if he could be as fortunate as his friend. But, he thought with a shrug of his shoulders, there was no sense in useless dreaming. And so he did his best to forget about it.

At night Lionel returned from the synagogue with a heavy heart. As much as he tried, he could not overcome the desire to have a real *Seder*. He entered the house and prepared to eat the meal that his aunt had set for him, trying to arrange it to resemble a *Seder* as best as he could. Just as he was about to wash his hands there was a hurried pounding on the door. He ran to open it; it was Michael.

He was panting from running, but he managed to gasp out:

"You are invited! Mother had been thinking of you all the time, but she was so busy with preparations, she clean forgot that she had not told me to invite you. When I came from *shul*, she asked, 'Where's Lionel?' And I rushed here without even taking off my coat."

Arm-in-arm the two friends walked briskly to celebrate the Seder. "Tonight *I* shall ask the *Four Questions*, but tomorrow night, it will be *your* turn! Do you know them?" Michael said.

Lionel smiled confidently, and warmly pressed his friend's arm in his own.

THE STORY OF ABRAHAM

THE VICTORS VANQUISHED

(*Continued*)

When the kings saw these miracles, they decided to rush upon Abram and seize him. Thereupon Abram took the sand and the straw and hurled it back at them. Lo and behold! The sand changed back to arrows and the straws again became spears. This was too much for the kings. They picked up their crowns and fled, leaving all their captives and spoils behind.

Lot was a free man again. But if he was grateful to his uncle for liberating him, he did not show it.

In the meantime, the king of Sodom, who had escaped from his first encounter with Chedarlaomer, came out from his hiding place, and met Abram with humility and gratitude. He had no claim upon his people or their possessions, for such was the law of war in those days, but he begged Abram to free the people of Sodom and allow them to return home, while keeping all their possessions.

A broad smile covered Abram's face as he told the poor king that he had already given orders to set all the captives free. As for their possessions and wealth, Abram said that he had already sworn to the Most High G-d that he would not touch of it as much as a shoelace!

Great was the rejoicing of the people of Sodom at regaining their liberty and wealth.

"Be thou our king!" they begged of Abram. But to their amazement they heard a reply quite different from the one they had expected.

"G-d forbid that I should rule over you. Who am I but dust and earth like all men? If you want to please me, just love your neighbor, live in peace, open your doors to the poor, and have faith in G-d, the Creator of heaven and earth, and worship Him alone with all your heart."

Very touching was the greeting of Malkitzedek, the king of Shalem (later to become the city of Jerusalem).

He was a peace-loving king, serving the right G-d. Malki-tzedek was overjoyed with Abram's victory over the tyrannical kings and praised the Lord for having helped Abram to overcome his enemies

This victory over the mighty kings of Babylon made Abram the most powerful man in the entire country. His advice and counsel was sought by everyone in need, and the fame of his wisdom and justice, as well as his great belief in one G-d, travelled far.

Soon after Abram had returned from the battle with Chedarlaomer, G-d spoke to Abram again and told him, as he had already promised him once before, that his descendants would inherit the entire country. But Abram replied that all the riches and power in the world would be of no avail to him as long as he had no children; he was now an old man, and there was little hope that anyone but his servants would inherit his possessions.

Upon hearing Abram's sad reply, G-d showed him the skies studded with millions of stars. "Thus," said G-d to Abram, "will be the number of thy seed."

G-d then went on to tell Abram of the glorious future of the people that was to come forth from him: That it would first be enslaved in a strange land, then be liberated with abundant wealth, and inherit the land of Canaan; it would become a strong and respected nation, a model to all other nations of the world.

(To be continued)

RUMORS

"I'll bet she cheated, that's why she got 100% in the test," exclaimed dark-eyed Ruth to a group of girls in the school yard.

"Yes, she thinks just because she lived in a different city she's smarter than we are," Naomi vigorously nodded her head.

"Did you see how she does everything just as the teacher says, and she's always studying. She just wants to be teacher's pet," said Hannah.

"I heard my daddy say, her brother is a wild bad boy," contributed Naomi.

"Girls, let's not play with her," Ruth decided.

As they turned homeward, quiet little Sarah's welcoming smile turned to anxious wonder as the girls, whose friendship she desired, passed her without a glance.

Hannah's parents were waiting on the porch.

"Well, Hannah," her mother greeted her, "how was school today? I see you walked home with your friends, but I didn't notice that new girl who had just moved here. She seems very sweet."

"Sure, she seems nice, but—" and Hannah repeated all the mean remarks the girls had made about Sarah, ending, "and so we're not going to play with her any more."

Hannah's parents exchanged glances, and then her father said: "Hannah, that doesn't sound like the daughter

I'm teaching to be fair and kind. You **and** your **friends are** being mean and vicious. You are certainly disobeying the laws of our Holy Torah!"

"What do you mean, father?"

"You are all acting jealous. Now don't look so surprised. You know that in your hearts you envy little Sarah her excellent marks. She is obedient and studious. She probably just wants to catch up to her new classmates, but you say she wants to be 'teacher's pet!'

Hannah looked guiltily at the floor. "I suppose you're right, daddy."

"Hannah, I've often told you that one of the worst sins the Torah names is the sin of repeating mean tales and gossip about people. Even if the things you said abut Sarah were true, it would be a terrible sin to repeat them. But you and your friends made up a bunch of jealous lies! Would you like such things said about your-self? What impression would a stranger get of poor in-nocent Sarah if he heard your cruel words?"

"Oh, daddy, we didn't realize what we were doing. I promise I'll never speak evil things about anyone again. Even if it's true, I'll seal my lips!"

"Good for you, Hannah. Don't you think Sarah feels lonesome in this new neighborhood? Forget what hap-pened, and try to be friends."

"As soon as I finish my homework, I'm going to visit Sarah," promised Hannah as she skipped into the house.

SGT. MARTY TAUB DISGUISED AS AN SS PARATROOPER ON A DANGEROUS MISSION, BEHIND THE JERRY LINES AT HEILBRONN, LOCATES THE HOME OF AN ERSTWHILE NURSE, ANNE, WHO HAD ONCE BEEN VERY DEVOTED TO HIS FAMILY. BUT NOW, WHO KNOWS...

Fln. Anne Bauerle

KNOCK! KNOCK!

FRAULEIN ANNE BAUERLE?

YAH! VON'T YOU COME IN, PLEASE.

MARTY, AS PART OF THE ACT, DOESN'T FORGET TO HEIL!

Barry

DIS MEDALLION, I TOOK IT FROM AN AMERIKANER SPY BEFORE EXECUTING HIM. HE ASKED ME TO DELIVER IT TO YOU, MIT HIS LOVE

(SOB) MY POOR BABY - (SOB)- MARTIN!!

BUT HE WAS A VER DAMTER JUDE

YOU MURDERER!

THIS PROVES TO MARTY THAT ANNE ISN'T A NAZI

OH, ANNE! DON'T YOU RECOGNIZE ME?

(To be continued)

שעורי למוד הדת

SHALOH

Published & Copyright 1945 by
MERKOS L'INYONEI CHINUCH, INC.
770 EASTERN PARKWAY
Brooklyn 13, N. Y.
PResident 4-0507 - 1866

No. 13

LAG B'OMER

"Don't turn the radio off, Pa, I want to hear the weather report."

"You've been rather interested in the weather lately, Dinah," father said, looking puzzled.

"If the weather is nice next Thursday, we will have an outing. I do hope the weather *is* nice."

"Of course, it's Lag B'Omer," father said. "I almost forgot."

"Yes, and Mommy promised to prepare some hard-boiled eggs for my Lag B'Omer lunch — *colored*."

" . . . *Further outlook unsettled*," the weather-man concluded his report.

« 1 »

"Oh, I do hope the weather will turn out nice for Lag B'Omer!" Dinah exclaimed.

Dinah's brother Sammy was too intent upon his work to join in the conversation. He was carving out a wooden sword for himself, and arrows for his bow. Dinah went up to him and watched him closely for a while.

Finally, Sammy was finished, and with a bright look in his eyes he asked father:

"Dad, may I borrow your air-warden's helmet for our outing on Lag B'Omer?"

"Yes you may, if you don't get lost in it. But you have to tell me first why you are arming yourself to the teeth and whom are you going to make war on?"

"Oh, it's all in fun of course," Sammy explained. "Here, I will tell you the story.

"Many many years ago, there lived a great rabbi in the Land of Israel whose name was Rabbi Akiba. He had 24 thousand students. They used to gather in the fields, spending half the time in study, and the rest of the time in training for war. They wanted to fight the cruel King Hadrian of Rome who closed down all the Hebrew Schools and Yeshivoth in the Land of Israel, and forbade Jewish children to study the Torah on penalty of death. And so, to remember the great Rabbi and his students, we celebrate Lag B'Omer in mock battle-dress in the fields. We don't really fight, but we play games and teacher tells us stories about those days."

"Makes me want to be a little boy again," said father. Then, turning to Dinah, he said, "Now it is your turn to tell us, why do you want to take colored eggs with you for your Lag B'Omer lunch?"

"Well, Sammy didn't tell you the whole story of Lag B'Omer. There lived another great rabbi during those days when the wicked Romans were the real masters of our Holy Land. His name was Rabbi Simeon ben Yohai, and he was very brave, too. He defied the Romans until they put a price on his head. Then he fled and hid in a cave together with his son Eliezer, and for many years they lived in the cave studying the Holy Torah. . . ."

"But what did they eat?" father interrupted.

"It was a miracle that saved them. For G-d made a carob tree grow near the cave, on which the most delicious carobs grew. G-d also made a well spring forth near the cave to give them fresh water."

Then Dinah, becoming a little sad, continued:

"This rabbi died on Lag B'Omer; and it is an old Jewish custom to eat eggs when mourning the death of a dear person."

"But why *colored* eggs?"

"I never thought of that," Dinah confessed. "Do you know why, Dad?"

"Well, Lag B'Omer is really a happy day. For as you know, the students of Rabbi Akiba of whom Sammy has told us, had been dying of a plague for many days, because they had quarreled among themselves. But on Lag B'Omer the plague ceased, and the rest of the students were spared. That's why Lag B'Omer is a holiday for all school children, a happy day. Now, the death of the holy Rabbi Simeon ben Yohai on that day does not make it any sadder, for he was very happy when the time came to surrender his soul to the Creator, because he knew that everlasting happiness awaited him. And so, while the Lag B'Omer eggs are to remind us of his death, their purpose is not to make us feel sad on this day. Lag B'Omer is a children's festival, and children love color. And so it became customary to paint the shells of the eggs in various colors to make the children feel very happy on Lag B'Omer."

"Thank you Dad!" both Dinah and Sammy exclaimed, as they bade their father "Good night," and retired with happy dreams about the forthcoming happy outing on the day of Lag B'Omer.

 ### THE STORY OF ABRAHAM

THE VICTORS VANQUISHED
(Continued)

Thereupon, G-d made a covenant with Abram and changed his name to "Abraham," which stands for "The father of many peoples." According to this covenant,

Abraham's children that would make up the Jewish nation must remain loyal to the idea of One G-d, which Abraham proclaimed to the whole world. For this they would be blessed by G-d, would multiply and become a princely nation among the nations of the world.

G-d also changed Sarai's name to "Sarah," "the princess," assuring Abraham that his wife Sarah would be the mother of that great nation.

HOSPITALITY TO WAYFARERS

Abraham built inns and hostels on all the main roads so that wayfarers should find food, water, and rest on their way. He charged no fees, and all were welcome. Many a weary and hungry wayfarer found food and shelter in these inns. "How can we thank you, Abraham, for your kindness and hospitality?", they said before leaving.

"Thank the Lord, the Creator of all these good things," Abraham would reply.

In Beer-sheba, where Abraham and Sarah lived, they built a very big house, with entrances on all the four winds. So anxious were they to show their hospitality that no matter from what direction the visitor came, he would always find an open door.

(To be continued)

« 5 »

"THEY'RE ALL G-D'S CREATURES"

A small group of boys stood on the corner. "Come on," one of them said, "let's find something to do. What are we standing around here for?"

"We could help Mr. Stein clean the snow off his walk," Leon suggested. "He's pretty old to be doing it himself."

"Oh, you and your crazy ideas," said Al, the 'tough guy' of the bunch. Just then the horse-and-wagon of the Silver Star Laundry stopped across the street. "I got an idea," Al said suddenly, and ran over to an empty lot nearby and gathered up two handfuls of stones. He returned and began handing them out. "Let's see whose aim is best. We all throw at the horse and see who can get three bullseyes out of four"

"But you're not allowed to do that," Leon protested. "Don't you remember what our rabbi told us about being cruel to animals? 'Do not harm animals, he told us, 'because they're all G-d's creatures. He made every one of them; therefore, we are not allowed to hurt them.' That's just what he said. I remember the exact Hebrew words: *Tzaar Baalei Chaim*."

"If you think that I'm going to worry about the rabbi you've got another guess coming," Al told him. "Come on fellows," he shouted, "one, two, three!" and he threw a stone at the horse. When he saw that no stone followed his, he turned around surprised. Then he saw that all the other boys had followed Leon's advice, and not one of them would join him in his cruel sport. "Ah, you're all cowards," he said to them angrily, and he walked away in disgust.

Winter passed and spring came 'round, and the boys went to the park. All day, despite his friends' protests, Al went around catching all kinds of insects, torturing those he caught and chasing and frightening those he could not catch. Even the pretty-colored butterflies, which everybody else admires, he did not spare. The other boys became so angry that they wanted to punish him, but Leon quieted them down. "Don't worry," he told them, "G-d will see to it that those who are unkind to the animals He created will get what they deserve."

Soon after, Al caught something, and proudly showed it to the boys. When they saw it they all ran, and a second later Al screamed with pain. In his eagerness to catch insects he had clasped a bee in his hand, and it gave him a painful sting. At first he would not listen to Leon's explanation that it was a punishment for his misdeeds, but later he realized that his friend was right.

From that time on, Wilbur, the Silver Star Laundry's horse, was able to go about his business without being molested.

PLEASED WITH HIS DISCOVERY ABOUT HIS CHILDHOOD NURSE, ANNE, RE-MAINING LOYAL TO HIS FAMILY AND NOT ADOPTING THE NAZI DOCTRINES, SGT. MARTY TAUB DECIDES TO STAY AT HER HOME FOR THE DAY.

Meanwhile MARTY IS RESTING ON THE COUCH DREAMING OF HIS PARENTS

AT THE SAME TIME A MAN IS STEAL-THILY APPROACHING ANNE'S HOUSE.

(To be continued)

« 8 »

Published & Copyright 1945 by
MERKOS L'INYONEI CHINUCH, INC.
770 EASTERN PARKWAY
Brooklyn 13, N. Y.
PResident 4-0507 - 1866

No. **14**

SHOVUOS

The seven weeks after Pesach passed very slowly for Danny, but finally Shovuos, the holiday that he so eagerly awaited, arrived. Every year he looked forward to its coming with growing anticipation, because every year he had a greater understanding of the significance of the holiday. Shovuos was the day on which G-d had shrouded Mount Sinai with clouds and fire, and there, after thundering and lightning and amid trembling of the earth, G-d's Glory descended upon the mountain and His voice was heard proclaiming the Ten Commandments. Danny knew that the day the Torah was given to our people on Mt. Sinai was the most important day of all.

In the morning of the first day of Shovuos, when he went to the synagogue, Danny heard the Ten Commandments read from the Scroll of the Torah. By now he knew the meaning of the words and his little heart throbbed with awe and excitement as he followed each word pronounced so clearly and slowly by the reader.

"I am the Lord thy G-d. . . ."

"Thou shalt have no other G-ds. . . ."

Before the Commandments were given man had worshipped the sun, the moon, animals, and other living or non-living forms. But at Mt. Sinai, the truth was revealed by G-d Himself, that there is only One G-d, The Almighty Creator of the world. To Him alone we owe our lives, to Him alone we must pray and Him alone we must worship.

"Remember the Sabbath day to keep it holy. . . . "

This fourth of the Divine Commandments was full of meaning to Danny. The Jewish nation was a Holy Nation and it was given a holy day of rest. On this day the Jew ceases his everyday pursuits and devotes himself to activities that raise him spiritually. If the other days of the week are spent in pursuit of the welfare of the body, the Sabbath is spent in pursuit of the welfare of the soul.

"Honor thy father and thy mother. . . ."

"Thou shalt not kill. . . ."

"Thou shalt not covet. . . ."

Danny knew that all the Commandments were connected together and formed one whole. One thing leads to another. There are, unfortunately, many people who do not recognize the first of the Ten Commandments. They do not worship G-d alone; some worship money, some worship power, some worship a dictator. Many people, sad to say, think only of the body and forget the soul. Those who start on such a path go down and down until they sink to a depth where they don't even respect their own father and mother. It is but one step further to rob and kill.

Danny felt very proud that he was a member of the Holy Nation which had accepted not merely the Ten Commandments but all the 613 Commandments of the Torah. Danny was determined to live up to them.

THE STORY OF ABRAHAM

HOSPITALITY TO WAYFARERS
(*Continued*)

Around his house Abraham planted a wonderful garden and an orchard in which grew the most delicious fruits and berries. Most wonderful of all, however, was a magnificent palm tree which seemed to know every wayfarer that came near it. If an honest and G-d-fearing man would sit down under its shade, the tree would spread forth its branches to shield the visitor from the sun or wind. But if the visitor happened to be an idolator, or dishonest man, the palm tree would lift up its branches disdainfully, and offer no protection. In this way Abraham knew at a glance what sort of visitor he had. Whenever he saw the tree act disdainfully toward the visitor, Abraham would come up to the man and show him especial kindness and attention. He would tell the visitor about the greatness and unity of G-d, and how silly it was to worship idols that were nothing but wood and stone, and the work of man. Abraham would thus open the eyes of the visitor to see the true light, and then the palm tree would spread forth its branches and give shelter to the man — and everybody was happy.

Sarah was also very generous and hospitable. She would take care of the women visitors in the same way as Abraham took care of the men folk. Sarah was even busier than Abraham. She would sit up late at night, making dresses and things for the poor and needy. When everybody was fast asleep, there was still a candle burning in Sarah's tent, where she was sitting and doing some needle work. So G-d sent a special Cloud of Light to surround her tent and illuminate it throughout the night. For miles and miles around the illuminated tent of Sarah was seen, and everybody said: "There dwells a woman of worth!"

Abraham and Sarah grew very famous. From near and far men and women made their way to Beer-Sheba to seek help, advice, and comfort from that wonderful couple. Weary and sorrowful they came, and happy and cheerful they left, laden with gifts and presents. The men and women wanted to thank Abraham and Sarah, but they were told to thank G-d. "But where is this G-d?" the astonished visitors would ask.

"His Glory fills the heaven and earth," came the reply.

Away went the visitors blessing the G-d of Abraham and Sarah.

ABRAHAM'S UNUSUAL GUESTS

It was a very hot day in the spring, unusually hot for that time of the year. Man and beast sought the shade of trees, barely able to breathe in the hot air. Abraham stood in the entrance of his tent, vainly scanning the horizon for a stray wanderer for whom cool, refreshing water, and a comfortable meal, were always ready in his tent. Abraham was feeling weary and faint, for it was the third day after he had circumcised himself according to the command of the Lord. Nevertheless he remained in front of his tent from where he could overlook all the ways leading to and fro. But the heat had chased all wanderers off the roads and Abraham was beginning to despair of finding a guest to share the dinner with him that day. He felt very sad.

Suddenly Abraham saw three men standing in the distance.

(To be continued)

« 5 »

FRIENDS

This is the sad story of Aby. It is not an unusual story, but that doesn't make it any less tragic. What happened to Aby could happen to anybody, and that is why it is so important. It is the story of a boy who could have become an outstanding scholar, a great "light" in Israel, but missed his chance. This is the story of a boy who could have enjoyed the respect and love of everybody but, instead, lost the respect of even his best friends. It is the sad story of a boy whose future was ruined by bad friends.

Aby had been a very good boy. He used to go to Hebrew School regularly, and studied diligently. He said his prayers every day and made the proper blessing whenever necessary. His family was very proud of him. People often went over to his mother or father and said, "What a wonderful child you have. Some day he will be a great man, I am sure." And indeed, it seemed that way.

Aby's teachers very often praised him for his remarkable ability and for his qualities of character. They were certain that Aby would be a great scholar one day. They had but one regret, Aby was so busy studying that he didn't have time to make friends. Both his teachers and parents told him that it was very important to have companions. At the same time they warned him to be careful about what kind of friends he chose. Aby listened to their advice, but he only took the first part of it.

So anxious was Aby to make friends, that he accepted the first ones he could find. This was very unfortunate, as they happened to be the worst boys in the class. But Aby, having always tried to be good, could not imagine that anybody else could be wicked.

It did not take long for the influence of the bad company to make itself felt upon our Aby.

Being a loyal friend, Aby called for his companions on his way to Hebrew School. But they were never ready on time nor in a great hurry, and Aby, too, began to come late. Then when he was playing a game with them and it was time to stop and do his work, Aby could not leave his friends until they were finished also. And so it was with everything else. Slowly but surely, Aby changed.

The change began to show in Aby's school record, and in his general behavior at home and at school. His parents and teachers became worried. Aby came under cross-fire from both. He was very unhappy and promised to reform. Once again he began to work hard for the scholarship of which he had thought so much at one time but had neglected of late. Unfortunately, Aby had lost too much ground and could not quite regain it. The scholarship went to a better boy.

WHILE ANNE IS OUT SHOPPING AND MARTY IS TAKING A WELL EARNED NAP A MAN SNEAKS IN THROUGH A WINDOW AND SEEING THE DISGUISED AMERICAN AND BELIEVING HIM TO BE A NAZI, DECIDES TO DO AWAY WITH HIM AND TAKE THE UNIFORM..

HOWEVER - HE DISCOVERS THE "NAZI" TO BE HIS VERY OWN BROTHER!

MARTY

"WAKE UP!!! MARTY!!!

MY G-D'! I ALMOST KILLED HIM!!

BENNY!! IT'S YOU

THAT'S A PRETTY SLICK GUN! - TELL ME, WHAT HAPPENED TO YOU! YOU WERE REPORTED KILLED WHEN YOUR PLANE WAS SHOT DOWN

WELL, I BAILED OUT AND LANDED SAFELY UNSEEN. NOW, I WORK WITH THE UNDERGROUND

JUST THEN 3 NAZIS BURST INTO THE ROOM

DON'T MOVE!

(To be continued)

« 8 »

Published & Copyright 1945 by
MERKOS L'INYONEI CHINUCH, INC.
770 EASTERN PARKWAY
Brooklyn 13, N. Y.
PResident 4-0507 - 1866

No. 15

WHO IS RICH ?

The teacher was reading from the "Ethics of the Fathers" that was resting on his desk. All the children were deeply interested in the sayings of the wise Sages who were the leaders of the Jewish people about two thousand years ago. Of the several selections that the teacher had read and explained to them that day, the one that impressed them most was that which said: "Who can be called rich? He who is content with his lot."

The teacher explained the meaning of the words. "What we are to learn from this," he said, "is that it pays to be satisfied with what we have, instead of always wanting more. Not only is one happier if he follows this principle, but also if one is always looking for more, he may even lose that which he already has."

Out in the street Esther and her brother Morris were discussing what they had learned that day. "What do you think of the quotation our teacher gave us today from the 'Ethics of the Fathers'?" she asked him.

"I don't know," he answered her. "But I think that if I had the chance to get more than I already had I would try to get it anyways."

"But you heard what he said. Sometimes you even lose what you have in the first place."

"I'd take the chance," he said, and they did not talk about it any longer.

It was a sunny day and Esther suggested they make a little detour and go home through the park. Passing the lake they stopped for a moment to gaze at their reflection in the water. Presently, a little poodle carrying a bone in his mouth waddled up to the water's edge. Seeing in the water another little dog with a bone in his mouth, the poodle began to snarl and then with a loud bark jumped into the water to try and wrench the bone from the other dog. Still barking fiercely the little poodle searched for the other dog in the water for a few minutes, and then thought better of it, and finally climbed out of the lake, drenched to the skin. With his tail down, the greedy little dog walked sadly home, for instead of getting the other imaginary bone, he lost the real bone which he had had, and got a wet ducking in addition.

The children laughed heartily. Suddenly Morris became very serious.

"You know, Esther, I think teacher was right after all."

Esther chuckled.

 ## THE STORY OF ABRAHAM

ABRAHAM'S UNUSUAL GUESTS

(*Continued*)

His sorrow vanished. Abraham cheerfully ran down the road to welcome the strangers. Greeting them very courteously and heartily, Abraham begged the men to turn into his tent where he would offer them a little water, and a little bread to refresh themselves before continuing on their way.

Near Abraham's tent there grew a big palm tree with many branches, thickly covered with leaves. Under this the visitors agreed to rest, while their host busied himself with preparing the refreshments for them.

Abraham's servants knew their master. They always hurried to prepare a meal whenever he had guests. But today they just could not be fast enough for their master. He was so excited about his unexpected visitors as if the king himself had honored the tent with his visit. The most tender meat, the finest oil and flour, everything of the best had to come on the table. And Sarah who, just as eagerly as Abraham, had been looking forward to having guests for dinner, was in the kitchen kneading the dough, with her own hands, for delicious cakes.

Abraham was personally waiting on his guests. He was not interested who they were, but he wanted to make sure they were comfortable and had enough to eat and drink. Presently the older one addressed him:

"I bring you a message from G-d," he said. "Next year on this day, at exactly this hour, your wife Sarah will give birth to a son."

Both Abraham and Sarah heard the good tidings and were very happy about it. Though Abraham was 99 years old, and his wife Sarah only ten years younger, they suddenly felt their youth come back to them and rejoiced at the news of having a child of their own.

Then the second stranger spoke: "I have been sent to destroy the wicked city of Sodom."

And the third one said: "I have been sent to rescue your nephew Lot dwelling in Sodom."

It then dawned upon Abraham that the three visitors were angels of the Lord.

The next moment they disappeared.

(To be continued)

PLENTY OF TIME

Excited whispers ran through the classroom of the Hebrew School. The teacher had just made an important announcement. He told the class that, since they had been doing such good work, he had invited the principal to come the next day to see how well they knew what they had learned. He wanted every student to study very hard so that the principal would be impressed by their excellence. The class promised that they would do as he asked.

Once outside the classroom, the boys gathered in little groups to discuss plans for studying that day. Several of them went over to Joseph, the best student in the class. "When are you going to study?" they asked him.

Joseph, overconfident of his abilities, said, "Oh, I don't know. I'm not going to worry about it too much now. I'll have plenty of time tonight."

"But we will be examined on the entire term's work," they told him. "If you don't study you'll never know it."

"Stop worrying about me," he answered, disturbed by their talk. "I told you I have plenty of time."

The boys saw that it was useless to argue with him any further, and left him. When they had gone Joseph realized that he really should study, but, he thought with a shrug of his shoulders, there was no rush. He would be able to play ball during the afternoon and study later in the day.

When Joseph came home that evening he was very tired. He had been playing all through the afternoon, and now he was beginning to feel the effects. But he did not let that stop him. He hurriedly finished his meal and sat down to study. Fifteen minutes later he heard his mother calling to him; she wanted him to go on an errand.

"But mother," he complained "I'm studying."

"If you really had to study," his mother answered him, "you could have done it all afternoon. Now no more excuses."

Joseph was ashamed to admit that he had wasted the entire afternoon playing in the park, and he did as his mother told him. He returned fifteen minutes later, only to find that the house was in complete darkness: a fuse had burned out. By the time a new one was installed half the evening had passed. With even greater vigor than before he returned to his studying, but slowly his eyelids began to close. The afternoon's activity had wearied him considerably. Although he kept fighting it off, sleep finally overtook him. He had only covered one-fourth of the term's work.

The next day the principal came to examine the class. Everybody except Joseph, whom the teacher had pointed out as his "prize pupil," was able to answer the questions. Even the things that he had studied were all muddled up in his head, and it was no wonder that the principal said, after the examination was over, "Except for one, you have a wonderful class. I am sure that if this student took the time to study he would be as good as the rest of the class."

Formerly the best student in the class, Joseph now suffered bitter disgrace. Never again would he put off studying because he had "plenty of time."

This is **SHALOH No. 15!** If you are missing any of the revious numbers write to the **MERKOS L'INYONEI CHINUCH, Inc.** (See page 1).

Tell your friends about the **SHALOH.**

Each **SHALOH** has **four** features marked by a Menorah, Torah, Stag, and, last but not least, the comic strip adventure.

THE UNEXPECTED BUT VERY HAPPY REUNION OF THE TAUB BROTHERS, MARTY WHO IS DISGUISED AS A NAZI SOLDIER, AND BEN WHO IS WITH THE UNDERGROUND, IS SHATTERED BY THE GESTAPO WHO TRAILED BEN TO ANNE'S COTTAGE..

MARTY THINKS FAST. DAT'S ALRIGHT, MEN. DIS DANGEROUS MAN IS MY PRISONER. I HAFF, TO CLEAR UP A FEW THINGS UND DEN I'LL BRING HIM TO HEADQUARTERS! MEANWHILE, GUARD DIS HOUSE UNTIL I WILL RELIEVE YOU!

JUST THEN ANNE RETURNS.. AH, I'VE BEEN VAITING FOR YOU, FRAULIEN! YOU'RE UNDER ARREST.

THEY SNEAK OUT SECRETLY ... WE MUST WORK FAST. ANNE! TAKE US TO MY PARENTS

WE FIND THE TAUB'S IN ANOTHER PART OF TOWN, IN HIDING! HERE IT IS THE FIRST NIGHT OF PASSOVER, FESTIVAL OF LIBERATION, AND WE HAVE NO MATZOTH, WINE, NOR FREEDOM!

At that very moment, THE GESTAPO! ANNE, YOU HAVE BETRAYED US!!

(To be continued)

שעורי למור הדת

SHALOH

Published & Copyright 1945 by
MERKOS L'INYONEI CHINUCH, INC.
770 EASTERN PARKWAY
Brooklyn 13, N. Y.
PResident 4-0507 - 1866

No. 16

THE HOLY SHABBOS

"Sorry, boys. I'll have to leave you now."

David had been playing with his friends all **day,** but now the sun had begun to set and he had to leave.

"Oh, don't go yet," Solomon said to him. "**You** have plenty of time. Stay around and we'll think **up** another game."

"I really can't," David replied. "You see, Shabbos will soon be here, and I have to get washed and dressed in order to go to the synagogue."

"Oh, all right," Solomon told him with disgust. "If you think that going to the synagogue on Shabbos

is more exciting than playing ball I won't stop you."
David felt hurt by these words, but nevertheless he left.

After David went away Solomon suddenly got a
bright idea. He gathered all his friends around him and,
in a low, sneering voice that gave away his evil intentions,
he told them his plans for that night. Some of them
wanted to disagree, but they were all afraid of the
husky Solomon and finally agreed to help him.

That night, after all the men had come home from
the synagogue, Solomon and his friends paid a visit
to David's house. They walked to the back of the house
and stopped under the window of the room where David
and his family were eating their Friday night meal.
Whispering to his friends to be absolutely quiet, Solomon
climbed up to the window. He thought that it would
be a big joke if he would knock on the window and
run away, disturbing the peaceful Shabbos meal.

Just as Solomon raised his hand to strike at the
window he stopped, as though paralyzed. The snowy
white tablecloth, the burning candles, the sparkling cups,
and the glittering silverware caught his eyes and held
them, and he could hardly tear himself away. He was
overcome with awe by the holiness that filled the room,
and now, for the first time, he understood why Shabbos
meant so much to David. Yes, this was much better
than just playing games in the street. He was now even
a little jealous of David. Without waiting another

second, he climbed down from the window and walked away slowly, followed by his puzzled friends.

The next morning, when David went to the synagogue bright and early, there, filling up a whole row, were Solomon and all his friends. They had come to the synagogue that Shabbos for the first time

 THE STORY OF ABRAHAM

(Continued)

THE FLOURISHING VALLEY THAT BECAME THE "DEAD SEA"

Everybody has heard about the "Dead Sea" in the land of Israel. It is called so because it is so thick with salt that there is not a living fish in it, and no life for miles around it. But many years ago, in the days of Abraham and Lot, there was a flourishing valley on that site. It was the most fertile place in the land of Israel and many people lived there. Five large cities dotted the valley: Sodom, Gomorrah, Admah, Zebaim, and Zoar, and many caravan roads led to them from all parts of the world. Many people came to gaze at the wonders of that valley where, as it was rumored, treasures of gold and precious stones lay buried under the roots of every tree and plant.

The people who lived in this valley were rich. They became fearful of the many strangers that flocked there like bees attracted to a jar of honey. So the people of Sodom got together to think of a way to stop the flow of unwelcome visitors and strangers. "Let us treat our visitors and guests in such a way that they should never want to come to us again," the Sodomites decided. Soon it became known everywhere that any stranger setting foot in Sodom did so at the peril of his life.

When an unwary wanderer came to Sodom he could get no food or water even if he wanted to pay for it. In addition to this there were torture chambers in Sodom for the unwanted strangers. One of the favorite sports of the Sodomites was to place the stranger in a bed which was either too short or too long for him. If the stranger was too short for the bed he would be "streched" out. If he was too long for the bed, they would "shorten" him by a head. He died, of course, in either case.

Perhaps the most peculiar law of the Sodomites was the one about paying for an injury. The injured party was, of course, the one that had to pay. The "reason" was as follows: Whereas many people suffered from high blood pressure, and it was a common practice to treat patients by letting some blood to relieve the pressure, now therefore, when anyone injured another person, causing him some loss of blood, the injured party had to pay the assailant a doctor's fee!

Such and similar laws and customs gave Sodom a hideous reputation, and strangers began to shun that fertile valley which turned into a death trap.

It was in Sodom that Lot, Abraham's nephew, decided to settle after he departed from his uncle. It was very foolish of Lot to live among such wicked people, but Lot wanted to be rich and he did not care about anything else.

(To be continued)

 ## JUST A PENNY A DAY

Hymie and Benny lived next door to each other. Every morning they went together to the synagogue to pray, and when they were finished they both walked towards the door. The only difference was that during the week, whenever Benny passed the charity box on the table in the middle of the synagogue, he would drop a penny into the box. Hymie, however, simply looked straight ahead and walked right past. He would wait for Benny at the door, and they would go home together.

"Benny," asked Hymie once, "why do you put your money in there? You don't even know who gets it, and even if you did how much good could it do? Just a penny a day!"

Benny would smile, and answer him: "But that is the way true charity should be given. Why should it make any difference who gets it as long as it is for a good cause? And don't think that my pennies are nothing. I have been giving a penny a day for almost a year now, and that is about three dollars. It may not sound like a lot to live on, but it sure means a lot to a person who needs it." But Hymie still couldn't see Benny's point, and he continued to ignore the charity box as before.

That night, Hymie had a strange dream. He saw himself in the Museum of Natural History with Benny at his side. They were gazing with fascination at the armor-clad figures in the museum, when suddenly an armored knight began to shift. Hymie became horrified as the figure slowly came to life. Looking very fiercely at Hymie, the knight began to draw his sword. Hymie wanted to run but he was paralyzed with fear and seemed nailed to his place. Hymie looked up appealingly to his friend, but Benny merely smiled and didn't seem frightened at all. The knight turned his gaze upon Benny and as though infuriated by his smile, he thrust his sword at Benny with all his might. To his amazement Hymie noticed that the sword bounced back without hurting Benny at all. He looked at his friend and suddenly noticed that Benny was clad in a coat of mail, consisting of many copper coins. He looked closely and saw that they were pennies! Benny was covered with lots of pennies hundreds of pennies, which sparkled brightly as though they had just come from the mint.

Then Hymie looked at himself and saw that he was quite defenseless. Here and there a few pennies were hanging on his coat, but he knew they could not give him much protection.

The fierce knight now turned his attention to Hymie. He raised his sword and was about to thrust it at him. Gathering all his strength Hymie shouted, *"Shema Yisroel,"* and then awoke with a start.

*   *   *

The following morning Hymie called for his friend to go to *Shul* as usual. This time passing the charity box Hymie, too, dropped a penny into the box. Benny was pleasantly surprised to see this, but he did not say anything. On the way home, Hymie related to his friend the dream he had had the previous night.

"Don't you remember?" said Benny excitedly. "The Rabbi once quoted from the Bible that charity is like a coat of mail. Each penny one gives for charity adds another 'scale' for protection. The beauty of giving charity continually is that it becomes a very fine habit, a second nature. To give is a very nice feeling, isn't it?"

Published & Copyright 1945 by
MERKOS L'INYONEI CHINUCH, INC.
770 EASTERN PARKWAY
Brooklyn 13, N. Y.
PResident 4-0507 - 1866

No. 17

THE DAY OF ATONEMENT

It was the eve of Yom Kippur—the Day of Atonement. Soon it would be time for *Kol-Nidrei,* the early evening prayer. At the synagogue on Bentley Street many people were passing through the wide open doors. They all carried *Machzorim* which contained the prayers of Yom Kippur. After they had entered, they walked down the aisles softly and with solemn expressions on their faces. A deep hush had fallen like a heavy curtain over the entire synagogue. The Day of Judgment would soon be here.

The boys and girls were also more serious on this day. They had been told in Hebrew School of the im-

« 1 »

portance of this great day, and they felt that it was not the time for amusements. They had come to the synagogue with their parents, and they were all perfectly quiet. The only one who did not act any differently was Sammy Blum.

"Why should I feel any different?" Sammy went around saying to all his friends. "I didn't do anything wrong this year. In fact, I was even better this year than last."

No one bothered to answer him because they all knew that Sammy would never admit that he was wrong anyway. The only one who spoke to him was one of the men in the synagogue who had overheard Sammy talking to his friends.

"Don't be so sure of yourself, son," the man said to Sammy. "Just think back a little. I'm pretty sure that you will find that you did something wrong. Isn't there something for which you feel that you ought to ask forgiveness?"

The man had said this in a very gentle voice, but still it made Sammy feel very uncomfortable. He walked away angrily. Why did people bother him? He hadn't done anything wrong as far as he could remember. Then he remembered what his teacher had said in Hebrew School. It did not matter if he forgot, because in Heaven there was a large book in which the good and bad deeds of every person were recorded. There was a page in that book for Sammy, too.

When he came to think of it, Sammy decided he

could not have been so perfect after all. He had told himself that he had forgotten all about it, and thought that that would be the end of it. But now he realized that even if he had forgotten, there would still be a record. He even began to think of what might be on that record. It would probably have every bad name that he had called his friend Joe in an argument the other week. And it would surely have a record of the time when he came home late one night and in his hurry he had eaten without saying a *berachah*. The man had been right after all. Sammy did have something for which to ask forgiveness on this day of Yom Kippur.

 ### THE STORY OF ABRAHAM

THE FLOURISHING VALLEY THAT BECAME THE "DEAD SEA"
(Continued)

Abraham was very worried about his nephew. He had brought him up to be kind and hospitable to all, friends and strangers alike. Abraham was afraid that his nephew might become cruel and hard like all other Sodomites.

One day Abraham sent his trusted servant Eliezer to visit Lot in Sodom.

The first sight that greeted Eliezer on arrival in Sodom was a Sodomite ill-treating a visitor who had just wandered into the city. Eliezer took up the cause of the poor stranger, whereupon the Sodomite grabbed a stone and flung it in Eliezer's face, which immediately became covered with blood. Seeing this, the Sodomite rejoiced. "Now pay me a doctor's fee!" he exclaimed.

"What wicked law is this?" cried Eliezer in amazement. "First you injure your visitor then you ask to be paid for it?"

"Live and learn!" cried the Sodomite. "If you don't pay me I will take you to the judge."

"To the judge I will gladly go," said Eliezer, hoping to get some justice in the court of law. He took the stone which the Sodomite had flung in his face as "exhibit one."

The judge listened to the case and passed judgment in favor of the Sodomite. "Such is the law of the land," he said, "and if you don't like it, nobody sent for you!"

"Is that so? Well here's where you get a taste of your own law!" Eliezer said, throwing the stone in the judge's face, and making his nose bleed profusely. "Now, your honor, you can pay my fee to the Sodomite," saying this, Eliezer strutted out.

*　　*　　*

Eliezer had quite a hard job trying to find Lot's house, for nobody was willing to help him. The people he accosted only jeered at the stranger who did not know that in Sodom people did not help unwelcome visitors.

Eliezer became weary. Nobody wanted to sell him any food or let him rest in the shade of a tree. Eliezer became very hungry and thirsty, too. Suddenly he heard music coming from a big house. Eliezer entered and found a party in progress. The people were sitting around a table which was richly covered with delicacies and refreshments. Eliezer sat down by the corner of the table and was about to help himself to some of the refreshments, when he was rudely asked, "Whoever invited you here?"

"The fellow sitting next to me is my friend," Eliezer replied. Thereupon the host and the guests set upon Eliezer's neighbor, beat him up and threw him out, for they thought he had invited the stranger.

Eliezer moved up to the next fellow and began to chat with him in a very friendly manner. He patted him on his back and said, "Thank you for your invitation." The startled guest took to his heels.

Once again Eliezer moved up and addressed himself to the next one in a like manner. This fellow, too, became frightened and fled for his life. Before long, Eliezer had the whole table to himself. He ate and drank to his heart's content and praised G-d who had not forsaken him.

(To be continued)

This is SHALOH No. 17. Have you the previous sixteen numbers? If not, write to:

MERKOS L'INYONEI CHINUCH
770 Eastern Parkway, Brooklyn 13, N. Y.

PRAYER

"Daddy, what are all these men doing?" Bennie asked.

"They are praying, my son, praying," his father answered.

Bennie looked about him in wonder. "Daddy, why do they pray?" he asked again.

This was by no means the first time that Bennie had come to the synagogue with his father. Every Sabbath and Yom-Tov (festival) he would accompany his father to Shul. There he would sit silently and watch the men wrapped in their prayer shawls as they swayed to and fro. He watched with fascination the holy Ark being opened and scrolls being taken out, from which the Reader read some words which little Bennie did not understand. Little Bennie knew that it was a holy place, where boys must be on their best behavior.

He had never before thought of asking questions about the meaning of what he saw. But as he grew older his curiosity grew, and now he had finally asked his father about it. He hoped he would hear something strange and wonderful.

"Do tell me, Daddy," Bennie urged, "why do they pray?"

The father looked at his boy with pride. He was so happy that he should be interested to know the answer to such an important question.

"My son," he began, "we pray for so many reasons. Some of our prayers are prayers of thanks to G-d. We thank Him for all the good things He has given us; our good health, nice peaceful home, good food, nice clothes, and so on. We also pray that G-d continue to grant us health and happiness and other kind blessings.

"There are also prayers in which we praise G-d for the wonders that He performs every day. For, my son, you know that it is G-d Who makes the sun rise every morning, to give us light and warmth. He keeps alive all living creatures, and makes things such as fruits, flowers and vegetables grow. I know you like all these things, and these also help you and me to live.

"All these prayers are the important duty of every Jew, for they teach him to be kind and gentle and grateful."

Bennie listened carefully to every word that his father said to him and now he realized why Jews pray so earnestly in Shul.

DEDICATION

This issue of the SHALOH is published through the generosity of

MR. MORRIS PERELMAN

in loving memory of his dear parents

מנחם מענדיל בר' אברהם משה ז"ל

שרה בת ר' פינחם ז"ל

Published & Copyright 1945 by
MERKOS L'INYONEI CHINUCH, INC.
770 EASTERN PARKWAY
Brooklyn 13, N. Y.
PResident 4-0507 - 1866

No. **18**

TWO LOAVES

Nathan and Moshe were neighbors, and they met very often, and even played together. But they did **not** go to the same school. In fact Moshe went to a Yeshivah Parochial School, and Nathan went to the nearest Public School.

One day Moshe asked his mother's permission to invite Nathan to dinner on Sabbath afternoon, and his mother gladly agreed. That Sabbath, both boys went to *Shul* to gether and returned after *Shul* together again.

On a white cloth that covered the entire table, still stood the Sabbath candle-sticks from the night before. At the head of the table, where Moshe's father sat, were set

« 1 »

two *Challahs* (Sabbath loaves) covered with a white cloth. The wine bottle was also on the table and a silver ·cup nearby. Everything was set for "Kiddush," which followed soon after everybody was seated.

Both boys received a taste of the Kiddush-wine, and Nathan was thrilled to see that in front of him, as in front of Moshe, were set two tiny loaves.

After Moshe's father had made "Kiddush" they all went to wash their hands, and then they began their repast with hearty appetites.

"I will probably appear very ignorant to you," Nathan began, "but this is the first time I have been invited to a Sabbath dinner at a home like yours. Could you explain to me a few things about today's dinner?"

"I shall be glad to, if I only know it. But at any rate, my father could always tell us."

"Well, first of all, what is the meaning of the double loaves? And why were they covered?"

"That's easy to explain," Moshe replied. "Teacher at the Yeshivah told us. One of the first laws our forefathers learned to observe soon after their departure from Egypt, was to keep the holy Sabbath. Now, when they wandered through the desert for forty years, they were sustained by the 'manna,' as you know. This wonderful food came down from heaven every day, except on the holy Sabbath day. But on Friday a double portion came down, to last them also for Sabbath. The Sabbath loaves remind us of the double portion of the 'manna.' "

"That's wonderful. I know, of course, the story of the Exodus from Egypt. But I still do not know why the loaves were covered?"

"I'm coming to that. This is again connected with the 'manna.' You see, before the manna came down from heaven, there was a layer of dew on the ground upon which the manna rested. Then another layer of dew covered it, so that the manna was kept very fresh, as though it came 'straight out of the oven.' Thus, the Sabbath loaves resting on the white table cloth and covered by another cloth on top, remind us of the manna."

"This is very interesting," Nathan exclaimed enthusiastically. "But there must also be a good reason for wanting to remember the 'manna' on Sabbath, isn't there?"

"There certainly is. Teacher told us there is a very good reason for everything we do. The 'manna' tells us how G-d takes care of us in time of need; that we must always have faith in G-d that He will sustain us. But more than that. The 'manna' tells us that G-d provides for the holy Sabbath day, when no work is permitted to be done. There is no need to go to business or do any work on th holy Sabbath day, for he who works on the holy Sabbath day shows that he has no faith in G-d. Surely, G-d can provide in six days enough for the whole week! Jews do not have to work on Sabbath; they can have a full free day for such things as going to Shul, studying the Torah, and otherwise having a complete change from the rest of the weekdays."

"Did you learn all that at the Yeshivah?" asked

Nathan in amazement, and with much greater respect for his young friend than before.

"Where else can you learn about these things? Why don't you join the Yeshivah too?"

"It is a good idea. I have been thinking about it for a long time, but couldn't make up my mind. But now, I'm definitely going to ask my parents to enroll me in the Yeshivah." Before leaving, Nathan shook his friend's hand very warmly.

"This has been a very good Sabbath day for me," he said, to the great delight of Moshe.

 THE STORY OF ABRAHAM

THE FLOURISHING VALLEY THAT BECAME THE "DEAD SEA"

(*Continued*)

Eliezer continued his search for Lot, finally found his house, and entered. Lot was very happy to see Eliezer. He always respected the honest and devoted manager of his uncle Abraham, and now greeted him very warmly. Eliezer was glad to note that Lot was still as hospitable and kind as he used to be in Abraham's house. His master would certainly be happy to hear of that.

Lot's married daughters gathered to honor the visitor,

for they too had inherited something of their father's hospitality and friendliness, but their husbands, who were Sodomites, stayed away.

Eliezer noticed that Lot's youngest and kindest daughter was missing.

"Where is Plitith?" Eliezer inquired.

Lot's face became very sad. "I am sorry to say that she is no longer among the living."

"What happened to her?"

"Well you know what a dear soul she was. . . . Once there came a stranger to Sodom, an old and frail man, and nobody gave him any food or water. Plitith used to take some food to him every night and so kept him alive. When the Sodomites noticed that the stranger took a long time dying, they suspected a 'dirty trick.' Well they caught my poor daughter red-handed, and she is no longer alive."

Lot shuddered as he thought of his daughter's cruel death.

"Take my advice, Lot," Eliezer said. "Get out of here before it is too late. This is no place for you. If you try to be honest among these crooked people you will die, and if you try to live the way these people live here, it is even worse than death. So clear out of here. I am sure Abraham will welcome you back."

"Sorry, Eliezer, old man," replied Lot. "I cannot go back to Abraham. You know the way our shepherds had quarreled. I was the cause of this strife, and I would again bring strife into the peaceful house of Abraham if I should return to live with him. Besides, this is a rich country, and I am growing richer every day. And here I am free from the ever-watchful eye of my uncle. Life is so much easier here. I think I will stay."

With a heavy heart, Eliezer bade Lot farewell and returned to his master.

(To be continued)

 THE POWER OF EVIL

There was a time when Ruth was the best student in the Hebrew School that she attended. All her teachers expected that she would grow up to be a clever, well-mannered girl. But that was some time ago. Since then a great change had taken place in Ruth.

It all began with a little white lie. Ruth was on her way to Hebrew School one day with some of her friends. On their way they passed a big department store that had many display windows. The girls stopped to admire the different articles that were being shown. Before they knew it, they were already late for Hebrew School. They ran the rest of the way, but when Ruth reached her class she was already fifteen minutes late.

Asked by the teacher where she had been, Ruth felt ashamed. She did not want her teacher to know that she had spent her time before a department store window. An idea came into her head. Suddenly she said, "My mother was sick, and I had to go to the drug store."

Ruth was not used to lying. But this was not lying, she thought. Not really lying. After all, she was not hurting anybody. It was just to save her from embarrassment. What could be so wrong about that?

When her teacher heard Ruth's excuse he said, "Well, in that case I suppose it will be easy for you to bring me a note from your mother?"

Ruth nodded her head slowly, and walked to her seat.

The next day Ruth brought the note in to her teacher. He seemed a little surprised to see it, but he did not say anything. When the class was over teacher called Ruth to him. "Ruth," teacher said, "there is something that I must tell you, although it makes me very sad to do so. Yesterday I met your mother in the street after class, and I inquired after her health. Then I learned from your mother that she had not been sick at all. That can only mean that you lied to me and also wrote this note yourself. You must promise me faithfully that you will never do such a disgraceful thing again, if you wish to remain at school! I will not allow anyone to spoil the other students!"

Ruth never went to Hebrew School again after that. Later in her life, she bitterly regretted having given up her Hebrew education, but then it was too late.

And it all had come about through a little lie. . . .

Published & Copyright 1945 by
MERKOS L'INYONEI CHINUCH, INC.
770 EASTERN PARKWAY
Brooklyn 13, N. Y.
PResident 4-0507 - 1866

No. **19**

GRACE AFTER MEALS

Nathan had not been very long in Hebrew school, but he was making very fine progress. Already he knew all the *Berachot* (Blessings). Whether he was eating cake, fruit or candy, he knew what blessings to make in each case. He always said the blessing in a clear voice, so that whoever was listening could say "Amen."

One day he was visiting his friend Moshe. This was his second visit. Nathan loved visiting his friend who was not much older than he, but much cleverer, for Moshe had been attending Hebrew school since he was five. So Nathan looked forward to learning something new from his friend. This was not the only reason why Nathan

‹ 1 ›

loved visiting his friend. To be quite honest, Nathan loved the delicious cookies and chocolate cake of which Moshe's mother always had a good supply. After Moshe and Nathan did their homework and managed also to have a game of draughts, they were called in to have "tea." As usual the cookies and cake were crisp and delicious, and the boys were permitted to have a second helping.

Finally it was all over, and Nathan was about to rise from the table when he saw his friend produce a little booklet. On the cover Nathan read "Blessings and Prayers."

"Let's say the *Berachah Achronah* (Grace after eating cake and certain kinds of fruit) together," Moshe said.

"I thought Grace was said only after eating a proper dinner, but not after a snack," Nathan said, somewhat surprised.

"Oh no. We say Grace after anything we eat or drink, just as we make a Berochah *before* we eat or drink anything. You are thinking of *Birchat Hamazon*, the longer 'Grace,' but there is a shorter one we say after eating cake and certain kinds of fruit. Here, read for yourself."

Nathan read the instructions: *"After eating cake made of wheat, rye, barley and similar grain, or the following fruits: olives, dates, figs, pomegranates, or drinking wine, the following is said. . . ."*

"Tell me, Moshe, why only these things, and not others?"

"When you learn more *Chumash* you will know. But I will tell you. Our Holy Land, the Land of Israel, was praised by G-d with seven kinds of produce which grow in abundance in the Land of Israel and are of an excellent quality: 'A land of wheat and barley, and wine and figs and pomegranate, a land of olive oil and honey (dates)'. Every time we eat cake, drink wine, or eat fruit of these kinds, we remember our Holy Land from which we were driven by a cruel invader about two thousand years ago. So while we thank G-d for not having forsaken us and for giving us these nice things wherever we are, we pray to G-d to take us back to our beloved native land where we could fully, and with gladdened hearts, enjoy G-d's blessings and worship Him in holiness and purity."

"Thank you so much, Moshe. You are really clever. Every time I talk to you, I regret more and more why I did not join Hebrew school earlier. I should then have known these things myself. . . ."

"It's never too late to learn, and teacher is very pleased with you, I know."

After Nathan and Moshe recited the prayer, Nathan said, "I'm going to say it so often that I will know it by heart before long."

"You must be very fond of cake," Moshe remarked with a chuckle.

THE FLOURISHING VALLEY THAT BECAME
THE "DEAD SEA"
(Continued)

Lot continued to live in Sodom. Gradually he became used to the way the Sodomites lived. Their cruel habits didn't shock him as much as before. The natives began to consider him as one of their own. When Lot became the richest man in Sodom, they elected him as their Lord Chief Justice. Lot didn't refuse the honor and took up his place near the gates of the city as was the custom of the Lord Chief Justice in those days.

All day long nothing special happened, but towards twilight Lot suddenly noticed two strangers approaching the gates of the city.

Now Lot did a very brave thing, which showed that he was, after all, made of a different clay than the wicked Sodomites. Disregarding his high position which he let fly to the winds, Lot ran to meet the strangers with a friedliness and hospitality which he had learned from his uncle Abraham.

The two strangers did not want to accept the sacrifice. They said that they would stay overnight in the open spring air. However, Lot begged them so long, that they finally accepted his invitation.

Now Lot didn't give them fresh water to wash

the dust off their feet, as Abraham always used to do. It was not because Lot was mean, but rather because he thought that should any Sodomite surprise them in his house, he would say, "They arrived only a moment ago. Look, the dust is still on their feet."

Then Lot called to his wife: "Edith, set the table for our guests, and don't forget the salt."

Edith was not very pleased with the guests. "You forget you are in Sodom and not in Beer-Sheba, my lord and master. Here it is not customary to entertain guests at all, let alone to offer them salt. It's high time you got out of those habits of your aged uncle."

Lot's wife stopped her protests abruptly as she noticed her husband's stern gaze, and she went out into the street in search of salt.

Going from door to door, she told her neighbors, "My husband must be out of his mind! He sent me out to borrow some salt for his guests. But keep it a secret. . . . "

By the time she came back with the salt, the rumor had spread in Sodom that Lot, the Lord Chief Justice himself, was entertaining guests in his house. Such an outrage!

The next moment all the Sodomites came running towards Lot's house. Those who could walk, came running, and those who could not were brought anyway. All the people of Sodom came, men, women, and children, and surrounded Lot's house.

"Surrender your guests to us at once!" they demanded.

(To be continued)

THE RETURNED THEFT

The day was cold but clear, and a group of boys were playing football in Madison Park. They had been heavily dressed at the beginning of the game, but after a while they had begun to shed some of their outer clothing. It was not long before a large heap of sweaters and jackets lay beside the wire fence that ran around the field.

A few boys, including Jackie Stein, had come too late to join in the game, and they stood watching from the sidelines. Jackie soon got tired of standing around and doing nothing, and he decided to have some fun. He knew that his friend Sol had put his jacket near the fence. Making sure that no one saw him, he sneaked over to where the jackets lay and found the one that belonged to Sol. He searched his friend's pockets, and when his hand finally closed around an object, he withdrew it. He looked to see what he had taken from Sol's pocket, and he saw that it was his friend's wallet.

"This will really be fun," Jackie thought to himself as he put the wallet into his own pocket. Of course he was not going to steal it. That would be wrong. He was just going to keep it so that Sol would be frightened when he would find that it was missing. It would be fun, he thought, to watch his face. Jackie stood by the pile of clothing, waiting for Sol to come over.

The game finally ended, and the players came over to the fence to get their things. Sol put on his jacket, and immediately he put his hand into the pocket where the wallet had lain.

Jackie smiled when he saw the look of terror that appeared on Sol's face. It was just what he had expected. Then he realized that his friend was worried about something more important thant just a wallet. Sol searched frantically through all his pockets, looking for the missing article. Before Jackie could tell him that he had taken it, Sol ran out of the park with tears in his eyes. Jackie went home.

A few hours later there was a sharp knocking at the door of Jackie's house. His mother opened the door. Mrs. Barofsky, Sol's mother entered, sobbing terribly with tears rolling down her cheeks. It seemed that Mr. Barofsky had told Sol to take a large sum of money out of the bank that morning, and he was to bring it home at night. It was nine o'clock already and Sol was not home yet. Something must have happened to him.

Immediately Jackie understood what had happened. He told Mrs. Barofsky to stop worrying, and he dashed out of the house. As he had expected, he found Sol near the bank searching for the lost wallet. Quickly Jackie explained to him what had happened, and he gave him the wallet which contained the money from the bank. Too happy to be angry with his friend, Sol quickly ran home. "Just imagine," Jackie said to himself, "I thought that the whole thing would be a joke, yet it could have turned into a real tragedy. No more such silly jokes for me!"

Published & Copyright 1945 by
MERKOS L'INYONEI CHINUCH, INC.
770 EASTERN PARKWAY
Brooklyn 13, N. Y.
PResident 4-0507 - 1866

No. 20

FENCES

It was Shabbos afternoon. Danny had just finished reviewing the lessons he had learned in Hebrew school the past week. Now he was in his back yard thinking what he could do until the time came for Minchah, the late afternoon prayer. His eyes turned upwards, and he saw the spreading branches of the pear-tree that stood just beyond the fence of his back yard. "I wonder if I can climb that tree," Danny thought.

Danny walked over to the fence. He sized up the branches that were partly overhanging into his yard. He would have to climb over the fence first and then try to climb up the tree trunk. As he was just about to swing himself over the fence, his heart began to beat quickly and a silent voice within him sounded a warning, "Don't!"

Danny remembered a long talk his teacher once gave the class on "fences."

"Fences are made to protect something or somebody," teacher began. "Especially where there is danger there is a fence. You find a fence near an electric power station, railway crossing, and the like. There is also a different kind of fence, for instance: In certain factories, on ships, in certain warehouses, and wherever there are so-called special 'fire-hazards,' you can see 'No Smoking' or 'Smoking Strictly Prohibited' notices. Now, it may be perfectly harmless to smoke in these places, except that once in a while a person might forget and toss a burning match onto or near inflammable things and blow the whole place up! These special regulations are made by way of precaution, but it is a very serious offense to disregard them. These regulations, or 'by-laws' are also 'fences' since they are intended to protect the safety of people and property.

"Similarly, our Sages of old, our great teachers who have taught us the true way of life, have given us certain laws which they called 'fences,' to keep us away from breaking serious laws of the Torah and causing ourselves great harm. For instance, we must not climb a tree on Shabbos, because if we were allowed to, we might forget and pick some fruit or leaves off the tree, which would be a very grave Shabbos desecration. . . .

"Not only must a Jew respect these 'fences' which our Sages erected for our benefit, but it is a good idea for every one to erect his own 'fences' around these 'fences' so as to make doubly sure that he would not break a law of the Torah. . . . "

These words now came to Danny's mind as he was about to swing himself across the fence which separated him from the pear-tree. "How fortunate I am to have remembered these words," Danny said to himself. "Think of it. I would have climbed the tree; I would surely have been tempted to pick a luscious pear off, which would have meant that I was breaking the Sabbath, and also stealing!"

Danny took another glance at the fence, and drew back a few paces. He shook his head at the tree, and turned back. "The best place on Shabbos is in the *Shul*; there I shall surely keep away from mischief," thought he, and off he went to *Shul*.

Q U I Z

Questions:	*Answers:*
What is *Kol Nidrei?*	*Shaloh* No. 17, p. 1
What is *Yom-Tov?*	*Shaloh* No. 17, p. 6
What are *Challahs?*	*Shaloh* No. 18, p. 2
Why do we have two *Challahs* on Shabbos?	*Shaloh* No. 18, p. 2
What is *Birchat Hamazon?*	*Shaloh* No. 19, p. 2
What is *Berachah Achronah?*	*Shaloh* No. 19, p. 2
Who was Eliezer? What was he doing in Sodom?	*Shaloh* No. 17, p. 3
Pick the father, mother and daughter: Plitith, Lot and Edith.	*Shaloh* No. 18, p. 5 *Shaloh* No. 19, p. 5

THE FLOURISHING VALLEY THAT BECAME THE "DEAD SEA"

(Continued)

Lot pleaded with the Sodomites to spare the guests who came under the protection of his house, but the mob would not hear of it. "Let's break in," roared the mob, and moved upon Lot's house menacingly.

Then a curious thing happened. The mob seemed to have been suddenly blinded. Everybody began to move in circles, without being able to find the door.

At that moment the two strangers said to Lot, "Have you got your entire family here? You must leave at once, for G-d has sent us to destroy this place because of the wickedness and cruelty of the people."

Now Lot realized that the two strangers were no ordinary people, but angels of the Lord. He began to pack his things at once. He even wanted to run outside to collect some of his debts. But the angels said to him, "Hurry, hurry, time is passing. Never mind your wealth if you cherish your life."

Lot's sons-in-law refused to believe that the end of Sodom had come, and decided to stay. When the angels saw that Lot was tarrying too long, one of them took him and his wife and his two daughters and carried them outside of Sodom. "Now flee for your lives," the angel said. "Never, never turn your head to look back upon Sodom. Were it not for your Uncle Abraham, you would have probably shared their fate. But you certainly don't deserve to watch them perish."

Meanwhile word spread in Sodom that G-d was about to destroy their land. But nobody believed it. Those who worshipped the sun said, "Soon the sun will come out and it will protect us." And the moon-worshippers said, "The moon will save us."

As it began to dawn there were both the sun and the moon in the sky, but neither, of course, could help the Sodomites. Hail and brimstone and sulphur swept down on Sodom, and devastated the entire province. One of the angels touched the rock upon which all the four Sodomite cities were built and turned them upside down. The once flourishing valley of Sodom now turned into a sea of salt — the Dead Sea.

Only Lot, his wife and two daughters escaped. With their hearts in their boots they ran on and on, away from the dying valley. But Lot's wife was very inquisitive. "I will have but one little glance," she said. But no sooner did she turn her head than she turned into a pillar of salt.

For many years, the salt figure that was Lot's wife stood near Sodom as an awe-inspiring monument.

Coming Next: THE GREAT TEST

THE SICK FRIEND

"Come on, fellows," Saul called to his friends who were about to begin a ball game down the block. "Let's go and see how Joe's getting along."

There was no answer to Saul's call, so he walked on alone. Joe was a sickly boy. He was never able to play with the other boys, and Saul was the only one that ever bothered to speak to him. Even this did not happen too often, since Saul had to leave his other friends whenever he did so. Now, too, although he had heard that Joe was very sick, he was not very anxious to leave his friends. Still, he went to see Joe because he had been told how important a "mitzvah" it was to do so. Even G-d visited the sick, as He had done when Abraham was ill.

A few minutes afterwards, Saul arrived at Joe's house. He noticed that a doctor's car was parked in front of the door. He rang the bell and Joe's mother answered. She seemed to be very worried. As he entered, he noticed that the entire house was filled with a strange silence. It was as though something dreadful were going to happen! Walking practically on tiptoe, Joe's mother led Saul to her son's room. The doctor was standing outside the door, a solemn look on his face.

"Could I go in?" Saul asked in a whisper. In the heavy stillness of the house, he did not dare to raise his voice.

At first, the doctor did not seem to hear his question. After a few seconds, he seemed to realize what he had been asked, and replied: "I suppose there is no harm in your going in to him. Perhaps you may even do him some good. But don't stay more than a few minutes."

Saul opened the door softly and stepped into the room. Joe lay on the bed, very pale, and his eyes shone with feverish brightness as he moved restlessly. He lay there, thinking there was no purpose in his trying to get well. No one had been to visit him. None of his friends had shown any interest in whether he were ill or well. He had no friends, he decided, as he turned wearily to the wall.

"Joe," Saul called to him gently, "this is your friend Saul. I have come to see you."

Joe turned around in surprise. He could hardly believe his eyes and his ears. But yes, it was true. There was a friend who cared about him! Great was the joy in his eyes! The next few moments were spent in eager conversation until the doctor came to remind Saul that his time was up, and he must leave.

The doctor followed Saul almost immediately, and as he caught up with him said, patting him on his back: "My son, you've done Joe more good than I. He's going to get well now, I can see." Saul smiled with pleasure as he walked home, so glad of the "mitzvah" that he had done in visiting his sick friend.

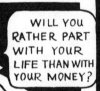

TO BE CONTINUED.

שעורי למוד הדת

SHALOH

| | Published & Copyright 1945 by MERKOS L'INYONEI CHINUCH, INC. 770 EASTERN PARKWAY Brooklyn 13, N. Y. PResident 4-0507 - 1866 | No. 21 |

DANNIE LEARNS SOMETHING

Dannie was playing in his back yard. The day before he had received a set of darts for his birthday, and now he was trying them out. On the wooden fence of the yard he had nailed up several pictures, which he had torn from an old geography book and he was using them as targets. While he was thus occupied, his friend Alex who lived across the street, came over to pay him a visit.

"Why, Dannie, what are you doing?" Alex exclaimed as he saw his friend throwing the darts at the strange targets.

"Oh, it's nothing," Dannie answered him. "I just

« 1 »

thought that these pictures would be just the right thing for a target."

"But you've ruined the book," Alex said.

"Well what of it? It's mine isn't it? It's not like spoiling something that belongs to someone else. That would be like stealing, but this book belongs to me."

Alex smiled. "You know, I once thought the same way," he said. "But yesterday," he continued, "my teacher in Hebrew school told us differently. He told us that it wasn't only forbidden to destroy something that belonged to someone else, but you are supposed just as well to take care of the things that belong to you."

"I still don't understand. This old geography book has no use for me now that I am in the fifth grade. Why cannot I do with it what I like?"

"Well for one thing destroying things is a very bad habit, teacher said. If you get into the habit of destroying things, you become wicked. You start by destroying old books, then you destroy plants or flowers in the meadow, then you go about hurting harmless animals, and finally you wind up by hurting other people!

"Besides," Alex continued, "there is always someone who could use something *you* don't need. You could give your old geography book to some poor boy of the fourth grade who cannot afford to buy a new one!"

"I never thought of that," Danny confessed.

THE STORY OF ABRAHAM

THE GREAT TEST

The destruction of Sodom *) instilled great fear into the hearts of all men. They saw that the mighty hand of G-d had finally overtaken the wicked people of Sodom. People began to fear the All-Powerful G-d who was stronger than all the forces of nature. At the same time the fame of Abraham as a true prophet of G-d spread far and wide. His wisdom, kindness, modesty, honesty, and all other traits of fine character, were the talk of everybody. Kings and princes sought his friendship and advice, and many seekers of truth and wisdom became his willing and eager students.

As for Abraham himself, he was truly as happy as only a true servant of G-d can be. He was blessed by G-d and had everything his heart desired. Abraham had riches, numerous flocks and herds, servants, precious stones and metals. But could there be anything more precious than his beloved son Isaac? A few years before, he would gladly have given everything he possessed for a boy of his own like Isaac. But G-d gave him Isaac as a blessing and fulfilled his greatest wish.

Yes, Abraham was a happy man and he was truly grateful to G-d. He was humble and modest; he despised

---

*) See *Shaloh* Booklets 16-20

« 3 »

power and honor, though he was the most powerful chieftain of his time. Abraham devoted his life to the service of G-d, teaching the true way of life to all who wanted to learn. He spent a great deal of time with his beloved son Isaac, who would carry on his work some day.

Even the angels in heaven began to take notice of Abraham. But there was among them a notorious troublemaker, who first invades man's mind and heart and settles there comfortably as man's "evil inclination." Then, after he seduces his victim into sin, he comes to G-d to demand that his victim be punished. This troublemaker was Satan.

"It is easy for a man in Abraham's position to be a true servant of G-d," Satan declared. He has riches, he has children, he has everything any mortal could desire. Why should he not be grateful? To give charity, and to be kind is no sacrifice for Abraham. But ask him for a sacrifice that is dearer to him than his own life, and see whether he would do it."

G-d knew Abraham's heart; He knew that no sacrifice would be too great for Abraham if only G-d requested it of him. However, in order to show to all earthly and heavenly creatures that there is no more faithful a servant than Abraham, and in order that Abraham's faith in G-d be forever a lesson to all men, G-d agreed to put his loyal servant Abraham to the greatest possible test.

Thereupon, G-d called to his favorite servant.

"Abraham, Abraham! Take your son and bring

him up as an offering upon one of the mountains which I will show you."

"Which son?" asked Abraham. "I have two sons, Isaac and Ishmael."

"The son you love so much," answered G-d.

"But I love both sons very much," replied Abraham truthfully.

"Your son Isaac, whom you love most," said G-d.

Was Abraham puzzled by the strange command of G-d? Was he crushed with grief at the thought of losing his dearly beloved son? Did Abraham plead for his son at least as much as he had pleaded for the wicked Sodomites?

Not at all.

Though Abraham could not understand why G-d commanded him to do such a strange thing, he was ready, nay, eager to fulfill it without delay.

Abraham's second thought was for his wife Sarah. He knew she was as faithful to G-d as he himself, but after all she was a woman and a mother, and he was afraid she might not be able to survive the shock in her advanced age. He had to take Isaac out of the house without alarming her. And so, that evening he said to his wife. . . .

"You know, Sarah dear, that our son Isaac is quite a young man now. He is already 37 years of age. We have kept him home all the time. He was short of nothing and he was never asked to make any sacrifices in the worship of G-d. It is high time I took him out into the world that he may learn to make sacrifices for the worship of G-d." Sarah readily agreed.

And so Sarah courageously bade Isaac good-bye, giving him her blessing.

(To be continued)

 ## THE UNLIKE TWINS

Joshua and Menachem were twins. They looked alike, they dressed alike, and even their voices were alike. People had often called Joshua by his brother's name, and similarly mistook Menachem for his brother. So closely did they resemble each other that even their parents made mistakes at times. However, it was only their outward appearance. The behavior of the two boys was entirely different.

Joshua was quiet, modest, and obedient. He never shouted or insulted anybody. If he got into an argument with his friends, he always settled it in a peaceful manner. Joshua never boasted, but praised the qualities of his friends. When his mother sent him on an errand he went gladly, and he always followed her instructions to the letter. It was easy to see why everyone liked Joshua very much.

Menachem was exactly the opposite of his brother. Whenever there was a fight, he was in the middle of it, and he called his friends names for no reason at all. Menachem went around boasting how wonderful he was, which was not only bad manners but also a falsehood. No one liked Menachem very much.

One day Menachem received a post card from his Hebrew School teacher. The card said that he should report to the principal's office half an hour before school on that day. Menachem, who thought that his teacher had told the principal about his bad conduct lately, expected to be admonished by the principal. Menachem did not want to be told about his shameful behavior, and an idea came into his head. He called over his brother Joshua, who was in a higher class.

"Look, Joshua," he said, showing the post card, "the principal wants to see me. I'm sure it's nothing bad, and I don't feel so well today. You go there today instead of me. Nobody will know the difference."

When Joshua came home from Hebrew School that day, his brother ran over to him and asked him what had happened. "I had a wonderful time," Joshua told him. "I had ice cream, cake, soda, and candy, and a lot of other things. You see, your teacher got married last week, and he sent post cards to the whole class to come and celebrate. Here," Joshua said, handing his brother a small package, "I saved a piece of cake for you. But if you had gone there yourself, you would have enjoyed the whole party! It was grand!"

Menachem decided he had not been as smart as he thought, and made up his mind that in the future, he would act in a straightforward manner and he would have no need to fear anyone or anything.

REFUSING TO DIVULGE THE HIDING PLACE OF HIS TREASURE, CORDOVERA IS KIDNAPPED AND HELD PRISONER.

THEY ARE COMING AGAIN.

THANK G-D I HAVE MY HOLY BOOKS TO STUDY. COST ME A LITTLE FORTUNE TO GET THEM HERE.

TOMORROW IS THE LAST DAY. IF YOU DON'T OPEN UP IN THE MORNING, YOU'LL BE BURIED DEEPER THAN YOUR TREASURE.

BRING ME QUILL AND INK.

WE KNEW YOU'D BE SENSIBLE.

LEFT ALONE, CORDOVERA BEGINS TO WRITE FEVERISHLY.

TO BE CONTINUED

שיעורי לימוד הדת
S.H.A.L.O.H.

Published & Copyright 1945 by
MERKOS L'INYONEI CHINUCH, INC.
770 EASTERN PARKWAY
Brooklyn 13, N. Y.
PResident 4-0507 - 1866

No. 22

FAIR PLAY

On his eleventh birthday Eli received a shiny, new pair of skates from his father. Eli had a pair of skates already, but they were a few years old, and now a little too small for him. Eli decided to sell his old skates. He knew that Gershon was looking for a used pair of skates, so the next time he saw him he said, "Hey Gershon, how would you like to buy my old skates?"

Gershon was happy to hear this. He wanted skate very badly, but he had not saved up enough money for a new pair. "Sure," he said eagerly, "how much do you want for them?"

"Oh, I don't know. How much do you think they're worth?"

« 1 »

"How should I know? I never bought used skates before."

"I'll tell you what," Eli finally said, "Let's ask Peretz. He knows a lot about these things."

"That's okay with me," Gershon replied. "We'll let him be judge."

That evening Gershon paid Peretz a visit. Gershon had an idea.

"Peretz, my friend," Gershon said affectionately, "will you do me a favor?"

"First tell me what it is, then I can tell you whether I'll do it or not."

Gershon told him about Eli's offer to sell him his old skates, and that they agreed that Peretz should suggest the right price. "Now," he concluded, "you see, you can save me some money. You can tell him that the skates are worth a couple of quarters less than they really are. If you do this for me, you can use my skates whenever you want to!"

Peretz drew back in indignation. After a moment he said, "Let me ask you something. Would you place a stone in the path of a blind man so that he should fall over it?"

"Who do you take me for?" replied Gershon, a little hurt. "You've got to be pretty mean to do such a thing."

"Well, you've just asked me to do just that."

"I don't understand," said Gershon surprised.

"Our Torah tells us that when anybody comes to you for advice in good faith, and you knowingly give him the wrong advice, it is just like tripping a blind man over. At the same time you offered me a bribe to do this dirty trick for you!"

Gershon lowered his eyes with shame. "I am sorry. I did not realize it was a mean thing I was asking you to do. Only I thought that to Eli the couple of quarters did not mean much. . . . "

"That, of course, makes no difference. But let's forget it. I know you did not give the matter careful thought, but that now you know better."

"You know, Peretz, now that I come to think of it, I should never have been able to enjoy the skates if I had come by them through such a mean trick. Thank you very much. All I want of you is your honest opinion what the skates are worth. Will you tell Eli what I had asked you before?"

"That would be just as bad as doing what you asked me to do in the first place. Don't be silly. Let's forget about it."

"Nice of you to forget about it. But I will never forget the lesson you taught me today, for which I am very grateful to you."

THE STORY OF ABRAHAM
THE GREAT TEST
(Continued)

Abraham's faith in G-d was so great that G-d's command to bring his son as a sacrifice to G-d did not even disturb his sleep that night. He rose up with the sun, roused Isaac, and told him to be ready for a long journey at once. Abraham himself saddled the asses, took some wood for a fire, a long knife for the sacrifice, and two loyal servants. Then the small caravan set out on their fateful journey.

While the angels in heaven admired Abraham's courage and loyalty to G-d, Satan got busy with his tricks. First he appeared to Sarah as a horrible thought. "Maybe I should not have let Abraham take Isaac away. Who knows if I will ever see my dear Isaac again?" But the good Sarah banished the horrible thought away. "Surely Abraham would not do anything contrary to G-d's wishes," Sarah decided.

In the meantime, Abraham proceeded on his way. Suddenly, he met an old man.

"Where are you taking your son at such an early hour?" the old man asked. "I see you are prepared for a sacrifice. Now I know it is not unusual for the heathens to sacrifice their sons, but surely *your* G-d would not require a human sacrifice? Besides, has not G-d promised you that your son would be the father of a great nation? What will happen to all your good work if you should sacrifice your son?"

"These are the words of Satan," Abraham said. "Nothing will stop me from fulfilling G-d's command, whatever it is. Be gone now!"

It was Isaac's turn now. It suddenly occurred to Isaac that it was strange his father had not taken a ram with him for a sacrifice. "Father," he asked, "I see

« 4 »

you have taken wood and fire with you for a sacrifice, but where is the ram for the burnt offering?"

"Don't worry, my son, G-d will provide me with a ram for a sacrifice. And if it be G-d's will, you may be the sacrifice, my son."

Isaac didn't become frightened. He was glad of the opportunity to show that he was ready to offer his life in the service of G-d, if necessary.

"Don't let the old man lead you to the slaughter like a lamb," Isaac heard an evil voice inside of him.

"You are wasting your time," Isaac's better self said in reply.

Father and son thus united in thought, continued their journey.

Suddenly, they found a stormy river barring their way. Once again they knew it was the work of Satan to prevent them from fulfilling G-d's command. Abraham and Isaac began to wade through the water, until it reached up to their shoulders. If they stepped further, they would surely drown. Then Abraham cried to G-d, "Spare us, O Lord, that we may be able to fulfill your wish." Immediately the river vanished and Abraham was able to continue his way again.

(To be continued)

THE HOLY NAME

Down the street a bitter dispute was going on over a game of marbles. Both Sammy and Eli were shouting at the top of their voices. "Come on, Sammy," Eli cried, "give me the marble. You know I hit."

"You did not," Sammy returned. "You missed by a mile."

"I did so. I swear to G-d."

At this very moment Eli's brother Joe passed by. He was shocked to hear the way his brother was speaking. Stopping near the two boys, Joe spoke to his brother.

"Eli," he said, "I'm surprised at you! Not only are you arguing and getting angry—which is bad enough—but you are also doing something even worse. You just mentioned G-d's holy name for no reason at all. That is a bad thing to do!

"Just to show you how wrong it is, I'll tell you what the Talmud says about it. It says that the whole world shook when G-d said at Mount Sinai, 'Thou shalt not take the name of the Lord in vain.' From now on you should be very careful not to utter G-d's name unless there is a very good reason for it; and not only in Hebrew but also in English."

Eli listened ashamedly to what his brother said to him. He had never thought how great a wrong he had been doing. He promised himself that from now on he would not use the holy name unless he was absolutely forced to do so.

A few days later, Eli had a chance to see how well he would keep his promise. It was during a baseball game. Eli had sent a grounder down the third base line, and he reached first just as the throw came in. Eli was sure that he was safe, but Danny, the first baseman, claimed that he was out.

"If you're so sure that you're safe," Danny said at last, "let's see you swear to G-d."

By this time many boys had gathered around to hear the outcome of the argument. When they heard Danny's words they nodded in approval. But Eli remembered his promise, and he refused to swear.

"You see," Danny jumped up, "he knows he's wrong, and that's why he won't swear."

When Eli heard these words he was sorely tempted to swear after all, because he knew that he was right. But he held firm. Finally he said, "No, I won't swear, even though I'm sure I'm right. I won't swear because it's not right to swear except for something very important."

All the boys, especially Danny, were impressed by Eli's answer. After thinking to himself for a few senconds Danny said, "I guess you were right after all, Eli. I was doubtful at first, but when you didn't want to swear I thought you were wrong. But now that you told us why you didn't want to swear, I believe you. I guess you can stay on first now."

TO BE CONTINUED.

שעורי למור הדת

SHALOH

Published & Copyright 1945 by
MERKOS L'INYONEI CHINUCH, INC.
770 EASTERN PARKWAY
Brooklyn 13, N. Y.
PResident 4-0507 - 1866

No. 23

THE SMART STUDENT

Everybody knew that Simon was the smartest boy in the Hebrew School. If no one else said it, Simon himself was sure to go around telling it to everybody. He boasted continuously. He had other bad traits, too. When a student would answer a question correctly, Simon would say, loud enough for everyone to hear, "Oh, that's nothing. Anybody knows that." If a student answered incorrectly, Simon would burst out laughing and embarrass the student even more. So far, nothing that anybody could say or do was able to change his bad habits.

There was one time during the term when Simon was even worse than usual. That was when the principal came to see how well the class was doing. Once a term this happened, and weeks before, the boys began to review their lessons so that the principal would not be disappointed when he asked them questions. While this eager studying was going on, Simon would go from one student to the next and say to him, "Why are you studying? It won't do you any good anyway."

So far this had happened every term in the past, and this term was no exception. There was nothing the boys could do about it. They would beg of Simon not to annoy them, but he only laughed. All they could do was to hope that something would happen to make Simon change his ways. This continued until the day finally arrived when the principal was to come into the class.

Rabbi Steinberg, the principal, walked into the room smiling cheerfully. He knew that the class had been anxiously waiting for this day to show him how well they knew their lessons. After greeting the class, Rabbi Steinberg began to ask questions.

"Michael," he said to a boy in the first row, "can you tell me the names of Noah's sons?"

"Shem, Ham, and Japheth," answered Michael promptly.

"Very good. And Ben," the principal turned to another boy, "can you tell me the meaning of the words *ve'ahavta lereiacha kamocha?*"

This was a difficult question, and Rabbi Steinberg did not expect Ben to answer immediately. While Ben was thinking, Simon suddenly blurted out, "He doesn't know,

Rabbi Steinberg. I know. It means 'Thou shalt love thy neighbor as thyself.' "

Ben's cheeks burned with shame, and Rabbi Steinberg looked at Simon disapprovingly. There was a heavy silence in the classroom. Finally the principal spoke.

"Simon," be began, "there is something very important that you ought to know. Just remembering what you learned is not enough. The important thing is to put into practice what you have learned. You just showed me that you knew the 'mitzvah' of loving your neighbor as yourself. At the same time you embarrassed one of your classmates. To me that means that your knowledge is worth very little."

Simon lowered his eyes. He felt deeply the importance of what Rabbi Steinberg had said, and that his actions had contradicted his knowledge. Simon decided it really was time he changed his evil habits!

 ### THE STORY OF ABRAHAM

THE GREAT TEST
(Continued)

On the third day, Abraham saw a mountain in the distance, upon which hung a cloud of fire with flames shooting up to the sky. Abraham turned to his son:

"Tell me, what do you see yonder?"

"I see a strange and wonderful sight," was the reply. "I see fire clouds and rainbows mixed in splendor atop that mountain."

Then Abraham turned to his servants. "What do you see over there?"

"Nothing, Master," they said. "We see nothing but a mountain, a mountain like all other mountains."

"Nor do the donkeys," thought Abraham, and then he said to his servants: "You had better stay here with the donkeys, while my son and I go yonder where we will worship G-d and return. Wait for us here."

Placing the bundle of wood on Isaac's shoulders, father and son went up the hill. There Abraham built a small altar and told Isaac to climb on it.

"Bind me tightly, father, so that I may not struggle and prevent you from doing your duty properly."

Abraham bound his son on the altar, then reached his hand for the knife.

At that moment, the angels in heaven began to cry. Their tears fell from heaven right into Isaac's eyes and dimmed them.

Suddenly, Abraham heard a voice from heaven, "Abraham, Abraham, lay not thy hand upon the lad, nor do thou any harm to him, for now I know that thou art a G-d fearing man, seeing that thou hast not withheld thy son, thine only son, from Me."

For a moment Abraham thought that he merely imagined he heard the voice. He decided that unless he heard it clearly again, he would continue with the sacrifice. Instantly he heard the voice again, and he knew now that it was all just a test. Abraham let his hand drop and looking around, he suddenly noticed a ram caught in a thicket by his horns. Taking Isaac down from the altar, he placed the ram in his stead, and offered it as a sacrifice to G-d.

Abraham then gave the place a special name in remembrance of the great event. He called the place, "The Lord Seeth; the Mountain upon which the Lord is Seen." This was Mt. Moriah upon which the Holy Temple was later built.

And of the ram, its two horns remained: one was sounded many years later when the children of Israel received the Torah on Mt. Sinai; the other will be sounded by Messiah, the Redeemer of Israel, who will gather the Jewish exiles from all parts of the world and lead them back to their Holy Land.

 THE TRUE FRIEND

Meir thought that Leon was a terrible pest. If Meir wanted to stay away from Hebrew School, Leon would not let him. If he was not in the synagogue on Shabbos, Leon would come to his house and take him along. If he ate a meal and was about to leave the table, Leon would remind him to say the *Birchat Hamazon* (Grace) It was only because they had known each other for years that Meir did not break his friendship with Leon.

Nor did Meir remain silent when Leon told him

what to do. One day, after one of these incidents, Meir became very angry. He shouted angrily at his friend and said, "Why don't you stop bothering me? Who are you to tell me what to do? It's none of your business!"

Leon answered him gently and said, "But it is my business. You know that every Jew is responsible for what his neighbor does. When I see you doing something that I think is wrong. I'm supposed to tell you about it. When you see me doing something that you think is wrong, you're supposed to do the same thing. Of course, there is a way of doing this—in a friendly sincere manner, and I don't intend to hurt your feelings."

Although Meir knew that his friend had spoken the truth, he was still angry. "Ah, you're just a nuisance," he said. "And you call yourself my friend."

"Don't worry," Leon said seriously, "some day you'll see that I'm the truest friend you have."

One day, not long after this argument, Meir and Leon were walking towards the Hebrew School. On the way they met several boys who had been expelled from Hebrew School because of their bad behavior. They were joking loudly among themselves and pushing each other around, often carelessly pushing a passerby. One of the "roughnecks" noticed the two boys with their books under their arms, and he called, "Hey, Meir, what do you want to go to school for? Come on with us. We're going to have a lot of fun."

Meir was not too anxious to go to Hebrew School anyway, and he was only too glad to accept the invitation. He turned to go, but Leon quickly gripped his arm. Try as he would, Meir could not tear himself free. Finally he said in a flash of temper, "Either you let me go or I'll sock you in the jaw!"

"I don't care," Leon said. "You can hit me if you want to, but I won't let you go with them. You know what kind of fellows they are."

Meir was much bigger than Leon, and he could easily have licked him. He realized that Leon was willing to be hurt just for his sake. "Oh, all right," he said at last, "I won't go with them." Turning to the boy who had called to him, he said, "Sorry, maybe some other time, but not now."

"Sissy, sissy," the boy jeered, but Meir ignored him. He continued with his friend towards the Hebrew School.

The next day the whole neighborhood buzzed with excitement. The boys whom Meir and Leon had met, had been caught stealing fruit from a truck. Every one of them was sure to be punished for the crime. When Meir heard the news, he realized from what a terrible fate he had been saved. If he had been there he knew that he would have done the same thing because the other boys did it. Walking over to his friend Leon, he said, "I'm sorry I got angry yesterday, Leon. I guess you're the best friend I have after all."

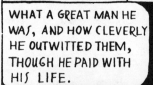

WHAT A GREAT MAN HE WAS, AND HOW CLEVERLY HE OUTWITTED THEM, THOUGH HE PAID WITH HIS LIFE.

AND YOU MY BOY HAVE THE SECRET OF THAT TREASURE. ALL YOU HAVE TO DO IS TO FOLLOW THE DIRECTIONS. I'LL HELP YOU...

IN THE CENTRAL LIBRARY YANKEL AND THE OLD MAN STUDY A MAP OF OLD NEW AMSTERDAM.

WHY, IT'S IDENTICAL!

I BELIEVE YOU'RE RIGHT.

IT'S SIMPLE: WE START FROM THE WEST SIDE OF THE EAST RIVER, FACING THE NAVY, YARD, AND FOLLOW WEST, NORTH AND WEST, ACCORDING TO THE INSTRUCTIONS!

NEXT SUNDAY, LAG B'OMER, YANKEL HAS A FREE DAY. MEETS OLD MAN NEAR WILLIAMSBURG BRIDGE AS ARRANGED, IMMEDIATELY AFTER AN EARLY BREAKFAST.

GOOD MORNING, SIR.

GOOD MORNING, YANKEL, NICE DAY FOR OUR WORK.

I BROUGHT MY COMPASS; WE CANNOT FAIL.

YOU HAVE NEVER FAILED BEFORE; WHY SHOULD YOU FAIL NOW?

FOLLOWING THE COMPASS, YANKEL AND THE OLD MAN FIND THEM-SELVES ON DELANCEY ST.

A. SCHOLZ

TO BE CONTINUED

Published & Copyright 1945 by
MERKOS L'INYONEI CHINUCH, INC.
770 EASTERN PARKWAY
Brooklyn 13, N. Y.
PResident 4-0507 - 1866

No. 24

REWARD

Shirley and Sarah were both good children. They were respectful of their parents and their elders. Whenever there was a chance to help, they would gladly do it. There was but one difference between them. When Sarah performed a good deed, that was the end of it. She knew that it was the proper thing to do, and that was enough for her. But Shirley was not like that. Although she was happy to do a good deed, she hoped for something more. She waited for the reward that would follow.

Of course Shirley, as well as Sarah, knew that all good deeds are rewarded. She had been told that many times. She knew that G-d did not forget what she had done. But she was very impatient. Shirley wanted her reward immediately.

One day Shirley and Sarah came home to find a surprise waiting for them. Uncle Sol had come to pay a visit, and they were delighted to see him. Whenever Uncle Sol came he told them funny stories, and it was no wonder that they liked him very much. Shirley and Sarah both threw their arms around him, and Uncle Sol embraced them warmly. He was very happy to see his two nieces. Soon he was sitting on his favorite chair, one niece on each of his knees, asking them about everything that had happened since he had seen them last.

After Shirley and Sarah had told their uncle everything that they could remember, Uncle Sol said, "Well, I am very glad to hear that you are both well and happy. Now I wonder which one of you would go out to get me some cigarettes."

"I'll go," both girls cried at once.

Uncle Sol smiled at their eagerness. "Very well," he said, "you can both go."

In a few minutes the two girls were back with the cigarettes. Uncle Sol thanked the girls very much, and lit a cigarette. "How about a tip, Uncle?" said Shirley, who was always impatient to get her reward without delay.

Uncle Sol dug into his pocket and withdrew two shiny nickels. The first one he gave to Shirley, who accepted it and politely thanked him. When he offered the second one to Sarah, however, she did not take it. "No thanks, Uncle Sol," she said, "it was a pleasure."

Later, when the two girls were alone, Shirley said, "See, you should have taken the nickel. Now you don't have anything."

"I don't mind," Sarah answered. "But I'm glad that I was able to do something for Uncle Sol anyway."

As they were talking, Uncle Sol walked in with a small box in his hand. Calling Sarah to his side, he said, "Here, Sarah, this is for you. It is not a reward for what you have done. It is just that I want to show you that I think that you are an unusually well-mannered girl."

Sarah excitedly accepted the box that her uncle offered. Even before she had opened it she thanked him again and again. "Oh," she gasped when she saw the contents of the box, "it's beautiful. Look what Uncle Sol gave me, Shirley," she said breathlessly, holding a shining silver bracelet in her hand.

Shirley, nickel in hand, looked at the bracelet, and a very sad look came over her face. Now she realized that in her eagerness to get her reward immediately she had forfeited a greater reward, which certainly would have been worth waiting for.

THE STORY OF ABRAHAM

ISAAC AND REBEKAH

When Abraham and Isaac returned home, they were very grieved to find that Sarah, their dearly loved wife and mother, had died, just before their return.

Isaac felt he must keep his mind very busy, so that he would not have time to think so much about his sad loss. He decided to study very hard, which would make him very clever at the same time as it would soothe his aching heart.

So he became a student in the College of Shem, and studied the Torah under him for many years. Isaac was a very good student and was beloved by everybody. They thought Abraham was very lucky to have such a fine son.

The time came when Abraham thought Isaac ought to get married. It was very important that a very good wife be found for him; he did not want his son to marry any of the heathen princesses in his own land. So Abraham decided to send his faithful servant Eliezer to his relatives in Aram Naharaim, his own birthplace. He then called Eliezer and said to him: "You are my good friend and servant, and you know and love Isaac very much. Go to my birthplace Aram Naharaim, and you will surely find a wife for Isaac from among my family there. I need not tell you what a fine young man Isaac is. In addition I am going to leave him all my land and possessions, so he will be very rich too. Then when you find a worthy young lady, it should not be difficult to persuade her to become the wife of such a splendid man as Isaac."

"Indeed, my master, I agree with all you say, and shall most gladly carry out your orders," replied Eliezer.

Abraham gave Eliezer a caravan of ten camels loaded up with all sorts of food, clothing and beautiful presents! You know of course there weren't any trains in those days, and whenever anyone wanted to travel, they always went "by camel," especially as the country was then mostly desert. That is why they called camels "Ships of the Desert."

Eliezer could have travelled with one or two camels, but he had so many things with him that he needed ten camels to carry them.

Now it so happened that Abraham had a nephew in a place called Haran, in Aram Naharaim, named Bethuel, who had a most beautiful daughter named Rebekah. Very often when people are beautiful, they become conceited, vain and selfish, only thinking how beautiful they are, and expecting everyone to make a fuss of them and pay them compliments. But Rebekah wasn't a bit like that. She was as good as she was beautiful, and as clever as she was good. She didn't care for the people who lived around her, for they prayed to silly wooden images, as if that would do them any good! Even her own father did so, and so did her brother Laban. The people of that place were dishonest also.

Rebekah prayed to G-d that some fine young man would come and take her away from that awful place!

(To be continued)

 ENVY

Some boys are unhappy for a reason. Some boys are very poor. Others are sick. You could understand why they are unhappy. But there are boys who are unhappy for no reason at all. Such a boy was Maurice.

Maurice came from a nice family. They were not very rich, but you could not say that they were poor. And Maurice was a healthy boy. He had hardly been sick a day since he was born. Yet he was terribly unhappy. It is very hard to understand why he should have been so.

The trouble was that he was terribly jealous. If one of the boys down the block got a new baseball, Maurice would cry himself sick until he had one too. Even though he did not need it, his father would have to buy one for him. It was the same way with everything else.

Many people had spoken to Maurice about the foolishness of his behavior. His father, his mother, his teachers, and even the doctor had been unsuccessful when they tried to show him that he was only ruining his life by being so terribly jealous. If this kept up, they warned him, he would never be happy. And the worst part of it was, there was no reason for him to be jealous.

Maurice listened to what each one had to say to him, but he did not change.

One day Maurice went to visit a friend of his, named Harry, who had a very expensive electric train. Maurice immediately fell in love with it and wanted one just like it! As soon as he got home, he told his father about it and insisted he must have one too.

It so happened that business hadn't been so good with his father lately, and he did not have enough money to spare for such a "luxury," but Maurice wouldn't hear of any refusal and became furious with rage and disappointment! If his friend Harry had one, then he must have one too. He refused to eat, and his eyes were constantly red with weeping. Finally he worked himself up into a high fever and the doctor had to be called.

The following day Harry came to visit Maurice and asked what had made him so ill. Maurice looked at him enviously as he replied: "I want to have an electric train like the one you have, but my father won't buy it for me!"

Harry's eyes suddenly filled with tears.

"You are a silly boy," he burst out. "Why I'd give away all my toys and everything if only I could have my father back again! You know I am an orphan, and having no father or mother is much worse than being without an electric train. You don't know how lucky you are really," he finished with a sad look in his eyes.

"What a fool I have been," exclaimed Maurice, now quite ashamed of himself. "I shall never be jealous again!

THE END.

VOLUME II

Nos. 25—48

THIRD PRINTING

Published & *Copyright* 1961 *by*
MERKOS L'INYONEI CHINUCH, Inc.
770 Eastern Parkway, Brooklyn 13, N. Y.

5732   1972

PREFACE

The present series (Nos. 25—48) is a continuation of the first 24 issues of *Shaloh* which first began to appear in 1945.

Designed for younger children to read independently or with the aid of parents or teachers, these publications contain four features: (1) A story with a moral related to good behavior and character training; (2) Biblical history in serial form; (3) a story the subject of which is a precept or a custom; and (4) a picture story. A detailed subject-index is provided.

The purpose of these publications is thus obvious: To provide interesting and useful reading material for the younger Jewish child in the fullest accord with our Jewish tradition, with a view to teaching the Jewish boy and girl, by means of an interesting though simple story, a practical lesson in the Jewish religion, history, and in the cultivation of good character traits.

The popularity and success of the previous series make a further introduction unnecessary.

THE EDITORS

TABLE OF CONTENTS

FEATURE I

GOOD BEHAVIOR AND CHARACTER TRAINING

FEATURE II

HISTORY (Continued from SHALOH, Nos. 1-24)

« v »

FEATURE III

PRECEPTS AND CUSTOMS

FEATURE IV

PICTURE STORIES

Published & Copyright 1961 by
MERKOS L'INYONEI CHINUCH, Inc.
770 EASTERN PARKWAY
Brooklyn 13, N. Y.
HYacinth 3-9250

No. 25

FIRST IN GREETING

The services were over. All the people in the synagogue were calling "Good Shabbos" to their friends as they prepared to leave.

"Wait a moment, David," Mr. Gordon said to his son. "Before we go home I would like to stop and greet that quiet man we saw sitting in the back. I've never seen him here before."

"Sholom Aleichem, friend," Mr. Gordon smiled and extended his hand. "My name is Moses Gordon, I'm glad to see you here. Welcome to our synagogue."

The stranger's face lit up. "What a mitzvah you have, Mr. Gordon. I'm new in the neighborhood and I was feeling rather lost, but you make me feel at home.

« 1 »

My name is Daniel Greenberg, and we've just moved to King Street."

"That's near us. Let's walk home together and get acquainted."

As they were strolling home together and exchanging information about themselves, a young man dressed in work clothes passed by.

"Excuse me," murmured Mr. Gordon. Turning to the young man, "Good morning, Tom Jones, how are you and your family?"

"Nice of you to remember," grinned Tom as he shook hands, "we're all fine, thank you."

"He's a very good plumber," remarked Mr. Gordon as they resumed walking.

When they arrived home, David turned to his father: "Dad, did you have a special reason for greeting Mr. Greenberg? And weren't you embarrassed shaking hands with Tom Jones in overalls, especially on the Sabbath?"

"Why, David, I see you have many important things to learn! No, I had no special motives for greeting the two men, and I certainly wasn't ashamed to greet Tom. I was only trying to do what we are taught in the Torah. It says, we must always greet every person in a friendly manner. Try to be the first to say "Sholom Aleichem" —Peace unto you—and mean it. Friendliness and good neighborliness should be the natural manners of a Jew."

That night, as the Gordon family sat enjoying their Saturday night Melavah Malkah meal, the phone rang. It was Mr. Greenberg. "Mr. Gordon, I'll have to ask you for a favor, since you're the only one in town I know and trust. Our sink is leaking and I remember you said hello today to a young plumber. Do you think he would come to fix my sink, even at night?"

"I've always been nice to Tom, and I'm sure he'll come help out in an emergency. I'll call him and I'm sure he'll be right over."

When Mr. Gordon had finished phoning Tom Jones, he turned to his family: "Tom said that he was sure Mr. Greenberg would be as nice and friendly as we are. He'll be there within the hour.

"You see, David, how wonderful friendliness is."

A SUCCESSFUL TRIP
(Continued)

Eliezer Abraham's servant, set out on his way to his master's birthplace, Charan. With him were ten camels loaded with gifts for the lucky girl that would be the bride of Isaac, Abraham's son.

Eliezer came to a small town. "Tell me," he asked of a stranger, "what is the name of this town?"
"Charan," was the reply.

Charan! Eliezer could not believe his own ears. All that great distance in only one day! It was surely a miracle! He knew that some heavenly angel had sped him on his way, and so he prayed to G-d. "O G-d of my master Abraham! Continue to help me! Send unto me the right maiden who will make a good wife for Isaac! So many maidens come to the well, how am I to know which is the one?"

Then a happy thought struck him. The maiden who will show a special act of kindness will be the one!

Bethuel, Abraham's nephew, was the best known man in Charan. He was famous for his great wealth, but even more for his daughter Rebecca. For she was fair and kind, and so very different from all the people surrounding her. Not only were the people of Charan wicked and unkind, but even her very family was not much better. Yet, Rebecca's heart remained pure and unspoilt. She was the very soul of kindness.

Rebecca would often go down to the well, outside the gates of the city, to draw water for the tired and thirsty travelers and their animals. Soon, she gained fame throughout the country for her good heart and kind ways. So unlike her wicked townspeople was Rebecca that many sang her praises, saying, "Rebecca is like a rose among thorns."

That evening Rebecca was happily going about her household chores, when a heaven-sent angel planted a desire in her heart to go down to the well, and fetch water for the travelers. Quickly completing her chores, she took her pitcher and hurried down to the well.

Just at that moment Eliezer was standing at the well. He saw a young maiden approach. Near the well stood a little boy who was weeping bitterly.

"Why do you cry, my lad?" asked Rebecca. "What's the matter?"

"I cut my foot upon a stone, and it's bleeding."

"Don't cry. We'll put it right in a minute."

Rebecca washed and dressed the boy's injury. "Go home to mother now, and don't worry about your leg any more. It will heal in no time."

Eliezer was a silent witness of this little scene. Rebecca's kindness to the little boy touched his heart. "Surely this is the maiden the angels have sent to me. G-d has answered my prayer!" he thought.

Eliezer approached Rebecca. "Will you fetch some water for me?"

"Yes, my lord, I will fetch some for you and some for your camels also. They too, must be thirsty!"

Eliezer had no doubt that this was the maiden for Isaac. Even before asking her name, he presented her with two lovely bracelets, and beautiful jewelled rings.

"Tell me, good maiden, who are you?" he asked.

"I am Rebecca, Bethuel's daughter "

"Have you room to lodge a weary traveler for the night?"

"Yes, my lord. You are welcome to our dwelling. We have room for you and fodder for your camels."

Eliezer rejoiced at the gracious words of the maiden. To him, they were a further proof that this was the maiden whom G-d had chosen as a wife for Isaac. And in his heart he whispered a silent prayer of thanks to G-d who had guided and helped him in his task.

Rebecca hastened to her parents to tell them of the arrival of the stranger. Breathlessly, she displayed the beautiful gifts he had given her. "And, mother, I have invited him to be our guest."

The table was set for the welcome guest.

"I will not eat until I have spoken," said Eliezer. "It is my privilege to be a servant of Abraham, whom G-d has blessed and prospered. He has sent me here to choose a wife for his son Isaac. And G-d has shown me that Rebecca will make a good wife for Isaac."

Even before Bethuel had a chance to reply, Laban, Rebecca's brother, disrespectfully said, "Here is Rebecca. You may have her whenever you wish."

Eliezer thought to himself: I will not heed the words of this fresh young man who speaks before his father. But Bethuel agreed to Laban's reply, and said, "You may take my daughter Rebecca to Abraham, for that is clearly the will of G-d."

(*To be Continued*)

 BRAVE AS A TIGER

"Do you miss Hebrew school, David?"

"Sort of, Jacob. I like Rabbi Weiss' stories."

"Say, look—there's Jackie, my neighbor. I just can't persuade him to join our Hebrew school. I wonder who that tough looking boy with him is?"

"Hello, Jackie. How are you?"

"Hi, David, this is my friend Dick."

"Glad to meet you, David. Say, why are you wearing that funny hat on such a hot day?"

"This hat is called yarmulke—a skullcap. I wear it because every Jewish male is supposed to keep his head covered all the time. That is one way we remember there is a G-d above, whose commandments we must obey."

"But why should you boys do this? Look at us—we're much more comfortable."

"We prefer wearing the caps," David answered with a smile. "So long, Jackie and Dick."

"Wait, we're going your way," said Jackie.

Dick kept arguing with his new friends.

"Come on, boys. Everybody stares at us. How about it, Jacob? Take off your cap."

Jacob sighed and put his skull cap into his pocket.

"Now, you too, David."

"Last week Rabbi Weiss taught us a lesson. We learned that we should be brave as a tiger to serve G-d. A tiger is never afraid. We, too, should never be afraid or ashamed to do what we know is right. Your laughing at me and nagging doesn't bother me one bit. I feel sorry for you because you don't have the understanding of what is right and what is wrong."

"I must give you credit," said Dickie. "From now on I'll have more respect for your beliefs."

Jacob replaced his cap on his head. "And I'll try to be stronger, like a tiger—and not listen to others."

בס״ד

A LUCKY FIND

LT. JOE BERG, FROM BROOKLYN, N.Y., A FORMER YESHIVAH STUDENT, IS SENT TO GERMANY WITH HIS OUTFIT, AND IS STATIONED WITH HIS TROOP IN THE SMALL CITY OF BAMBERG. AS AN ADMINISTRATION OFFICER, IN CHARGE OF THE ACCOUNTS OF HIS TROOP HE HAS MORE LIBERTY THAN THE AVERAGE SOLDIER, AND CAN MOVE ABOUT MORE EASILY, AND PROVIDE FOR HIS KOSHER FOOD.

OR TO SPEND SHABBOS AND HOLIDAYS AWAY FROM THE BAMBERG BARRACKS IN THE HOME OF SOME DP FAMILY.

ON ONE SUCH TRIP TO THE OUTSKIRTS OF THE CITY HE IS SURPRISED BY RAIN.

IT'S A GERMAN FARM BUT I'LL BE ABLE TO TAKE COVER TILL AFTER THE RAIN

SEVERAL CHILDREN CROWD ABOUT HIM.

BUT ONE YOUNGER GIRL, APPARENTLY SHY, DOES NOT COME CLOSE.

(To be Continued)

Published & Copyright 1961 by
MERKOS L'INYONEI CHINUCH, Inc.
770 EASTERN PARKWAY
Brooklyn 13, N. Y.
HYacinth 3-9250

No. 26

AT HOME

As Mrs. Greenman walked out of the kitchen, she turned anxious eyes to the front door. Where could the boys be? She looked into the living room.

"Dina," she called, "please come right down here and put away your school books; take your hat and coat off the sofa, too. A thirteen-year old girl should know enough to put away her things neatly and in order."

"I'm sorry, mother. I'll do it immediately."

Mrs. Greenman's thoughts returned to Jacob and Daniel, her adopted sons. They were her nephews, orphaned in Europe by the war. She had brought them to her home, and was trying her best to give them a normal, happy life.

« 9 »

"The boys are rather late coming home from school," remarked Dina.

"They should have been home some time ago."

"I hear them coming now, mother."

As Mrs. Greenman ran to the door, it was opened by a blond ten-year-old Jacob. "Hello, Aunt Rose," the boys chorused.

Daniel, who was twelve, noticed the anxious look on his aunt's face. "I hope you weren't worried, Aunt Rose. We forgot to tell you that our teacher asked us to stay a little later for extra lessons to help us catch up with our classmates."

"That's all right, my children." She never reproached the boys as she did her own daughter—she was afraid to hurt them. Dropping their books, the boys followed their aunt into the kitchen, where they removed their outer clothing.

Mrs. Greenman set a tray of milk and cookies before her nephews. Gathering their clothes and books, she went up to the lovely room she had furnished for them.

"I do hope they are happy here," her thoughts ran as she put the things in place. "They seem to like this room—they certainly mess it enough playing here every day. But I don't mind cleaning up after them if only they learn to love their home, and me, too."

She was really very good to them. No effort was too great for their sakes. Mrs. Greenman, trying to make her nephews forget their unhappy past, tried to satisfy their every wish.

"Aunt Rose," a shout interrupted her thoughts, "may we go out to play now?"

"Of course, you may."

A few hours later, Mrs. Greenman was returning from a shopping trip. Her good friend Mrs. Cohen was with her. As they walked into the house, Mrs. Greenman gasped! What a sight met her eyes! Hats, sweaters, balls and skates were strewn over everything. In the center sat Jacob and Daniel reading.

"Boys, couldn't you have put your clothes away just once?" The moment the words were out, she was sorry.

As the children hurriedly gathered their things, Mrs. Greenman wondered, "Will they ever forgive me for scolding them? What can I say to them now?"

Mrs. Greenman trudged up the steps. "Will they kiss me good-night as usual?"

"Is that you, Aunt Rose?" asked Jacob.

"Yes, dear, it is. Children, about that scolding—"

"Oh, Aunt Rose, you were very right, and we were wrong. From now on we'll try our best to keep things neat."

"I'll tell you something else," said Daniel. "You know, you have always been very good to us and given us everything we want. So, although we love you very much, we never felt as if we really belonged here."

"We were like guests," said Jacob.

"But tonight, when you scolded us, I felt as if you're a real mother, and we were really your children."

The tears came to their aunt's eyes, but she smiled as she said, "Okay, from now on I'll be as strict with you as I am with Dina. You'll have to keep your room and your things very tidy, go on errands, and be really helpful sons."

"We will, we will," they promised as they kissed her good-night.

THE BRIDE SAID "YES"
(Continued)

"Eliezer, make haste, and return to Abraham's house. This is a place of evil men. Depart lest any harm should befall you." These were the words an angel spoke to Eliezer when he slept that night.

The next morning, Eliezer arose and informed Rebecca's family of his desire to depart, but her family wished her to stay for at least another year to prepare some beautiful clothes for her wedding.

Eliezer, however, was impatient to return home. For one thing, he did not want to stay any longer among wicked people, and for another, he was anxious to bring the good news and the fair maiden, to old Abraham, who was surely waiting for him impatiently. He insisted that they leave at once.

"Let Rebecca decide!" the family said.

"I want to go with Eliezer now!" Rebecca said, and the question was settled.

Bidding her family "good bye," Rebecca departed, in the company of her faithful servant.

She was very happy indeed. But none was happier than Eliezer. "I never thought I could be such a fine matchmaker," he said delightedly.

JACOB AND ESAU

Twenty years had passed since Isaac and Rebecca were married. To their great sorrow, they had not been blessed with children. Finally, G-d answered Isaac's prayers, and Rebecca gave birth to twins. The first child to be born was covered with hair like a grown person. His parents called him Esau (from the Hebrew word "*asso*," finished). The second child was born holding on to his brother's heel, and Isaac called him Jacob (Hebrew "Yaakov," one that takes by the heel).

It was a strange thing, the way they grew up: twin boys, both children of perfect, holy parents, and yet they were so different. Jacob spent all his time at home, studying with his father and grandfather Abraham. Not only was he studious, he was truly like his father and grandfather: honest, trusting and sincere.

But his brother Esau was just the opposite. He was always finding a new trick to avoid studying. Instead, he spent most of his time in the fields. He enjoyed hunting and killing, and was often absent from home for many days. But he was clever enough to pretend to be interested in certain studies so his parents wouldn't realize how different he was.   (*To be Continued*)

BEHIND THE IRON CURTAIN

Mrs. Levy didn't even try to hide her great excitement as she stood by the window. It was a day the whole family had been waiting for, a long time. After many negotiations and delays, their little orphan cousin from behind the Iron Curtain was finally here. It was truly a miracle that they had been able to bring him to the U. S.

There was her husband's car! Mrs. Levy ran out as her husband, then her eight-year-old son Daniel, came out from the car, followed by a small, shy looking boy. Jacob Kaplinsky looked younger than his ten years.

"Sholom Aleichem. We're so happy to have you here," she exclaimed as she led the boys into the house.

During the delicious dinner, Jacob watched Daniel as he washed and said a prayer before the meal and said grace afterwards. Jacob haltingly did the same. "We were not allowed to go to Hebrew school to learn," he explained, "and I only know what my dear parents taught me before they died."

"Don't worry, Jacob. You will go to Yeshivah Day School with me, and you'll soon catch up," Daniel comforted him.

"Oh, I can't wait! My father always spoke about how wonderful it was to be free to learn Torah. How he prayed that some day, somehow I would have the opportunity to learn as a Jew should! How often he spoke about this!"

"We are anxious to hear about your parents and life across the ocean."

"My father would explain to me that it was a great privilege and duty of every Jew to study the Torah as much as he is able. Because the Torah is our dearest heritage, our most sacred possession! Even under the most terrible circumstances, Jews have always sacrificed much in order to fulfill the commandment to study Torah.

"Do you know, my father used to meet secretly with several of his friends to study, but they didn't have the proper books, and they were always afraid of being discovered."

"And to think," burst out Daniel, "that some of the boys are always complaining that they'd rather play ball, and they hate studying."

"I can't believe it!" replied Jacob. "I think I will never forget for one minute how lucky I am to be able to study Torah. Why, how can you know how to behave as a good Jew, if you don't learn? There is so much to know: The Bible, the Talmud, the laws, the prayers. My father told me all about them. And that's what I want to do! That was my father's last wish: that I get a chance to study Torah, and now that G-d had brought me to a place where I am free to learn, I will try with all my heart to make my father in heaven happy."

A LUCKY FIND (2)

(To be Continued)

ש עורי למור הרת

SHALOH

**Published & Copyright 1961 by
MERKOS L'INYONEI CHINUCH, Inc.
770 EASTERN PARKWAY
Brooklyn 13, N. Y.
HYacinth 3-9250**

No. 27

BENEFIT OF A DOUBT

"A dozen eggs, 2 quarts of milk, a loaf of bread—5 lbs. of sugar—that will be $1.74," said Mr. Cohen, the grocer.

"Mr. Cohen," stammered David, "could you please do me a favor? I haven't the money now. I'll pay you tomorrow."

"Certainly, I'll just put $1.74 on your mother's bill."

"Um— I know it sounds funny, Mr. Cohen, but please don't add it to my mother's bill."

"What's this, David? You're hiding something from your mother? Did she give you the money and you spent it elsewhere? It's hard to believe!"

« 17 »

Poor David looked all confused. "I know it sounds awful. Honestly—I didn't spend the money for myself. I can't explain. I promise to pay tomorrow." The tears swelled in David's eyes.

"You'll have to explain your behavior tomorrow as well as pay. I feel it is my duty to tell your mother what's going on. But I'll wait till tomorrow."

Red and embarrassed, David took his package and left the store. At the door a neighbor, Mr. Klein, greeted him very happily.

After David left, Mr. Klein exclaimed: "Now there's a wonderful boy!"

"Wonderful?" snorted Mr. Cohen. "I used to think so too, but not any more!"

"What made you change your mind?"

"He just bought some groceries for which he promised to pay tomorrow, but begged me not to add to his mother's account. He didn't even bother to explain when I accused him of using the money for himself. That I should live to see David fooling his mother!"

"You should not judge David without knowing all the facts. David was too modest to talk about it, but I saw what he did with the money with my own eyes. Listen! Do you know the widow—Mrs. Glass on my block? This afternoon her little girl Sarah, four years old, was crying, 'Mommy, buy me these cherries in the store, please, I love them.'

" 'Cherries are too expensive for us,' answered the poor woman.

" 'Then let's have that large cake in the bakery window,' said her other daughter Rachel, who is six.

" 'My poor babies, we are lucky we can buy bread and milk.'

"David was on his way here when we overheard this conversation. I saw him go and buy two pounds of cherries and the layer cake. He brought it over to Mrs. Glass and shyly said: 'Here's a little present.' You should have seen the tears of joy in those little orphans' eyes."

Mr. Cohen stroked his chin thoughtfully. "It is written: 'Judge every man with a good eye.' I have made a great mistake."

When David came to pay his bill the next day, he was greeted with a big smile. "Forgive me, David, for my mean talk. I was thrilled when I found out how you spent the money."

"This is my own money that I saved up," said David. "I didn't have time to go for it yesterday."

"Here's a dollar back," said Mr. Cohen. "Please do me a favor and let me share in giving the orphan girls a gift!"

PARTING OF THE WAYS

(Continued)

Abraham reached the ripe old age of 175 years. He felt that the time had come for him to leave this world.

He sent for his son Isaac, who was then 75 years old and the father of the twins, Jacob and Esau, who were then 15 years old.

All through the years, Abraham had taught his beloved son Isaac to love G-d and to fear Him, and to practise the love and fear of G-d in his daily life. This meant to walk in G-d's ways, the ways of justice and kindness, helping others in their need, and teaching them to know G-d. Abraham was happy to know that his son would continue to spin the golden thread which he had begun and would hold holy the covenant agreements which G-d had made with him.

Indeed, Abraham was a happy man even on this last day of his life. Looking back upon his long life, ever since he was three years old, he knew that it was a full life, every moment of which was spent in the service of G-d and mankind. His beloved son Isaac was at his bedside. So was also his son Ishmael. Ishmael, who was like an untamed animal in his youth, was now a changed man, worthy to be known as Abraham's son.

All the people of the land of Canaan, young and old, with their kings and princes, came to pay their last respects to Abraham, the greatest prince of them all. They were all very sad, and many wept when they heard that the great and beloved Abraham, the G-dly Prince, had passed away.

※　　※　　※

Abraham had been laid to rest in the Cave of Machpelah, next to his wife Sarah, and Adam and Eve. Isaac was in mourning, and Jacob was preparing some food for him. But where was Esau?

Esau had slipped out quietly and gone off to the fields and woods to do some hunting!

Until that time, Esau had been trying to be a good boy, although it was very difficult for him. He had tried his best not to upset his father, nor did he want his grandfather to know that he was not all that was expected of him.

But now that his grandfather was dead, and he was fifteen, Esau decided that he was quite a man, and could take care of himself. From now on he was going to do as he pleased, and first of all, he decided, there would be no more studies for him.

(To be Continued)

 THE MEANING OF TEFILLIN

Mr. and Mrs. Gordon tried to hide their smiles as they watched their six-year-old son Joseph. He held a block tied around with an old belt. He rolled up his left sleeve, placed the block on his left biceps, then carefully wound the belt around his left arm. Joseph was obviously imitating his father putting on "Tefillin." He took another block and another belt and began placing it on his head.

"What a little monkey!" said Mr. Gordon. "He's been watching David."

"Joseph has learned the rules very well, too. He is placing the make-believe 'Tefillin' exactly as I've taught

David. One on his left biceps and one just above the forehead between his eyes. And he's winding his old belt around his arm and fingers just the way I've shown David to wind the leather thongs of his Tefillin."

Just then David, their older son, entered the room. When he saw his little brother, he couldn't stop his laughter. Joseph looked up, startled.

"All right, laugh, just because you'll be thirteen soon and a Bar Mitzvah and you'll be allowed to wear real Tefillin. It's not my fault I'm smaller."

"Now, boys, don't tease and bicker," said their father. "A quarter to the one that answers my questions correctly. What are Tefillin?"

"I know," said David. "Tefillin are a set of two small black boxes to each of which is attached a long piece of leather about half an inch wide. Inside each box are four portions from the Holy Torah, hand-written by a learned scribe on special parchment."

"Good for you, David. Do you know who must put on the Tefillin?"

"Yes. Every Jewish boy and man must put on the Tefillin every morning except Saturdays and Jewish holidays. They usually start a few weeks before their thirteenth birthday, when it becomes imperative. If you didn't manage to put them on in the morning, you may do so later in the day, but not after sunset."

"Correct. You mentioned portions from the Torah. Which portions?"

"In the Tefillin are written the first two chapters of the prayer 'Shema Yisrael'—'Hear O Israel'. These two chapters contain the basic principles of the Jewish belief in G-d. The other two chapters in the Tefillin tell about the exodus of the Jews from Egypt. This is the history of the beginning of the Jewish nation and of the Almighty's great miracles in their behalf."

"Do you know why we don Tefillin?"

This time father himself replied: "First of all—it is commanded to do so in the Torah, 'And you shall tie them for a sign on your hand and they shall be a symbol between your eyes.' Besides, it shows that a Jew should be prepared to serve G-d with every part of himself. We tie the Tefillin on our left hand—on the side of our heart—our heart must be filled with love of G-d. We tie the leather around our arm and hand—we must perform the commandments with our hands and all our body. We put Tefillin on the head—we must use our brains and thoughts for G-d's commandments. In other words, we must 'Think, Feel, and Do G-d's will.' That is what we are showing when we put on Tefillin."

"That is why we start the day by putting on Tefillin. To show that if we start the day right, G-d will help us behave as good Jews all day," Joseph added.

"I'm proud of you, my boys. Here are your quarters. I hope you'll never forget these things and put on Tefillin every day of your lives."

A LUCKY FIND (3)

(To be Continued)

Published & Copyright 1961 by
MERKOS L'INYONEI CHINUCH, Inc.
770 EASTERN PARKWAY
Brooklyn 13, N. Y.
HYacinth 3-9250

No. 28

THE WINNER

Shy little Hannah edged over to the circle of girls surrounding Rebecca. They were all listening.

"Besides this new coat, my mother got me a suit and hat. They're very expensive. My mother says, a pretty girl like me deserves only the best," Rebecca said as she proudly tossed her blond curls. "Think how nice I'll look at the Purim party after the play!"

"Are you sure you'll get the part of Queen Esther?" one of her friends asked.

"Well, all I know is that I'm the prettiest in the class and one of the smartest. Besides, my parents are pretty important people in the school. Who else would the teacher choose?"

"Well," said another girl hesitatingly, "Hannah here has had dramatic lessons, and everyone says she's a good actress."

Rebecca smiled at the blushing Hannah. "You're a nice girl, and I like you. But I'm afraid I'm too much competition for you. There's the bell." The girls marched into class.

"Good morning, girls!" Miss Levy greeted them. "I'm glad to see you all looking well. Today is the big day. Today we decide who gets the most important part in the Purim play."

After they had done some work, Miss Levy said, "Put down your books now. Who would like to try for the Queen Esther part?" Rebecca raised her hand. "Is that all? I want more volunteers." Slowly Hannah raised her hand too.

"Here, take this page, read through your part and study it and then you will read it out loud." Miss Levy handed Rebecca a sheet to study.

As Rebecca read, she sounded just like what she was: a proud, bright girl reading a part in a play. Her speech was good, her expression too. She returned the page with a look that said, "I know I did well."

"Now I'd like to hear you do it," Miss Levy turned to Hannah. Hannah took the part and read it with concentration. Then her voice rang out. She was a changed girl—she seemed suddenly taller and more stately. Her face glowed with goodness, with conviction.

As she read, it was easy to feel she was *really* Queen Esther.

When Hannah finished reading, the class spontaneously applauded. Miss Levy came over: "Hannah, the part is yours! If you do as well with all of it, you will make us all very proud."

"As for you, Rebecca, I couldn't help overhearing you boasting to the class before. You are a nice girl, but I'm afraid a girl who is always boasting about how much better she is than others will soon find herself without friends. Every one has good points and bad, and a nice person doesn't brag. I can see on your face that you understand and have learned a lesson."

PARTING OF THE WAYS
(*Continued*)

Out in the woods Esau hid in the bushes waiting for game. Suddenly he saw a royal party in the distance. He recognized Nimrod, or Amraphel, the king of Babylon, surrounded by a group of his mighty warriors and best hunters.

Esau knew that Nimrod hated him. Ever since Abraham walked out of the burning furnace without a hair singed, and beat him later in the Great War, Nimrod watched with worry the rising sun of Abraham. But he was soon satisfied that Abraham, as well as his son Isaac, were peaceful men. Esau was quite different. Esau could become a dangerous enemy some day. No wonder Nimrod hated and feared Esau.

Esau watched the royal hunting party like a spider waiting to jump at a fly caught in his web. His heart began to beat faster as he saw most of the hunters scatter through the wood. Only two hunters stayed with Nimrod, and they were coming nearer to his hiding place.

When Nimrod came close enough, Esau darted from his hiding place and struck a mighty blow at Nimrod, cutting his head off outright.

Now the two warriors rushed at Esau with a loud yell. But Esau was strong, skilful with his sword, and light on his feet. He fought the two warriors with all his might, and finally killed one, then the other.

At this time, he saw Nimrod's men rushing toward him from all directions. They had heard the cries of the fighting men and sped to the scene of action.

Esau saw that he was hopelessly outnumbered. He quickly managed to strip the headless body of Nimrod of his royal robe and run for his life as fast as his feet would carry him. He was lucky enough to escape Nimrod's men, and he came home panting. He was frightened, tired and hungry, more dead than alive.

He found his brother Jacob still busy with the dish of lentils of which he had served his father, as was usual in a house of mourning.

Esau dropped to the ground of the tent, opened his mouth wide, and called out: "Pour down some of that red stuff into my throat! I'm so tired, I'm dying!"

Jacob was quite disgusted with his brother. He saw the stains of blood on him, and he knew that his brother was up to no good. Jacob felt very sad that on this day of their dear grandfather's death, Esau had nothing better to do than to go hunting, and killing people. For Esau had boasted of his great feat in murdering Nimrod and slaying two of his bodyguards.

"Shame on you, Esau, for the way you behaved to-day!" Jacob scolded his brother. "How lucky for our grandfather that he passed away before he saw you turn to this evil way," he added.

"Stick to your books, Jacob, and don't mix in my affairs!" Esau replied angrily. "Besides, don't try to teach your older brother and First-born!"

"You seem to forget that the First-born has duties and responsibilities. As the head of the family it is his duty to keep the traditions of the family, and as a priest to G-d it is his duty to lead a holy life," Jacob said very earnestly.

"You can have the Birthright with all its responsibilities and duties! I want to be a free man, to do as I please," Esau retorted.

"Do you really want to give up your Birthright, Esau?" Jacob asked unbelievingly.

"Sure! A bit of this lentil soup is worth more to me than the whole Birthright," Esau replied, and laughed very loudly.

"Would you sell me your Birthright, then?" Jacob asked.

"It's yours for the asking. I'm a hunter, not a priest."

"Let's make a real bill of sale," Jacob said.

"Gladly," Esau replied. Soon he signed the contract of sale which Jacob had drawn up.

"Some bargain you've got," Esau mocked as he filled himself with the red pottage. When he could not eat any more, Esau rose, and pouring some more abuse on the Birthright and Jacob's foolishness, he finally called out:

"Good-bye, Big Brother. Be a good boy now, for you have the Birthright. As for me, the sword is my Birthright. Good-bye!"

Jacob knew that from that day on they had parted ways. They were worlds apart, as far from each other as heaven was from the earth.

(To be Continued)

 ## STRONG AS A LION

"It's too hot to walk," said Leah to her friend Sarah. "Let's just sit down on this bench."

"Ouch, even the bench feels hot," exclaimed Sarah. "I imagine what it must be like in the city if it's 95° here."

"Why does it have to be Shabbos," sighed Leah. "What I wouldn't give for a nice dip in the pool—I could cry when I think of it. I'm so uncomfortable."

Just then Janet and Roslyn passed by carrying their bathing suits. "Too bad you can't joint us, girls," they called. "This Saturday isn't a very pleasant rest day for you."

"I can't stand this heat another minute!" Leah jumped up. "It can't be such a big sin to want to cool off a bit. I'm putting on my suit and taking a dip."

"What will your parents say?"

"They are taking their usual Saturday afternoon nap. They may be a bit angry at first. But I'm sure they'll relent when they see how much better I feel."

"Please, Leah, don't go. You may feel more comfortable for a while. But is the comfort worth breaking the Holy Sabbath Laws for? Do you want to spoil it all because of a few hours' comfort?"

Leah hesitated. "But—but it doesn't seem so bad."

"Think," Sarah leaned forward in great earnestness. "Didn't we learn that we should be strong like a lion to do G-d's will? Strong like a lion to fight doing wrong? Do you have any courage? Do you hesitate at the first test of your faith in Shabbos?"

"I guess you're right. But I'm still hot and uncomfortable," protested Leah.

"You know what, the porch on my cottage is pretty cool. I'll bring out some ice-cold soda and watermelon and something to read. That will make the time pass quickly. When Sabbath is over we'll have nothing to be ashamed and sorry about."

"You're a good friend, Sarah. I'll try to learn from you to be strong in fighting temptation."

A LUCKY FIND   (4)

LT. JOE BEGINS TO MAKE SOME CAREFUL INQUIRIES ABOUT THE FARM.
ALL HE FINDS OUT, THAT IS OF ANY INTEREST TO HIM, IS THAT ANDREAS HOFER WAS
ONE OF THOSE WHO WAS GIVEN JEWISH PRISONERS AS FARM HELPERS DURING THE
WAR, AND THAT THEY WERE TREATED AS CRUELLY THERE, AS ANY PLACE ELSE.
HE INQUIRES AT AN AGENCY

WHAT CAN I DO ABOUT LITTLE MOLLIE? JUST BECAUSE A LITTLE GIRL WHOSE HAIR IS DARKER THAN HER BROTHER'S AND SISTER'S LOOKS AT YOUR RING WITH A STAR ON IT, IS NO REASON FOR YOU TO DO ANY THING

ON THE CONTRARY THE AMERICAN AUTHORITIES WILL DEAL HARSHLY WITH YOU. IF YOU BOTHER THE HOFERS.. LISTEN TO ME, YOUNG MAN, AND FORGET YOUR SILLY IDEA ABOUT THE GIRL

No! I CAN'T JUST LET THIS GO, I'LL HAVE TO SEE MOLLIE AGAIN WITHOUT HER MOTHER, AND SEE IF I'M RIGHT

HE RETURNS TO THE NEIGHBORHOOD OF THE HOFER'S FARM SEVERAL TIMES, UNTIL BY GOOD PROVIDENCE HE SEES MOLLIE ALONE

HELLO MOLLIE! WOULD YOU LIKE A BAR OF CHOCOLATE CAN I SEE YOUR RING AGAIN

SURE

SUDDENLY, IN A PURELY YIDDISH PRONUNCIATION...

MAMME, MAMME!

(To be Continued)

Published & Copyright 1961 by
MERKOS L'INYONEI CHINUCH, Inc.
770 EASTERN PARKWAY
Brooklyn 13, N. Y.
HYacinth 3-9250

No. 29

A SCRAP

Sara sat at the desk doing her homework. This was an important report. Junior High School meant a lot of hard work. This scrap book had taken weeks to assemble. But if she thought so herself, it was very good. Sara was proud of it and was sure the teacher would admire it and give it a high mark.

"Sara, Sara, isn't it gorgeous?" her little sister Rebecca danced into the room. She was wearing her new dress and twirled around. "I couldn't resist trying it on! I just can't wait to wear it! Do you like it?"

"It's beautiful, Rebecca. But can't you see I'm busy?" Sara waived her sister away without turning her head.

A second later she looked up startled as her sister began to scream and cry.

"How could you do that, you mean thing! I hate you! I'll get even with you!"

"Oh, my dear, I'm sorry," Sara gasped as she saw that when she had waved her hand at Rebecca, the pen between her fingers had splashed some ugly blots of ink on the beautiful new pink dress.

"What's the good of saying you're sorry? You spoiled my dress, you nasty thing! I'll fix you!" Rebecca was so angry she didn't know what she was saying, or doing. She grabbed Sara's scrap book and began to rip it up. She would have destroyed it completely if Sara hadn't grabbed it quickly away.

Just then their mother came into the room. "What on earth is happening here, children?"

The girls tearfully related to their mother the thing that had just taken place. "Now calm down," she ordered, "Rebecca, go change your dress. It was an accident, and I know your sister is sorry. I'm sure I can remove the ink stains. Come right back here."

"Now let me see that scrap book.—H'm, I'm afraid you'll have to rewrite this page, and replace this torn picture. But these two pages can be neatly mended with some cellophane tape. Don't cry, Sara, I'll help you and your work will not go to waste. Your teacher will never know."

"But I must have a talk with Rebecca." She left Sara trying to repair her precious scrap book.

"Well, Rebecca, what do you have to say for yourself? The ink on your dress was an accident, but Sara's ripped scrap book was not!"

"But mother, I just got so upset and lost my temper and I just couldn't stop myself."

"Exactly," nodded her mother. "Because an angry person loses his self control and can do something terrible while he is angry, something he wouldn't think of doing when calm, something he would always regret, our Torah teaches us that anger is a very grave sin. It can cause a person to commit a terrible act because his anger blinds him!

"A person must learn to control his anger, to be master over his temper before it becomes master over him and makes him act in a way that shames him."

"You're so right, mother," sighed Rebecca. "If I ever feel angry again, I'll remember what happened today, and control myself. I think I'll go apologize to Sara now and help her fix the scrap book. Yes, Mother?"

THE BLESSING

It was the night of Passover when Isaac called his elder son Esau and told him: "This is a night when all the world sings G-d's praises, for the stores of dew are opened to bring blessing to the fields and meadows. Go and bring me dainty meats, and I will bless you!"

As Esau departed, a thought came to Isaac. "Eat not the bread of him that has an evil eye and desire not his dainty meats." Strange that this saying should have occurred to him just then! Could it be that Esau, because of his old father's failing sight, was fooling him all the time?

Meanwhile Rebecca was trying to persuade her younger son Jacob to disguise himself and get the blessings from his father. Jacob pleaded with his mother, but to no use. "The blessings are yours, and if you do not listen to me, I shall have to go to Isaac and tell him who is the worthy son. Shall I break your father's heart?" Rebecca said.

With tears in his eyes Jacog went to do his mother's bidding.

When Jacob came in, Isaac felt the perfume of the Garden of Eden in the room. It pleased him greatly, but the next moment he was startled to hear the soft gentle voice of Jacob. "Please, father, arise, I pray thee, and eat of the meat, for G-d, your G-d, sent me good speed."

Isaac never heard such words as "please" from Esau, and the name of G-d was never on Esau's lips. The dreadful moment came when Isaac called the disguised Jacob to come near, so that he might feel him. Jacob's knees became very weak and he would have surely fallen had not the unseen hand of an angel grabbed him at the back of his neck, held him up and pushed him to Isaac.

The hands of Isaac felt the hands of his son and

his neck, and they were not smooth, for he was feeling the skins of the baby goats which Rebecca had cleverly put on Jacob. "The voice is the voice of Jacob, but the hands are the hands of Esau," Isaac exclaimed. And he blessed Jacob.

"May G-d give you of the dew of heaven, and of the fat of the earth. . . ."

Jacob was thinking of the gentle drops of the dew that have such wonderful refreshing power. Surely his father must have had in mind the words of G-d that bring life, strength and blessing to mankind, as the gentle dew brings life to the parched earth. And when the blessings were concluded and Jacob took his leave, the words "dew of heaven and the fat of the earth" continued to ring in his ears.

(To be Continued)

    PREPARING FOR PICNIC

The four boyish heads were close together in conference. David, Abe, Sam, and Nathan were planning their club's picnic. They were the Refreshments Committee, and it was quite a job deciding what, and how much of it, would satisfy thirty hungry boys.

"Let's have plenty of hot dogs—with mustard," said Abe. "I can get them cheaper in my uncle's store."

"If it's a hot day, everyone will expect ice-cream," was Sam's opinion.

"Now hold on," said David, the chairman of the committee. "We can't have both delicatessen and ice-cream. Let's come to order and decide things seriously."

"First, whatever we serve, we must be sure that it it absolutely kosher according to our laws."

Nat chimed in, "It's best to buy in Sabbath-observing stores. Then we're sure we can rely on the kashruth of everything."

"Now," said David, "shall we serve meat or dairy foods?"

"Everybody likes delicatessen." It was Abe again.

"I know," said Sam, "but think of the disadvantages. Where would we get it?"

"What's wrong with the store on the corner?" asked Abe.

"Since he doesn't observe the Sabbath, can we trust that he observes the laws of kashruth strictly?" asked Dave.

"Just what could he have done wrong?"

"Well, for one thing, Jews can only eat certain kinds of meat: lamb, veal, and beef. No pigs' meat: pork, bacon, or ham. Then the animal has to be slaughtered according to the laws of our Torah, by an ordained 'shochet'—slaughterer—who has studied these laws."

"Like my grandfather," interrupted Nathan.

"Right. Then within three days after it's been slaughtered, the meat has to be soaked for half an hour in cold water, salted for an hour, then the salt is rinsed off—"

"And if any one of these rules is omitted or changed, no Jew may eat the meat," concluded Nathan, as David paused for breath.

"I can see where we have to be careful where we shop for meat," was Sam's opinion. "But even if we have a reliable butcher, I'm still not in favor of hot dogs for our picnic."

"Why?"

"Well, it's July, and it's hot, and we'll have to wait six hours after our hot dogs before we can drink milk or eat ice-cream."

"We'll also have to be very careful about the cakes and candies we buy, to make sure they contain no milk or cream."

"But what could we have instead?" asked Abe.

"What about sandwiches like cheese and jam, salmon, egg salad, plenty of fruit, cake, candy, and cookies, ice-cream and milk?" David asked.

"I'm for it," said Nathan.

"So am I," said Sam.

"I still prefer hot dogs, but you're right, I guess," said Abe.

"Okay, boys," said David. "Sam and Abe will take care of the sandwiches, cakes, and cookies—all in a kosher bakery, please. Nathan and I will take care of the rest. Here's hoping we have a good time!"

A LUCKY FIND (5)

(To be Continued)

Published & Copyright 1961 by
MERKOS L'INYONEI CHINUCH, Inc.
770 EASTERN PARKWAY
Brooklyn 13, N. Y.
HYacinth 3-9250

No. 30

WITHOUT PERMISSION

"Dave, I've got it! Come take a look!"

David Gordon put down his book and ran to the window. There was his best friend and neighbor Aaron beside his shiny new bicycle. Aaron was grinning and jumping with excitement. And well he might. His new bike was a beauty! David knew how long Aaron had dreamed of owning a bicycle; how hard he had worked at being helpful and well-behaved at home to earn it. He shared his friend's joy.

"It's too late now to take a ride, but I've brought it over to leave in your garage as we agreed."

David slowly inspected the bike, admiring every feature, then wheeled it into the garage. He went back to his book, but now he found it hard to concentrate. "Oh, I might as well go down and look at it again," he slammed down his book, "then maybe I'll be able to study."

In a moment he was in the garage, turning the bars, patting the seat. "I think I'll just ride up and down the driveway," thought David to himself. "I know Aaron would never object—we've always shared everything, and he has always said he would let me ride his bike when he finally got it. . . . On the other hand, I really don't have his permission now that the bike is a reality not a dream. He's trusting me to watch it for him carefully, and I am responsible for whatever happens.

"Oh, how silly I am! Aaron would laugh at my doubts. What can happen riding up and down the driveway?"

So thinking, David jumped on the bike and began pedalling down the driveway. My, how good it felt! As he neared the end, he steered to turn back. Alas! David had never steered such a bicycle. It was an awkward turn and he smacked right into the side of the house.

Poor Dave! He found himself sitting on the ground. He was shaken up and bruised, but not really hurt. But his heart fell as he looked at the dented and misshapen bicycle.

"Just a minute ago it was so new and beautiful, and I knew I shouldn't ride it. We've learned so many times that when we watch something for someone else, we have to be even more careful than with our own possessions. We are not permitted to use something left with us for safekeeping without the owner's express permission.

"How can I face Aaron? Oh, of course he will be kind and forgiving. And I will certainly pay for fixing the bike. But it will never look so new and shiny! I've spoiled the pleasure of the very first ride! Aaron will forgive me, but can I forgive myself? I will have to work very hard to make him trust me again!"

Such were David's repentant thoughts as he trudged slowly to Aaron's house to break the sad news.

THE HOLD-UP

Hardly had Jacob left Isaac, when Esau returned from the hunt. He prepared the meat and brought it to his father. He soon learned that Jacob had already received a wonderful blessing, and Esau cried with anger and disappointment. Isaac blessed him, too, giving him the right to throw off Jacob's rule whenever his brother strayed from the path of G-d. But Esau hated Jacob, and day and night he brooded over a plan to kill Jacob. Yet he feared his father too much, and he decided to wait with his revenge till after Isaac's death.

But Rebecca observed Esau and understood that no good could come from his mood.

"Go to my brother Laban in Paddan-Aram," Rebecca told Jacob, "and stay with him until your brother will forget his anger, and then I shall send for you."

His father Isaac also urged him to go there, but warned him against the wicked people he might come across in strange lands. "Be faithful to the teachings of your family wherever you go," his father warned him.

And so, having kissed his beloved father and mother, Jacob set out upon his long and tiresome journey. He was richly loaded with presents for his uncle and cousins.

The sun was about to set when Jacob heard the galloping of horses behind him. Presently he recognized his nephew Eliphaz, Esau's oldest son, riding at the head of ten horsemen.

"Are you in peace, my nephew?" Jacob asked him.

Eliphaz lowered his head and did not answer. Jacob repeated his question.

"My father sent me to kill you," Eliphaz replied. "I hate to do it, uncle, but I must obey my father." Saying this, Eliphaz drew his sword.

"Wait," Jacob pleaded. "Would you murder your uncle in cold blood? What have I done to you that you want to take my life? It isn't only my life that I plead for, but the holy teachings of our fathers Abraham and Isaac which I have to carry on. If you kill me you put an end to all that they have built up and given their lives to. . . ."

"But my father commanded me to kill you," Eliphaz said.

"Look here," Jacob said, "I have lots of riches with me:—gold, jewelry and precious stones. Take it all away and bring it to your father. He will be pleased with all this treasure. As for me, a penniless man is no better off than a dead man. It is almost the same as if you had murdered me."

Eliphaz was moved by Jacob's pleas and agreed to spare his life. He took away everything that Jacob owned, and rode off with his men.

When Eliphaz told his father what happened, Esau flew into a rage. But there was nothing to be done, for Jacob was far away.

In the meantime Jacob went on his way. He was grateful to G-d for saving his life, but his heart was heavy. Would Esau's anger always follow him? Was it not enough that he was driven from home, stripped of all he owned, that Esau should seek to take his life as well?

JACOB'S DREAM

The day was gone, and night found the wanderer in an open field before the town of Luz, still within the territory of Canaan. Weary from his journey, he took stones for his pillow and lay down to rest. With the earth for his bed, and the bright starlit heavens for his roof, he fell asleep. And in his sleep he saw a marvelous dream. A big ladder seemed to rise beside him, the foot of which rested upon the earth, and the top of which reached the heaven. Up and down this ladder went the angels of G-d. From above came the voice of G-d: "I am G-d, the G-d of Abraham your father, and the G-d of Isaac; the land whereon you rest, to you shall I give it, and to your children. And behold I am with you, and I shall guard you wherever you go, and shall bring you back into this land; for I shall not leave you until I have done that of which I have spoken to you." Jacob rose up a new man, full of hope and courage. He knew that he was not alone in the world.

(To be Continued)

 SWIFT AS AN EAGLE

The group of whispering boys opened to include Sam.

"There's a terrific picture tomorrow at the movies, with special cartoons. Only twenty cents for children at 1 P.M. We're all meeting in front of the movies after lunch. You'll come too, won't you?"

"Play hooky, you mean?"

"Don't be a sissy, Sam! Your mother will think you're in school. Sleepy old Mr. Jacobs won't even notice we didn't come to class after lunch. If he does notice, we'll give him some excuse. Colds or sore throats or something."

"I'll think it over."

The next day after lunch, Sam met them at the movies. "Good, we're glad you decided to join us."

"I'm not going with you. I think you should change your minds too. Our seeing this movie is leading us to playing hooky and telling lies. Let us flee like eagles from doing wrong."

"Don't be such a wet blanket and preacher. If you don't want to have fun, go back to school. Leave us alone."

The next day in school his friends cornered Sam.

"Did Mr. Jacobs notice our absence? Did we miss any work?"

"Mr. Jacobs didn't mention your absence. But you did miss an important new lesson. We're getting a test on long division today. We reviewed all day yesterday. Mr. Jacobs will collect the reports the first thing today."

"Oh, oh! Am I in trouble! My mother warned me if I fail one more arithmetic test I lose a month's allowance."

"My father will give it to me when he finds out I didn't do my homework," said a second boy.

"The picture wasn't even worth it," added a third.

"Sam, you were right after all. We fooled our mothers and Mr. Jacobs about playing hooky. But the movie wasn't worth it if we get poor marks today."

"You're an eagle all right, Sam. Smart and swift. From now on we'll call you 'Eagle Sam.' "

A LUCKY FIND (6)

LT. JOE CONFIDES IN HIS BEST PAL, SGT. BARRY BERGER, ANOTHER YESHIVAH BOY FROM A DIFFERENT OUTFIT STATIONED IN BAMBERG, WHOM HE HAD MET AT THE IMPROVISED SHUL.

WE MUST DO SOMETHING ABOUT THIS CHILD.

OH, JUST FORGET ABOUT IT. YOU HAVE NO PROOF THAT SHE'S JEWISH.

BUT I HEARD THE GIRL CALL "MAMME, MAMME". HOW CAN YOU AND I PERMIT A JEWISH NESHOMOH TO BE LOST, BECAUSE OF THAT BIG BRUTE OF A FARMER WHO HATES THE JEWS AS MUCH AS HE DID BEFORE, DURING HITLER'S DAYS.

YOU'VE GOT TO GET SOME REAL EVIDENCE

AND IF NOT...

THE FOLLOWING SHABBOS LT. JOE IS INVITED TO THE HOME OF A YOUNG DP COUPLE, BY THE NAME OF MOSES AND MIRIAM SCHARF IN THE CONVERSATION AT THE TABLE, THEY SPEAK OF THEIR OLD HOME IN POLAND, AND OF THE REST OF THE FAMILY THAT HAS COMLETELY BEEN DESTROYED

A FRIEND BROUGHT WORD BACK THAT MY SISTER WORKED IN THIS NEIGHBORHOD AS A SLAVE LABORER, MY SISTER, I AM SURE, IS LONG DEAD. SHE WAS TOO WEAK, TO STAND THE HARDSHIP LONG.

IN FACT WE ALREADY HAVE OUR PAPERS TO GO TO THE U.S. THE ONLY THING THAT KEEPS US HERE IS THE HOPE THAT PERHAPS, IF G-D HELPS US WE CAN FIND A TRACE OF MY SISTERS LITTLE GIRL.

BUT WHAT WOULD I NOT GIVE TO FIND HER LITTLE MALKELE, THE THING DEAREST TO HER IN HER LIFE! BY NOW SHE OUGHT TO BE ABOUT EIGHT YEARS OLD. IF SHE IS ALIVE...

(To be Continued)

Published & Copyright 1961 by
MERKOS L'INYONEI CHINUCH, Inc.
770 EASTERN PARKWAY
Brooklyn 13, N. Y.
HYacinth 3-9250

No. 31

THE TEST

The class sat very still as the teacher handed out the test papers. He called out the names of those who had received the highest marks. Aaron swelled with pride as he smiled in his direction:—"Aaron Cohen—98. Well done!" Then he came to the poorer papers. "David, I'm afraid your mark is rather low. I'm disappointed in you. You'll simply have to work harder to get good marks again."

Poor David hung his head and blushed. As the two friends walked home together, Aaron kept talking about the test and how proud he was of his mark. "My mother promised me a fifty cent bonus for every mark over 90," he boasted, "boy, it's easy for me to save this way!"

He glanced at his friend. David was glum and silent. His eyes were downcast, his face pink. Seeing Aaron's glance, he tried to make conversation. "Speaking of money, I'm saving to buy my mother a birthday present. Got any ideas?"

But Aaron ignored his friend's embarrassment and attempts to change the topic, and returned to his boasting. "It was as easy as pie, that test! I'm sure I'll do just as well next week even if I don't open my book. But I'll bet your mother makes you buckle down and study every spare minute from now on! You'll be lucky if you get nothing worse than a lecture from your father."

It was the next week. Again the teacher was returning test papers. "Aaron, I'm very surprised! You barely passed. I'm afraid you became too proud and confident. You'll have to improve."

"David, congratulations. You show a wonderful improvement. I can see you are really trying. A score of 90 is excellent."

David smiled gratefully. As they walked home together, Aaron waited for his friend's teasing. But all David said was, "Aaron, would you like to do homework and study together tonight?"

Aaron burst out, "David, I wish I could be like you. I was sure you would tease and taunt me as I did last week when I did better."

"But don't you remember how our teacher explained that it is cruel and sinful to boast and seek praise at the expense and shame of someone else?"

"I'm afraid it didn't penetrate until now," sighed Aaron. "I'm sorry I embarrassed you last week. Forgive me, and now let's help each other!"

A THANKLESS UNCLE

When Jacob arrived in Charan he went to his uncle Laban, his mother's brother. Not wanting to be a useless guest, he began tending Laban's sheep. By the time a month had passed, Laban knew he was lucky. Not only was his nephew an excellent, devoted shepherd, but he seemed to have brought great blessing to the house. Laban was afraid to lose Jacob, so he said to him: "Tell me, dear nephew, what payment do you want for your work? Because you are my relative is no reason to work for nothing."

Now Laban had two daughters. When Isaac sent Jacob to Charan, he had advised him to seek a wife, preferably one of Laban's daughters. So Jacob replied: "I am willing to work seven years for the hand of your younger daughter Rachel." This suited Laban very well.

Finally the seven years were over and the wedding day was at hand. But Laban made Leah, his older daughter, take her sister's place. Jacob had been afraid of this, and had arranged certain signals with Rachel when she would be veiled. But the sweet, good Rachel could not stand to see her sister Leah shamed and embarrassed, so she taught Leah the signals. Jacob did not discover that till after the wedding. He demanded an explanation from Laban, who said: "We do not allow the younger sister to marry before the older one. But I will let you marry Rachel, too, if you promise to work another seven years for me after the second wedding next week." (In those days men could marry more than one woman.) What could Jacob do, but agree?

JACOB'S FAMILY

Besides Leah and Rachel, Jacob married Zilpah and Bilhah, two members of Laban's household. Leah bore him seven children: Reuben, Simeon, Levi, Judah, Issachar, Zebulun, and a girl, Dinah. Rachel, who was childless till the seventh year of their marriage, finally was blessed with a son, Joseph, and shortly before her death, with another boy, called Benjamin. Jacob's two other wives also bore him children: Bilhah, gave him Dan and Naphtali, and Zilpah bore Gad and Asher. From the twelve sons of Jacob were to come the twelve tribes of Israel.

After the birth of Joseph, Jacob planned to return to Canaan. During the fourteen years he had worked for his uncle, Laban's house had been blessed, and his wealth had increased. Jacob now felt that the time had come for him to return to his parents: he was ninety-one years of age and still a servant. So he begged Laban to let him go; but Laban could not bear the thought of losing him, knowing of the Divine blessing that rested on everything

Jacob touched. Therefore, he promised him part of his flocks as a reward for his services, so that Jacob could make his own fortune. Jacob stayed on for an additional six years. However, Laban tried all kinds of tricks to cheat Jacob out of the payment due him by their agreement. But G-d blessed Jacob, and his flocks multiplied rapidly, until he became a rich man.

JACOB RETURNS TO CANAAN

Laban's sons envied Jacob because of his good luck and wealth, and Laban too, seeing all his evil plans to deprive Jacob of the just reward for his services, come to nothing, became unfriendly towards his son-in-law.

Then G-d spoke to Jacob: "Return to the land of your fathers, and I shall be with you." One day, when Laban was away, Jacob left for Canaan with his wives, children, and everything that belonged to him. As soon as Laban heard of Jacob's departure, he gathered his men and pursued him.

Catching up with Jacob on the border of the Land of Canaan, Laban planned to attack his son-in-law the following morning. However, that night Laban had a strange dream in which G-d warned him not to do any harm to Jacob.

Instead, Laban made a treaty with Jacob, and then kissed his daughters and grandchildren, blessed them and returned home. Jacob, too, continued his trip and the angels of G-d were with him wherever he went.

(To be Continued)

THE JEWISH CALENDAR

"Happy Birthday, Dear Eva, Happy Birthday to you!"

The guests sat enjoying their slices of birthday cake. Suddenly they heard a knock at the door. Eva's mother opened it.

"Hello, Miriam, I didn't expect you today."

"I was shopping nearby. What's all the noise about?"

"Why, that's Eva's birthday party. I thought that was the reason you came."

"How can you say today is Eva's birthday? I distinctly remember the day she was born, May 30th. Today is May 19th."

"I'll explain in a minute. Girls," Mrs. Levine turned to the guests, "meet my sister, Mrs. Gross."

"I'm so glad to see you, Aunt Miriam," exclaimed Eva.

"Let's clear up this mystery about your birthday."

"There is really no mystery, Auntie," said Eva. "We reckon my birthday according to the Jewish calendar, and today is the day I was born according to the Jewish calendar: the tenth day of Iyar."

"I'm ashamed to admit that I know very little about the Jewish calendar. Could you explain some more about it?"

"Certainly. The Jewish calendar counts the years since the creation of the world, as our Holy Bible teaches us. The beginning of the year is in the fall."

"Well, even I know the holiday Rosh Hashanah— the Jewish New Year!" exclaimed Mrs. Gross. "I always go to the synagogue to pray for a good year."

"Did you know," said Eva's mother, "that in the Torah Nissan is called the first month of the year?"

"I know why," said Deborah, one of the guests. "Nissan, in the spring, ushers in the holiday of Passover. That is the festival when the Jews celebrate their freedom from the Egyptians. That month started a new life for the Jewish nation."

"Do tell me more!"

"The Jewish year is divided into 12 months of 29 or 30 days. But every few years we have a 'leap year,' a year in which there are 13 months—the extra month comes just before the month of Nissan."

"This year is a leap year," said Deborah.

"In school we learned the names of all the Jewish months," said a brown-eyed girl, "and our teacher looked up the Jewish birthday of every one in the class. He has a special calendar that goes back many years."

"I wish I knew mine," sighed Mrs. Gross.

"The first day of every month is a sort of holiday, 'Rosh Chodesh,' on which special prayers are said," contributed Esther, another guest.

"I think it's fun to know the exact Jewish date of holidays like Passover, Purim and Chanukah," said Eva.

"I do too," said her aunt. "I must get a Jewish calendar!"

DO YOU HAVE A PICTURE OF MALKELE?

NO, WE ONLY HAVE A PICTURE OF MALKELE'S MOTHER IN HER YOUNGER YEARS AT HOME IN WARSAW.

I DON'T WANT TO GIVE YOU FALSE HOPES, BUT I HAVE COME ACCROSS A YOUNG GIRL IN A GERMAN FARM, THAT SEEMS TO HAVE A JEWISH BACKGROUND, HER NAME IS MOLLIE, THE GIRL STARED AT THE MOGEN DAVID ON MY RING AND CALLED, "MAMME! MAMME!"

SHE MUST BE THE CHILD!! MR. JOE DO YOU SEE THIS BROCHE? MY SISTER HAD JUST THE SAME, MY FATHER HAD BOTH MADE FOR US BY A JEWELER, AS A PRESENT FOR YOMTOV ONCE, WHEN BUSINESS WAS GOOD, AND WE WERE YOUNG GIRLS.

NOW THERE WAS NO LONGER ANY DOUBT ABOUT THE IDENTITY OF THE LITTLE GIRL. LT. JOE TURNED TO HIS FRIEND BARRY BERGER.

BARRY, YOU'VE GOT TO HELP ME. IF I AM SEEN NEAR THE HOFER FARM, THEY'LL SUSPECT ME AND KEEP THE GIRL AWAY, YOU'VE GOT TO STAY NEARBY, KIDNAP HER, AND BRING HER TO THE SCHARFS FOR A FEW MINUTES, IF WE MADE A MISTAKE, WE'LL RETURN HER AT ONCE.

SGT. BARRY BERGER CONSENTS TO DO HIS SHARE TO SAVE THE JEWISH GIRL, HE SETS UP A PRACTICE STATION FOR HIS COMMUNICATION UNIT NEAR THE FARM. THUS HE CAN FIND OUT ALL ABOUT THE SCHEDULES AND ROUTINE OF THE CHILDREN ON THE FARM.

(To be Continued)

**Published & Copyright 1961 by
MERKOS L'INYONEI CHINUCH, Inc.
770 EASTERN PARKWAY
Brooklyn 13, N. Y.
HYacinth 3-9250**

No. 32

ONE FOR ALL

Miss Gross called the fourth grade to order.

"Children, I would like to plan tomorrow's party now. The end of the term party is always lots of fun. Who would like to decorate the room? All right— 'arah, Leah, Rachel and Miriam will be the Decorations Committee. You'll find plenty of crepe paper and other material on these two shelves."

"Now for refreshments: Shall we each bring something from home, or shall we each give some money and appoint a committee to buy the refreshments?"

Leah raised her hand. "Miss Gross, I think it's better to have every one bring something from home. It's a lot of work and bother for the committee to collect the money, and buy and carry enough food for the whole class."

Rachel raised her hand. "I agree with Leah. Some children always forget their money. We end up with more refreshments when we bring them from home."

"Then that's settled," said Miss Gross. "Who will bring cake? What is it, Sarah?"

"Miss Gross, we must make sure that the food is strictly kosher. I volunteer to bring all the refreshments for the whole class tomorrow. I know where to buy kosher cake, kosher candies and other treats."

"I wouldn't let you go to such an expense.—Besides, as Leah said, it's a big job just to carry it all."

"My parents would be very glad to help me. I'm sure my father will gladly bring it to the school in his car. My mother will help me shop for the food. They would do everything in their power to make sure that no Jewish child will eat what is not allowed."

"I think you and your parents are wonderful, Sarah. But I want every child in the class to bring 20 cents tomorrow to pay for the refreshments. We're grateful that Sarah is willing to go to such trouble to provide us with kosher food."

"It's no trouble. It's a pleasure to know that I helped my friends do what is right. I'd do it any time."

THEY MET AND PARTED

Jacob was now looking forward to the time when he would see his beloved father and mother again, in Hebron. In his mind he went over all those long years he had been away from home. At the age of eighteen, his father sent him to the great academy of Shem (Noah's son) and Eber, while Esau chose to lead a carefree and wild life, hunting and fishing. For thirty-two years Jacob stayed with the aged and wise Shem and Eber, learning from them heavenly wisdom. The more he studied, the stronger his thirst for knowledge grew, and even after he returned home at last, he continued to study with his father for some years. Then came that fateful day, when he received his father's blessing, and he had to leave home again, to escape Esau's anger. Jacob remembered that day clearly. He was 63 years old then, and now he was 97! For thirty-four years he was away from home this time, of which fourteen years he had again spent at the seat of learning, in care of Eber (Shem had died long before). Thirty-two and fourteen!

Forty-six years of study! Yes, those were pleasant and happy years. But not so the twenty years in Laban's house. Jacob frowned as he thought of those years of work, under the burning sun by day, and the freezing wind by night! Laban would not let him go, so that he had to make his escape like a thief! Indeed, Laban had followed him as if he really were a thief.

Thank G-d, the wicked and sly Laban was gone, and good riddance. . . .

NEW PERILS

The sun was almost on top of the hills one late afternoon, when Jacob was making preparations to break up his camp and continue on his journey home. Suddenly he noticed a band of horsemen coming down the hill. Shielding his eyes from the sun, Jacob tried to make out who they were, but any suspicion he might have had was soon gone when he heard the friendly sound of their horns and cheerful waving of their hands. When they finally halted in front of him, Jacob recognized their leader as his mother's most trusted servant.

Jacob was delighted to see him. He immediately inquired after his dear parents, and was soon satisfied that all was well at home. Then he noticed that all the men were armed, as if they were about to go to battle.

"What's the meaning of this armed force?" Jacob asked in surprise.

"You are in grave danger, my lord," the chief servant answered, and then went on to explain:

"The sly Laban has sent his son Beor with ten men to Esau, to inform him that you were coming laden with wealth, and now was the time to avenge himself! From there those evil messengers hurried to your mother Rebecca, telling her of Esau's plans to attack you and wipe out your entire family. Your mother sent us to help you, should there be a battle between you and Esau."

Jacob became very sad. It was clear that Laban desired to bring about a violent battle between him and Esau that might possibly destroy them both. That must never happen.

"What is my mother's advice?" Jacob asked.

"Your mother said you must do everything possible to avoid a battle. Send messengers of good will to Esau, with a rich present to please him. But should he turn down your peace offers, we are ready to defend you and your household to the last drop of our blood. There are seventy-two men here, my lord, and though not experienced in the art of warfare, they are brave and true to the last man and, with G-d's help, we shall defeat our enemies."

(To be Continued)

 INSIDE THE MEZUZAH

Mr. Levy sat at the table. Before him were several small scrolls of parchment with Hebrew writing. He was carefully inspecting each one. Sometimes he would pick up his magnifying glass to see the small writing better.

"What are you doing, daddy?" asked Daniel. "What's that?"

"Come here, my son, and I will explain. These are *Mezuzos* and I am inspecting them to make sure that they are in perfect condition."

"I thought mezuzos were little metal things on doorposts."

"Actually, Danny, the word mezuzah means door post. In the Bible, we are commanded to affix to the right doorpost of every door, in every Jewish house a mezuzah scroll. The scroll must be made from parchment of a kosher animal. On it must be written, by hand, the first two chapters of the 'Shema,' one of our holiest prayers taken from the Bible. The verses must be written in the special script that is used in our Holy Sifrei Torah. That is why the mezuzah scrolls are written only by learned scholars who can write this script carefully and correctly.

"I am replacing some of our worn out scrolls. You see, here are the new ones in perfect condition. I roll them up so, and I put them in the special holder, and now I am ready to put them on the doorposts. Do you want to watch me?"

"Oh, yes! But could you please answer one more question first?"

"Of course."

"For what reason does the Torah command us to put a mezuzah on our doors? Of what use is it?"

"An excellent question! Before I answer it, see if you can answer my question. What do the words of the 'Shema,' which are written on the mezuzah, mean?"

"I've learnt that. 'Hear, O Israel, the L-rd is our G-d, the L-rd is one!' The rest of that paragraph tells us how much we should love the Almighty and learn His Torah, night and day. Wherever we go, whatever we do, Torah should be uppermost in our minds. Then the prayer goes on to tell of the many blessings that G-d sends the Jews when they obey His commandments."

"Right! We affix these words to our doorposts to proclaim that this is a truly Jewish home. That the people who live here believe in our Almighty G-d and love Him. We always try to remember to do His will. Every time we enter our door we glance at the mezuzah."

"And kiss it."

"Yes, to remind us to live as good Jews who love G-d. To remind us to keep our home a proud and happy Jewish home. That is one of the reasons why we are commanded, in the 'Shema' itself, to have mezuzos on our doors. Come, listen to me say the special blessing that is said when one affixes a mezuzah."

Daniel watched fascinated as his father proclaimed: "Blessed art Thou, O L-rd, our G-d, King of the universe, Who has sanctified us with His commandments and commanded us to affix mezuzos."

"Amen," responded Daniel heartily.

A LUCKY FIND (8)

AFTER A FEW DAYS, SGT. BARRY IN CIVVIES WAITS WITH A RENTED CAR

THE CHILDREN ARE RETURNING FROM SCHOOL NOW

AS USUAL LITTLE MOLLIE WALKS BEHIND

LIGHTNING FAST, SGT. BARRY PULLS HER INTO THE CAR

DON'T WORRY LITTLE GIRL, I'LL TAKE YOU TO A NICE PLACE IT WON'T TAKE LONG, JUST A FEW MINUTES

AS THE GIRL WALKS INTO THE SCHARF'S HOME....

OH! MY MALKELE! THIS IS MALKELE

MAMME... MAMME,

FOUND AT LAST! FOUND!

AT ONCE LT. JOE AND SGT. BARRY DRIVE THE SHARFS WITH THE GIRL TO THE HEADQUARTERS OF THE AMERICAN AUTHORITES.

(To be Continued)

שעורי למור הדת

SHALOH

Published & Copyright 1961 by
MERKOS L'INYONEI CHINUCH, Inc.
770 EASTERN PARKWAY
Brooklyn 13, N. Y.
HYacinth 3-9250

No. 33

AT YOUR SERVICE

The two friends, David and Jacob, were returning from school.

"Go home, drink your milk, and then come over with your bike," said Jacob to David.

"Fine."

A half hour later David called Jacob on the phone: "Sorry, but I can't come this afternoon. I have to do some errands for my mother."

"What kind of errands?"

"My mother is in charge of the rummage sale for the Ladies' Aid Society. She has a list of people who want to donate packages to the rummage sale. I have to go and collect the stuff. It will take me till dinner-time."

"You know what, David, I'll help you. If my mother gives me permission, I'll be at your house in ten minutes on my bicycle."

"You're really a pal, Jacob."

True to his word, Jacob came over very shortly. Each boy took a list of names and addresses and started on his way. Back and forth they went, bringing the packages to David's garage.

It took a while, the pile grew, and finally the boys had each finished his list.

"I'm really tired," said David. "I don't know how to thank you, Jacob. You didn't have to help and get yourself so tired, too. If not for you, I would have worked twice as hard."

Jacob shrugged. "I'm tired, it's true. But I believe that's what friends are for—to help each other. Come, let's relax with some nice cold soda pop and a quiet game till dinnertime."

 THREE STEPS IN AN EMERGENCY

Jacob thanked the men for their loyalty. "But there must be no bloodshed among us," he added, and immediately chose a few men to go to Esau, with a messeage of brotherly greetings and humble respects. The messengers were to tell Esau of the hard years Jacob had spent living with the wicked Laban. His father's blessings had not come to pass and the little he owned was earned through hard work. Esau, on the other hand, was a powerful chieftain, and really had no reason for hating him. Jacob therefore asked his brother Esau to make peace with him and forget the past.

The report for which Jacob waited so anxiously came at last, but it brought no comfort. The messengers did not succeed in winning Esau's favor. He was already on his way, in an ugly mood, with a powerful force of four hundred trained warriors.

Jacob's heart was filled with fear. It wasn't so much that he feared for his own safety and the safety of the people with him, for he trusted in G-d to save them all. But even the thought that he might be forced to kill in self-defense filled him with pain.

With a broken heart and with tears in his eyes, Jacob prayed to G-d. Of course, he knew that G-d had promised to protect him and bring him home safely. But he might have lost G-d's favor through failing in his duties without even knowing it! Jacob's prayer was therefore full of repentance and humility, as well as thanks for past favors. He ended with a moving plea to G-d to save him and all his people from the pitiless massacre that Esau was planning.

Jacob felt much better after his prayer. However, there were two more steps he had to take yet. He would make a bid for peace but at the same time would prepare for the last possibility—war.

Thereupon Jacob began to prepare the present for

his brother, in the hope that Esau's heart might soften at the sight of his brother's generosity. Choosing hundreds of sheep, and many heads of cattle, camels and mules, Jacob divided them up into herds, and placed each herd in charge of shepherds. Having told them exactly what to say when they should meet Esau, Jacob sent them off.

Jacob now turned his attention to war plans. He divided his people into two camps, placing the women and children in the second. He, himself, would stand at the head of the first camp which was to hold back the enemy, and should the fortune of the battle turn in favor of the enemy, the second camp would be able to make its escape in the meantime.

ESAU ON THE MARCH

From Seir, Esau's country, a company of fierce warriors set out, intent upon dealing a death blow to Jacob and his handful of people. Esau with his sons confidently rode at the head of the force, four hundred strong, all fearless and reckless warriors, who delighted in fighting and robbery, and in massacre of the weak and defenseless.

Suddenly a huge army swept down from the hills with their swords drawn and with a battle cry that chilled Esau's blood.

Frightened to death, Esau and his men jumped off their horses, and knelt before the onrushing army, begging for mercy.

"We are children of Isaac and Abraham," they begged, "O spare our lives."

Their pleas seemed to have no effect, however. Then Esau exclaimed: "I am Jacob's brother! I am on my way to welcome him with honor and love, have pity. . . ."

As soon as Esau mentioned Jacob's name, the captain of the strange army nodded and led his terrible warriors away.

With their hearts still beating with terror, Esau and his men proceeded on their way, now and then turning their heads back to assure themselves that those terrible-looking warriors were not pursuing them.

When they reached the top of the hill, another strange sight caught their eyes. But how different this sight was from the first!

They saw a big herd being driven slowly and peacefully across the plain, coming toward them.

"Who are you? Where are you going? Whose are these herds?" Esau asked the chief herdsman, as he drew up his horse in front of the herd.

"I belong to your humble servant Jacob, and these are a present sent to my lord from his brother," the herdsman answered.

Esau smiled happily. Jacob was truly generous, he thought; but wouldn't it be better to attack and destroy him, and carry off his entire wealth?

No sooner did the thought flash through his mind, than down from the hills swept another huge army of warriors, even fiercer looking than the first one, and armed to their teeth. The very sight of them threw Esau and his men into a terrible panic. Once again they begged for their lives, but not until they mentioned Jacob's name and asked to be spared for his sake, did the terrible warriors show any mercy, turning round and disappearing as mysteriously as they had come. Little did Esau know that those terrible looking warriors were heaven-sent angels, in order to frighten him out of his evil plans.

The next moment Esau and his men again beheld a beautiful sight. A big herd was being driven toward them, consisting of many camels with their colts, beautiful ewes and rams, asses and foals.

Much to his surprise, Esau learned that this herd, like the first, was a gift sent to him by his brother Jacob.

(To be Continued)

ROSH CHODESH

The Rubin family was eating dinner.

"I hope tomorrow is a nice day," said Mrs. Rubin. "I want to wash some clothes."

Her husband smiled. "Do you know that tomorrow is Rosh Chodesh?"

" I was in the synagogue this Shabbos too! How absent minded I am. I won't do the laundry. I never do heavy work on Rosh Chodesh unless it's urgent."

"Why?" Sarah asked her mother.

"Rosh Chodesh is the first day of every Jewish month. Rosh Chodesh may be one day, or two days. On the Shabbos before the beginning of each new month special prayers are said in the synagogue. They are called 'blessing the New Month.' We ask the Almighty to make it a happy, healthy month for all."

"When the Jews had their beautiful Beth Hamikdosh in Jerusalem," said Mr. Rubin, "Rosh Chodesh was a holiday. There were special sacrifices, feasts and prayers."

"So far I see that Rosh Chodesh means the beginning of a new month. We have special prayers the Shabbos before. Oh yes—and mother doesn't do any hard work. Anything else we do?" asked Sarah.

"Yes. In the morning prayers, we add the special prayers of 'Hallel' and 'Musaph.' We also read from the Torah a special portion which tells about the special sacrifices that were offered, when we had our Beth Hamikdosh."

"We also add a prayer to our Grace after meals. It is called "Yaale v'Yovo." Men have a beautiful ceremony in connection with the New Moon.

"On a clear night about a week or so after the beginning of the new month, we go outdoors. We go after the evening services to a place where we can observe the new moon. It is better to do it on a Saturday night, when we are dressed in our best and still feeling happy. We then recite some grateful prayers to our Father in Heaven. This is called 'Kiddush Levono.' He has given us many happy ceremonies and holidays. One of the nicest is the celebration of each New Month."

A LUCKY FIND (9)

THE HOFERS ARE CALLED AND QUESTIONED

IS IT YOUR CHILD?

YES SIR!

BUT AFTER THE GIRL TELLS HER MEMORIES OF HER MOTHER

WHAT DO YOU SAY NOW, IS IT YOUR CHILD?

NO SIR, THE CHILD'S MOTHER WHO WORKED AT OUR FARM DIED, AND WE KEPT THE CHILD

A SEARCH OF THEIR POSSESSIONS BRINGS OUT MANY BELONGINGS OF THE FORMER JEWISH SLAVE LABORERS, AMONG OTHER THINGS THE BROCHE OF MALKELE'S MOTHER

IN FACT AS THE AUTHORITIES INVESTIGATE FURTHER, IT IS FOUND THAT MANY A JEWISH SLAVE LABORER HAD DIED ON THE HOFER FARM BECAUSE THEY WERE MALTREATED. THE HOFERS ARE CONVICTED AND PUT INTO PRISON

A FEW MONTHS LATER THE LITTLE GIRL LEAVES WITH THE SCHARFS FOR AMERICA. LT. BERG AND BERGER ARE AT THE TRAIN.

NOW WE KNOW, WHY G-D MADE US COME TO THIS FORSAKEN PLACE. WHEN I LEFT AMERICA MY REBBE SAID: "THERE MUST BE SOMETHING IN STORE FOR YOU, PROVIDENCE, THE HASHGOCHOH HO-ELYONO, HAS ITS OWN WAYS TO MAKE US WORK ITS PLANS. SEE TO IT THAT YOU DON'T FAIL THE CHANCE HERE INDEED WAS THE CHANCE OF A LIFE TIME FOR ME TO SAVE A JEWISH NESHOMOH FROM BEING LOST, THANK G-D.

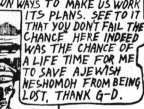

THE END

Published & Copyright 1961 by
MERKOS L'INYONEI CHINUCH, Inc.
770 EASTERN PARKWAY
Brooklyn 13, N. Y.
HYacinth 3-9250

No. 34

BAD EXAMPLE

"Oh, oh—it looks like that ball is going across the street."

Crash, bang, right into Mr. Gross' window it went.

Mr. Gross rushed out to survey the damage—the window shattered, a few clothing models knocked over.

He crossed the street to the sand lot where the boys were playing. "Who broke my window?" he asked angrily.

"What's the difference?" argued Jacob Green. "You have to expect broken windows where kids play ball!"

"That window costs a lot of money. If one of you broke it, either he should replace it—or you can all share the cost. You surely don't expect me to have a loss because of your game?"

"You're rich enough," sneered Jacob. "We buy all our clothes from you. So you'll spend some money—you'll still be rich."

Mr. Gross was so surprised, he could only stare.

"Is that what your parents teach you? Is that what you learned in school? Are you the one that broke the window?"

"Yes, I'm the one. What are you going to do about it?" I'll bet even my rabbi in Hebrew school will say my parents don't have to pay."

"You go to Hebrew school?"

"I go to the Sons of Israel Hebrew school, and I'm the smartest boy there."

"Really?" Mr. Gross seemed to have forgotten the broken window. He looked very thoughtful as he walked away.

A few days later Jacob wondered why he was called to Rabbi Fisher's office.

"Tell me, Jacob," said the principal—"Are you a good baseball player?"

Jacob was puzzled. "Yes—I can hit very well."

"Tell me, did you break Mr. Gross' window playing ball?"

"Did that guy come to you to tattle?"

"Listen, Jacob. You have done something far more serious than break a window. Mr. Gross is an important person in our community. He is very generous and helpful. He was planning to give a large sum of money for our new school building. But now he is not so sure."

"Just because I broke his window?"

"No. Because you were very rude and fresh to Mr. Gross. You refused to bear the cost of the damage you caused. You insulted Mr. Gross to the bargain. Mr. Gross came to me and asked me if you were an example of our good students. He asked me, if that is how we teach our students to be good Jews? What could I have answered him?"

Jacob hung his head.

Rabbi Fisher continued: "Every Jew, boy or girl, man or woman, must always watch his every action. Never, never can he do something to make others say: 'See how that Jew behaves? See what their religion teaches them?' You bring shame on yourself, all Jews and our Almighty Himself!"

"I'll apologize to Mr. Gross, Rabbi Fisher—and pay for the window."

"And learn a lesson for other times, too."

THEY MET AND PARTED

By the time Esau reached Jacob, he had seen so many warriors, who seemed to be Jacob's and so many domestic animals who became his own, that Esau thought it wiser to forget his evil ideas and make peace with his brother.

When Esau finally saw his brother Jacob coming toward him, seemingly still uncertain whether Esau would greet him with open arms or drawn sword, Esau ran toward his brother and embraced him. He fell on his neck and kissed him and they both wept with feeling.

Jacob knew then that G-d had accepted his prayers and turned Esau's hate to love.

With the usual courtesy so common in the Orient, Esau seemed reluctant to accept Jacob's gifts, but finally accepted them. Then he suggested that they join up and form one kingdom and live together, in one land. But Jacob almost shuddered at the idea, knowing full well what would become of his children if they mixed freely with Esau's. Jacob knew how far apart his views and ideas were from those of Esau. His was a life dedicated to G-d, while Esau's was a life based on the sword.

Of course, Jacob could not tell Esau what he was thinking at that very moment, but refuse Esau's suggestion he most certainly did. "My children are still too young to acquire your habits and customs and way of life," Jacob said, trying not to arouse Esau's displeasure.

Esau then offered to leave some of his men with Jacob in order that they might later lead him to Seir, when the children would have grown up. Again, Jacob declined Esau's offer with thanks, knowing that there could be no question at all of his ever joining Esau.

And so the brothers parted. Esau returned to his land Seir: he went back to his way of life, to live by the sword. But Jacob went to Succoth, the place he named after the "Succoth" (tents) he built there, perhaps with the intention of showing that he did not rely on his own power, and felt quite safe even in a frail Succah, because G-d was his real protection.

(To be Continued)

 ## THE MEANING OF KIDDUSH

"Here we are, mother," called Sara as she entered the house with her friend Leah.

"I'm very happy that you are able to spend the Sabbath with us," Mrs. Kahn welcomed the fatherless little girl. "Now, girls, there isn't too much time till I have to light the Sabbath candles. I would like you to help me tidy the kitchen, and then we will get washed and dressed for Shabbos."

The chalah and wine were set on the snowy white tablecloth, the candles were lit. Now the girls were setting the table as they waited for Mr. Kahn to return from the synagogue.

"I'm getting hungry," said Sara, "but we can't eat until my father comes home and makes Kiddush."

"It's been a long time since I heard a Daddy make kiddush," sighed Leah.

"Good Shabbos," just then Mr. Kahn opened the door. "My, how nice the table looks, and the whole house is really sparkling for the Sabbath Queen!"

He began singing the lovely song greeting the Sabbath, Sholom Aleichem. As he finished the prayers, he brought to the table a beautiful silver goblet. "Here, Sarah, rinse out the cup. We must make sure that the cup over which we make kiddush is very clean."

Then the whole family stood quietly while Mr. Kahn filled the goblet with wine and began to recite the kiddush. They saw how Leah was drinking in every detail of the scene, as if her eyes and ears were anxious to preserve every detail in her memory.

"Blessed art Thou—Who sanctifies the Sabbath," Mr. Kahn ended the prayer, drank from the cup, and then filled small cups for the rest of the family.

After they had drunk, Mr. Kahn turned to Leah. "Leah, dear, do you know the meaning of Kiddush?"

"I'm not too sure, Mr. Kahn."

"You see, my child, the Sabbath is very dear to us. It is a holy day, a day in which we proclaim our belief that G-d created the world in six days. If we rest on the seventh day as He has commanded us to, G-d will take care of us. Shabbos is a day of joy, of devotion.

"Just before we sit down to the meals of this special day, we want to show how different and dear it is to us! So we take a cup of wine."

"Must it be a silver goblet?" inquired Leah.

"Not necessarily, but we should always observe a commandment with the nicest things we own. We take wine, which is a sign of festivity and holiness, and over it we say a prayer declaring the special meaning and holiness of the Shabbos. Even if we have previously heard kiddush in the synagogue, we must still say it before our meal."

"I'm lucky I was here to listen to you say it and explain kiddush to me."

"You know, Leah, you should say kiddush every Friday night, and holiday night too. Even if there is no father in the house, another member of the family may say it. Kiddush may also be said over chalah instead of wine. Here, let me show it to you in the prayer book."

"Show her the short kiddush prayer you say before the midday meal on Shabbos and holidays, too," said Mrs. Kahn.

"A good idea!"

"From now on," resolved Leah, "we'll always recite kiddush in our house every single Shabbos and holiday!"

THE SILVER RINGS

DON'T EVER LOSE YOUR RINGS, IT MAY BE THE ONLY THING TO TIE YOU TO YOUR FAMILY, FOR ONLY G-D KNOWS WHAT MAY BE IN STORE FOR US.

YES FATHER

WHEN IZCHAK LUMBROZO LEFT SPAIN DURING THE HATEFUL REIGN OF THE INQUISITION, HE HAD ABRAHAM DA BURGOS, THE FAMOUS JEWISH SILVERSMITH, MAKE THREE IDENTICAL RINGS FOR HIS THREE SMALL SONS, ABRAHAM 8, JOSE, 10, AND LEON 12 YEARS OLD, ALL OF WHICH BORE THE INSIGNIA OF THE LAVER FOR THE LUMBROZOS WERE LEVITES, AND VERY PROUD OF THEIR HERITAGE.

LIKE THEIR UNCLE JACOB DEL MENDEZ, WHO HAD TRAVELLED NORTH TO BELGIUM, AND FROM THERE TO THE FREEDOM OF THE NETHERLANDS, THE LUMBROZOS JOINED A GROUP OF MARANOS THAT TRAVELLED NORTH ON THE LAND ROUTE

MOST OF THE SHIPS THAT HAD LEFT SPAIN RECENTLY WERE CAUGHT BY PIRATES, AND THE TRAVELERS SOLD AS SLAVES. THE LAND ROUTE, HOWEVER, WAS NOT VERY SAFE EITHER. THE BITTER COLD, AND HARD PASSAGE OF THE PYRENEES MOUNTAINS WAS ENOUGH TO CLAIM SEVERAL LIVES OF THE REFUGEES.

REBECCA LUMBROZO, THE TENDER BUT BRAVE WIFE OF IZCHAK, WAS ONE OF THE VICTIMS WHOM THE MARRANOS HAD TO BURY HIGH UP IN A MOUNTAIN PASS.

(To be Continued)

Published & Copyright 1961 by
MERKOS L'INYONEI CHINUCH, Inc.
770 EASTERN PARKWAY
Brooklyn 13, N. Y.
HYacinth 3-9250

No. 35

A FRIEND INDEED

"Hello, David. Where are you going with your record player?"

"I'm going over to Jacob's house, Dan. I'm spending the day with him."

"To Jacob's house? Why aren't you coming to the school field day? Such a beautiful day, and we always have such a wonderful time! How come you and Jacob don't want to go?"

"Oh, we would love to go. But Jacob's mother is in the hospital. She had an operation. Usually his aunt takes care of his little sister. Today his aunt has to go away and Jacob must mind his sister."

"What's that got to do with you? We need you

to run for us. Leave your record player with Jacob and come with us. It's selfish of Jacob to make you keep him company."

"Jacob isn't making me stay home. He doesn't even know I'm coming to spend the day with him.

"But he is my best friend. I know how he is feeling. He is very worried about his mother's health. It's very hard for him to manage his sister by himself. We've always helped each other out. I wouldn't even have a good time at the track thinking of Jacob at home with so much trouble. I'd much rather go and try to help Jacob and try to cheer him up."

"David—you're proof that a friend in need is a friend indeed."

THE INHERITANCE

It was a black day when Isaac died. No man was ever mourned more sadly than Isaac. The birds did not sing, the sun did not shine, on the day that that great man passed away. Kings and princes of all the lands paid their last honor to the noble man. His two sons, Jacob and Esau, cried most of all for their dear father.

When the time came for the two sons to divide their father's wealth, Jacob said to Esau, "You know that G-d promised the land of Canaan to our father, and his children. If you want the land, I shall take his other possessions and I will be content. However, as you know, together with the Land of Canaan that G-d promised our ancestors, there goes the treaty that G-d and Abraham entered into. This agreement demands of the dwellers of the land, the children of Abraham, to follow the ways of G-d. If you choose the Land of Canaan you must accept also the other part of the bargain."

Now Esau was puzzled and didn't know what to do. "I will ask someone's advice," he thought to himself.

He hastened to talk with his cousin, Neboyoth, Ishmael's son. "What shall I take, the land or my father's other possessions—his gold and silver, and flocks?"

"I will tell you, dear cousin," replied Neboyoth. "The land of Canaan is inhabited by a race of terrible giants. They will overcome you before you have a chance to settle down there. Take my advice, and tell your brother that you want your father's possessions, and he may have the land. Besides, in this way you will also be rid of the difficult responsibilities attached to the Land."

Esau hurried back to tell Jacob of his decision. "But," Esau said, "there is one possession that belongs to both of us. The Cave of Machpelah was bequeathed by Abraham to our father Isaac, and I will not give up my share in it."

When Jacob heard these words, he was upset. How could he allow Esau to spoil the holy resting place of Adam and Eve, Abraham and Isaac? He thought hard until he finally hit upon a plan. "I will blind Esau's eyes with gold and silver," he thought.

Jacob took part of his own precious treasures of gold and silver, and brought it before the Cave of Machpelah.

"Esau," he said, "you may choose whatever your heart desires from my treasures, instead of this cave."

Esau was overwhelmed by the sight of so much splendor. When he heard Jacob's words, he greedily pounced upon the gold and silver. After taking all that his heart desired from the vast treasure, he turned to Jacob, and said, "For all these wonderful jewels, I will gladly let you have the Cave of Machpelah forever."

So Jacob kept the holy Cave, because he treasured, more than gold or silver, the memory of his holy forefathers, and hoped to rest there, too, when his soul would be recalled to the Creator.

JOSEPH

Jacob loved his second youngest son Joseph very dearly. Even when he was a young boy, everybody saw that Joseph was very good as well as very clever. He also was as beautiful as his mother Rachel had been. She had passed away while the family was returning to the land of Canaan. It was therefore not surprising that Joseph was his father's favorite son. Jacob spent much time teaching Joseph everything he had learned. His eleven brothers were jealous of Joseph, because of the special attention he received from Jacob their father.

Once Joseph told his brothers that he had dreamed they were all binding sheaves in the field, when suddenly their sheaves bowed down to his. Another time, he related that he had dreamed that the sun and the moon and eleven stars had paid him honor.

When they heard these dreams, his brothers were sure Joseph wished to rule over them. Jacob warned him not to tell any more dreams, even though in his heart Jacob believed the dreams were true, and that some-day Joseph would be a great ruler.

The brothers were once tending their father's flocks of sheep in a certain place while Joseph stayed and took care of his father. Jacob had had no news of his sons for some time, and he was getting worried. "Go Joseph, find your brothers and bring me word of them," he ordered his beloved son.

From afar, Joseph's brothers sitting at their meal saw him coming. There was no mistaking the beautiful coat of many colors their father had given Joseph. That coat brought back all their feelings of jealousy. They became so aroused that they lost their heads and threw Joseph into a nearby pit!

Just then, a caravan of Ishmaelite merchants passed by. The brothers went to the pit, took Joseph out and sold him as a slave to the merchants. This way, they thought, they would be rid of him, but his life would be saved. *(To be Continued)*

 WHEN SHABBOS ENDS

Sarah and her guest Leah had spent a wonderful Shabbos together.

"You must come again," said Sarah to her friend as they sat chatting in the gathering dusk.

"Oh, I will. I'll never forget it. The sparkling house, your father's singing the Kiddush and Sabbath songs, the services in the synagogue, the delicious meals, the pleasant walk in the park, the Bible stories—I don't know which I've enjoyed most."

"I hate to see Shabbos end, too. Every Jew hates to see such a lovely day end, I guess. That is why we are told to wait till it is fully dark before Shabbos is over. But my father will soon be home from the synagogue, and say Havdolah."

"I wonder what Havdolah means?" mused Leah.

"Well, I know it's a prayer we say at the end of Shabbos or a Jewish holiday. It's said over a cup of wine. Maybe my father can tell us more," said Sarah.

So they sat chatting and singing till Mr. Kahn came home. "A good week," he greeted them. "Did you enjoy your Shabbos?"

"So very much," exclaimed Leah.

"I'm happy to hear that. Sarah dear, please get out everything we need for Havdolah now."

Sarah ran to get the beautiful Havdolah candle—a long braided one, and imported wooden spice box while her father took out the wine and the silver goblet.

"I usually hold the candle, but this week I want you to, Leah, because you're my guest." Then Sarah turned to her father. "Could you tell us what it means?"

"Why, surely! The word Havdolah means separation. Havdolah proclaims the end of our special, beautiful Sabbath day and the return to the everyday week. The word separation is important. We thank G-d for creating special holidays and ordinary days, for giving us a *separate* day of rest. We thank Him for making the Jews a special *separate* nation that is different from all other nations because we learn and obey the Torah."

"What about the Havdolah candle?"

"We light that in memory of the fact that Adam discovered fire and its power the very first Sabbath night after Creation. The Havdolah candle must be braided of at least two candles to make a large flame. We say the blessing, "Who creates light." We also have a beautiful custom of making a special 'brochah' and smelling fragrant spices during the Havdolah prayer.

"We'd better start already." Mr. Kahn lit the candle which Leah held up high. Then he recited the prayer, saying the special blessings over the light and the spices as usual.

When he had ended the prayer and drained the cup of wine, he took the candle from Leah's hand and extinguished it in the dregs of the wine. Then he dipped his fingers in the dregs and passed his fingers over his eyes.

"That's for G-d's blessings," explained Sarah.

"I must go pack now," said Leah. "Let's hope we have a blessed week after this happy Shabbos."

THE SILVER RINGS (2)

DESPITE IZCHAK'S COURAGE AND CARE HIS MIDDLE SON, JOSE, TOOK ILL WITH PNEUMONIA

YOU WAIT HERE WITH RABBI MOSE MADEIRA AND THE REST WHO ARE TOO WEAK TO COME ALONG NOW, TILL YOU WILL BECOME WELL. THE ABLE ONES MUST GO NOW AND WHEN WE PASS THROUGH SAFELY, WE WILL LET YOU KNOW.

AND WATCH YOUR RING MY SON, ALWAYS CARRY IT WITH YOU.

YES FATHER I WILL WATCH IT

UNDER THE GOODCARE OF RABBI MOSE, JOSE RECOVERED, AND THE TWO TOGETHER WITH ONE OLDER WOMAN AND ANOTHER EVEN YOUNGER BOY, AKIBA LOPEZ, SET OUT TOWARDS THE COAST OF THE ATLANTIC OCEAN.

IT IS SAFE FOR YOU TO TAKE THE ROUTE WHICH WAS TOO DANGEROUS FOR THE LARGER GROUP, WITH DON IZCHAK

THEY HAD BEEN ADVISED BY A SPECIAL MESSENGER

A SMALL FISHING BOAT COULD EASILY BE FOUND, AND, AT LITTLE COST WOULD CARRY YOU NORTH, WITHOUT DRAWING THE ATTENTION OF PIRATES AND OTHER ENEMIES

(To be Continued)

Published & Copyright 1961 by
MERKOS L'INYONEI CHINUCH, Inc.
770 EASTERN PARKWAY
Brooklyn 13, N. Y.
HYacinth 3-9250

No. 36

PAINFULLY YOURS

Jacob was happily riding along on his bicycle when suddenly he swerved. He strained to keep from falling. He managed to stay on the bicycle but the twisting had made his arm and shoulder feel very painful.

"I must get home somehow," thought Jacob as he slowly pedaled. Every movement of his hands and arms was torture.

Then he saw a brown-jacketed boy coming towards him. "There's David. If he doesn't start a fight as usual, I'll ask him to help me home."

"Hello, David," Jacob smiled in a friendly way. "How've you been? You haven't come around to play with me for days."

"Well, if it isn't big shot Jacob on a fancy bike!" sneered David.

"You have a lovely bike, too, David. I'd ask you to take a ride with me now, but I twisted my shoulder a few minutes ago. It hurts me to move. Could you, please, help me home?"

"You look perfectly well to me. I have no time to play with you now," said David as he went on his way.

It took Jacob fifteen minutes instead of the usual five to get home. His mother called the doctor immediately.

"That's a bad strain," was the doctor's verdict. "I'll have to bandage your shoulder and arm tightly. Keep your arm in a sling for a few days at least."

"How will I do my homework? How will I take notes in school?" wailed Jacob.

The next day in the schoolyard all his friends sympathized with Jacob's plight. As they comforted him, David arrived.

He stared at Jacob with his hand in a sleeve while his face turned brick red. Finally he came over to Jacob and said, "Jacob, I'm sorry to see your arm is really hurt. Um-ah—could I speak to you for a minute?"

Very puzzled, Jacob walked aside. David looked him in the eye and said, "I want to apologize. When I think how nice and friendly you were to me yesterday, even though you were in pain, I'm ashamed of the way I spoke to you."

"Don't worry, I'll just forget it," said Jacob. "My mother has always insisted that I greet and speak to everyone pleasantly. How I feel and how the other person acts should never affect my pleasant greetings."

"That's a good thing to remember. Jacob, would you please let me help you now? I'll make copies of all the notes in school. Every night I'll come over to help you with your homework till your arm is better."

"You're really a friend. You guessed what I was worrying about. Thanks for helping!"

JOSEPH'S ADVENTURES

Joseph's brothers returned to their meal in grim silence. What had they done? Had they gone crazy? They looked at each other secretly and noticed that none of them was eating anything. They had lost their appetites; their consciences were troubling them. . . .

"Why are we sitting here doing nothing?" one of them suddenly burst forth. "Let us chase after those Ishmaelites and get our brother back!"

As one man they rose and hurried out, but the fastest runner among them had to turn back, as they could see no trace of the Ishmaelite caravan, nor had they any idea in which direction to look. Joseph, their brother, had disappeared as completely as if the earth had swallowed him up.

Meanwhile Reuben, who had gone home to take care of his father Jacob, returned, not knowing that his brothers had sold Joseph. "Now is my chance to free Joseph from the pit and take him home," he said to himself. "My brothers are not so bad; I am sure they will realize that they don't really want to harm Joseph, and they'll be glad I saved him." But imagine his horror when he reached the pit, called Joseph's name and got no answer. Had a snake killed poor Joseph, he thought with a shudder. Quickly Reuben let himself down into the pit, and was sadly convinced that Joseph was not there. Somehow he managed to climb out of the deep pit and hurried off in search of his brothers.

As soon as Reuben came within calling distance of them, he called out in a fearful voice, "Where is Joseph? What have you done with him?" As he came nearer, Reuben saw that his brothers had been crying, and they all looked very sad.

"It was all Judah's fault," they cried out together. "He was the one who suggested we should sell Joseph!"

"But I meant to save him! It was you who wanted to kill him!"

"No, it isn't so. If you said: 'Let him go,' we would have listened to you. It's all your fault!" Thus it went, back and forth.

"That's enough quarreling," interrupted Reuben. "Don't you see what terrible things come from quarrels between brothers? Let us make up our minds from now on never to quarrel amongst ourselves any more, and let us all swear that, as long as we live, we shall not cease in our search for our brother Joseph, until we find him and set him free. Meanwhile, we must keep the secret of our shameful deed from our dear father.

"For, heartbroken as he surely will be at the loss of his beloved son Joseph, he will at least be spared the shocking thought that we, his sons, Joseph's own brothers, sold him into slavery."

All Joseph's brothers swore that each would be ready to give his life, if only Joseph would be found.

The brothers took Joseph's beautiful coat and dipped it into the blood of a goat. They showed it to Jacob when they returned home. For many years Jacob mourned the loss of Joseph who, he thought, had been killed by a wild animal.

(To be Continued)

 ROSH HASHANAH

The lunchroom was very noisy. No wonder! After the summer vacation and the High Holiday Season, there was so much the children had to tell each other.

David and Jacob were busy comparing adventures like all their schoolmates.

"I had a wonderful time in camp. Those baseball games were terrific," said David.

"Give me swimming any day," said Jacob.

"What I really liked most was our daily Jewish

lesson. This Rosh Hashanah was the best ever. I can thank what I learned in camp for that."

"You should see the new suit I got for Rosh Hashanah," said Jacob. "My mother got me a complete new outfit for the New Year."

David shrugged his shoulders. "My mother always buys us new clothes for the New Year. She says we want to dress up to show how important the holiday is. But the new clothes are not what I meant when I said it was the best New Year ever. This year I was finally old enough to appreciate that Rosh Hashanah means more than new clothes."

Jacob laughed. "My mother sure went to town with the meals, too."

"Didn't you go to the synagogue? Weren't you impressed by all the people praying? Didn't you feel a shiver of fear as you realized that at that moment the Almighty was deciding the fate of each and every person for the coming year?"

"No, I didn't," said Jacob. "This is interesting. Please tell me more!"

"I learned that on Rosh Hashanah, the first day of the New Year, G-d weighs each person's deeds of the past. Then He decides what will happen to the person during the new year: riches or poverty, good health or bad, and so on. Naturally, every person begins to weigh his deeds. Most of the time he realizes how often he has done wrong, either to G-d or to other people."

"I'll say! Then he's doomed to a bad year and punishment from G-d?"

"Not necessarily. Our G-d is very kind. If we repent and make a strong resolution to mend our ways, if we make amends to anyone we wronged, then He forgives us. In fact, the whole month of Elul, which comes before the New Year, is a month of sincere prayer and atonement."

"Now I understand why everyone was so solemn during the New Year prayers in the synagogue. I saw a lot of people crying when the Rabbi was blowing the Shofar. Why do they blow the Shofar?"

"It is blown on Rosh Hashanah to rouse the people to atone for their sins before it is too late. We pray and call the L-d's attention to our prayers. We beg Him to write our names in the Book of Life for the coming year."

"I'm sorry," said Jacob, "that I didn't know all this. Now I know there's more to Rosh Hashanah than a new suit and good food, even the honey into which we dip our bread."

"Which, by the way, expresses our hope that the New Year will be a sweet year for all Jews!"

THE SILVER RINGS (3)

AFTER WEEKS OF STRENUOUS AND HAZARDOUS TRAVEL, RABBI MOSE AND THE TWO BOYS REACHED A SMALL HARBOR. THE WOMAN HAD NOT BEEN STRONG ENOUGH EVEN FOR THIS PART OF THE JOURNEY.

THINGS SEEMED TO GO WELL FOR A CHANGE. A FINE, OLD MAN AGREED TO TAKE THEM ON HIS BOAT, AS FAR NORTH AS HE WOULD FIND ENOUGH FISH FOR HIS TRADE. HE AND HIS SON WERE THE ONLY ONES RUNNING THE BOAT.

I DON'T KNOW HOW LONG I CAN HOLD OUT, BUT YOU TWO MUST LEARN AND TRY TO REMEMBER AS MUCH AS POSSIBLE, FOR ONLY G-D KNOWS IF, AND WHEN, YOU WILL AGAIN GET TOGETHER WITH YOUR FAMILIES AND HAVE A REGULAR SCHOOLING AS BEFITS YOUNG JEWS.

RABBI MOSE AND THE TWO BOYS WERE HAPPY WITH THE SMALL CABIN AND THE WOODEN COTS AS LONG AS THEY SAW THAT THEY WERE DEALING WITH A TRUSTWORTHY MAN.

HIS WORDS WERE ALMOST PROFETIC. AFTER TWO WEEKS OF FISHING IN THE SMALL BOAT, RABBI MOSE SUDDENLY BECAME WEAK, AND PASSED AWAY, LEAVING THE BOYS ALL HIS POSSESSIONS AND LAST BLESSINGS.

G-D IS WITH US, AKIBA, HE WILL PROTECT US EVEN THOUGH WE ARE NOW ALL ALONE. LET'S BE BRAVE AND TRUST IN HIM.

(To be Continued)

SHALOH

Published & Copyright 1961 by
MERKOS L'INYONEI CHINUCH, Inc.
770 EASTERN PARKWAY
Brooklyn 13, N. Y.
HYacinth 3-9250

No. 37

A PLEASURE SHARED

"Good news," Mrs. Greenberg called out to her sons when they returned from school.

Three pairs of brown eyes eurned to her in wonder. "What is it?" Jacob, Dan and Abraham asked as one.

"It's definitely decided that Jacob will be the one to go to camp this year."

"Yippee!" yelled Jacob as he danced around the room.

"I'm glad," Abraham smiled and nodded. "I'll bet you'll have a wonderful time."

Dan was quiet and grim. Suddenly he burst out: "It's not fair! Why should Jacob be the one to go? Why can't I? I want to go, too!"

"But Dannie," his mother pleaded, "remember, we said that only one of you could go. Remember how we discussed it and decided that since Jacob is the oldest, it's fair that he should be the one."

"Don't be jealous," said Abraham to Dan. "Let's be glad for Jacob, glad that he has a chance to have such a nice vacation. I hope you write to us, and tell us all about it."

"Of course, I will," Jacob promised. "I'll write about every ball game, every swimming meet. You'll feel as if you know every one in camp personally."

"I'd like you to have my tennis racket and baseball glove—they'll come in handy," said Abraham.

"You're too good to me."

"I'm just happy for you. And you, Dan, cheer up. We have each other for company. We'll do lots of interesting things together."

Mrs. Greenberg rushed over and hugged Abraham. "I'm lucky to have such a good, generous son!"

"I'm lucky to have such a brother," agreed Jacob.

"I guess I'm lucky to learn to be happy when someone else has good luck," said Dan.

AT RACHEL'S TOMB

"Quite a nice-looking boy, this Joseph, don't you think?" one of the Ishmaelites remarked to the leader of the caravan.

"What use is his beauty to us?" retorted the leader. "He doesn't look like a slave, and no one will pay much for him. He is too fine and gentle-looking. We'll do well to get rid of him and trust to make our profit on the spices we are carrying."

"This boy certainly is a lucky one. He is riding among the spices like a little prince. That is surely his good fortune, for he'd hardly be as comfortable riding among the barrels of kerosene and tar which we usually carry."

As soon as they met another caravan of camels, driven by some Midianites, the Ishmaelites were glad to sell Joseph to them at a "bargain-price."

When poor Joseph saw the mean, cruel faces of his new "masters," he began to plead with them to take him home to his father Jacob, who, he said, would gladly pay them his weight in gold.

"And why should we believe you? If you have such a rich father, how is it that your brothers were willing to sell you for a mere twenty pieces of silver? Think up some more funny stories," they sneered at him.

Joseph broke down, shaking with sobs. But, instead of arousing any pity in the leader of the caravan, it only seemed to anger him. The cruel Midianite struck at him with his whip, until Joseph had to cry out, twisting in pain. At the same time he threw Joseph off the mule on which he had been placed, and made him go along on foot.

As Joseph dragged himself along, trying to keep

pace with the caravan of camels and mules, he suddenly recognized that they were turning into the road to Ephrath. His heart began to beat faster as he thought that they would pass the place where his mother Rachel was buried. Soon he saw his mother's tomb from the distance. Paying no attention to his weariness and footsoreness, he rushed forward and flung himself down on the earth near her grave.

"Mother! Dearest Mother!" Joseph called out in heartbreaking sobs. "Have pity on your poor son! See what these wild men are doing to me, so far away from my dear father. Please pray to G-d for me. I want to go home to my father, please, please, Mother!" Joseph sobbed and sobbed, until he had no more strength left. . . .

Suddenly, Joseph lifted his tear-stained face and listened. His mother's voice came clearly to him from her grave:—

"My soul weeps with you, dear son. But do not give up hope. It is G-d's will that you go through hard times now, so that you will thereby learn to feel for those who are poor and those who suffer and are persecuted. My son, always remember who your father is, and what sort of a home you come from. Always be a faithful Jew. Turn away from evil and do good al-always. G-d will have pity on you and protect you even though you be among strangers. Have faith in G-d and He will never desert you. He will return you safely to your father and brothers in His own good time."

Joseph was a broken-hearted boy when he threw himself on his mother's grave, but he now rose a man. With self-control and confidence he walked back to the caravan, ready for whatever strain and suffering the future might hold for him. He was determined to live up to the teachings of his father Jacob, and mother Rachel, handed down by his grandfather Isaac and great-grandfather Abraham. Nothing would make him forget who he was, even though he lived among strangers.

(*To be Continued*)

 ## THE MEANING OF THE SUCCAH

It was a lovely September evening. Eight-year-old Joel sat very quietly, looking a little sad.

"Lonesome for home, Joel?" inquired his Aunt Sarah in a sympathetic tone.

"Not too much," Joel smiled a little at her as he sighed. "I love it here on your farm and I know that I'm getting stronger and healthier here, just as the doctor promised. And I did speak to mother on the phone last night. It's not exactly homesickness."

"Then why are you looking so blue? Did the Yom Kippur services yesterday make you sad?"

"It's just that at home in the city things are so different. You know, here we had to spend Rosh Hashanah and Yom Kippur in town in order to be able to attend the services in the synagogue. That was really wonderful. But you see, at home right after Yom Kippur we start getting ready for Succos. I guess here on the farm, Uncle Dan is too busy."

Aunt Sarah laughed. "It's always good to tell the truth. In all the excitement we forgot to mention Succos. Do you really think we don't have a Succah?"

"You do?" Joel's face was all alight.

"Of course we do! In fact, most years Uncle Dan starts putting up the Succah when we return from Yom Kippur services, just as most Jews do. It shows we meant what we resolved on Yom Kippur to observe as many 'mitzvos' (commandments) as possible. This year Uncle was rather busy and he won't have time to start building the Succah till tomorrow."

"May I watch?" asked Joel.

"Watch! Why, we expect you to help!" exclaimed Aunt Sarah as Joel jumped and clapped his hands for joy.

The next day it seemed to him forever before his uncle was finally ready. They chatted as they worked. Joel kept busy handing his uncle nails, holding sides in place, and generally making himself useful.

"Did you know," asked Uncle Dan, "that the commandment to live in a Succah is in memory of the Almighty's wonderful protection of our ancestors for the forty years they spent wandering in the desert after they left Egypt till they arrived in the Land of Israel?"

"Yes," answered Joel, "G-d surrounded the Jews with seven miraculous clouds, which protected them from the heat of day, the cold of night and all the other discomforts of the desert. To show our everlasting thanks for

His kindness and wonders, every year, we build an enclosure, a Succah, and eat our meals there for seven days. At every meal we say the blessing: 'Blessed are You, O L-d our G-d, King of the universe, Who has sanctified us with his commandments and commanded us to dwell in the Succah.'

"I know that the first two nights of Succos we must eat at least part of the meal in the Succah, even if it is raining hard. In any case, we should try to spend as much time as possible in the Succah, and treat it as our home."

"How does your father cover his Succah, Joel?"

"With evergreen branches. But our neighbor covers his with bamboo rods. The Succah is only a temporary dwelling."

"My, but you know a lot! Do you also know that we celebrate Succos in the fall when the days are cooler and damper to show that we leave our comfortable homes to stay in a hut not for comfort, but to obey the Almighty's will? And one of the things a Succah should teach us is that our comfortable home, like everything else we have, is a gift from G-d and not something we own that we have earned. We must always be grateful for what we have, and behave in a way to show the L-d we appreciate His kindness."

"Yes—there is much that the holiday of Succos teaches us. Come, let's go gather the branches to cover our Succah while Aunt Sarah decorates its walls with fruits and pictures."

THE SILVER RINGS (4)

I WOULD BE GLAD TO KEEP YOU, YOU COULD LEARN MY TRADE AND WORK WITH ME AS LONG AS YOU WANT OR I WILL TAKE YOU NORTH AND PUT YOU OFF IN A HARBOR WHERE OTHER BOATS COULD HELP YOU CONTINUE YOUR JOURNEY.

THANKS FOR YOUR KINDNESS TO US, BUT I AM SO ANXIOUS TO GET TOGETHER WITH MY FAMILY....

HE HAD OUTFITTED THEM WITH SOME OF HIS SON'S CLOTHES, AND HE HIMSEF SOUGHT OUT ANOTHER FISHERMAN.

TWO WEEKS LATER, THE FISHERMAN TOOK HIS BOAT, NOW LOADED WITH LOTS OF FISH, INTO THE PORT OF ST. GILLES ABOUT HALF WAY UP THE COAST OF FRANCE.

WELL, YOU SPEAK FRENCH WELL ENOUGH BY NOW, SO THAT FEW PEOPLE WILL SUSPECT YOU AS BEING SPANISH

I WILL PAY YOU TO TAKE THESE TWO CHILDREN TO LORIENT

BUT THE OTHER FISHERMAN PROVED TO BE A DRUNK WHO MADE THE TWO BOYS WORK HARD BEAT THEM WHENEVER HE WAS NOT SOBER, AND SIMPLY SET THEM OUT AT THE COAST, WHEN HE HAD SPENT THE MONEY WHICH HE WAS PAID FOR THE BOYS.

HA-HA-HA HO-HO-..

GIVE ME ALL YOU HAVE GOT WITH YOU, OR ELSE I'LL DROWN YOU

JOSE HAD HIDDEN THE SMALL LEATHER BAG WITH THE RING IN THE HEEL OF HIS SHOES

(To be Continued)

Published & Copyright 1961 by
MERKOS L'INYONEI CHINUCH, Inc.
770 EASTERN PARKWAY
Brooklyn 13, N. Y.
HYacinth 3-9250

No. 38

LOST AND FOUND

"Oh boy! Are we lucky!" exclaimed David as he pointed to the ten dollar bill on the sidewalk. "In front of the synagogue, too! It shows it pays to go to Hebrew school."

"Maybe it belongs to someone who came to pray here, or perhaps to speak to the rabbi. Maybe a passerby dropped it," said Jacob.

"There's no one in sight," said David as he looked up and down the street. "I'm sure it's all right to keep it."

"I'm not so sure," answered Jacob. "My father told me a very interesting story last Shabbos. Let me tell it to you.

"A long time ago there lived a great Rabbi and teacher whose name was Rabbi Simeon, the son of Shetach. He became the leader of the Jewish people of his time. But he was a very poor man. He worked hard for his daily bread, in addition to his holy studies with many students and scholars.

"One day Rabbi Simeon bought a donkey from a gentile farmer. As his students were bringing the donkey to the barn, one of them noticed a little bag tied around the donkey's neck. He opened it and gasped!

"Quickly he ran to Rabbi Simeon: 'Rabbi Simeon! Your troubles are over!' he shouted. 'G-d has rewarded you! The donkey was carrying a large, brilliant diamond in a bag around its neck. When you sell the diamond, you will be able to sit and study Torah and never work for a living again!'

" 'You are mistaken, my son,' Rabbi Simeon answered. 'I must return the diamond to the gentile from whom I bought the donkey.'

" 'How can that be? The owner sold the donkey to you this way. If he gave you the donkey as is, aren't you then entitled to keep whatever was on the donkey?'

" 'But think of the poor man who probably didn't realize he had forgotten to untie that precious bag. Come' — and Rabbi Simeon led his students back to the gentile.

" 'Here,' said Rabbi Simeon to him, 'you forgot to remove the diamond from the donkey's neck.'

"The farmer grasped Rabbi Simeon's hand and he wept as he said, 'That diamond is my life's savings. How kind and generous you are to return it to me. How great are your Torah and your G-d that teach you to act so righteously.'"

Jacob turned to David: "Let's learn a lesson from that story. Let's bring the $10 to the synagogue office."

As they entered the office, they saw their friend Sam with his mother. Sam's face was red and tear stained.

"Anything the matter?" they asked.

"I lost ten dollars I was bringing to the synagogue," said Sam as the tears started again.

"This is your lucky day. We just found your $10 in front of the synagogue."

As Sam hugged them for joy, his mother exclaimed: "What wonderful, honest Jewish boys! They bring respect and credit to their parents, themselves—and their school!"

 ## JOSEPH AS A SERVANT

The caravan of merchants came to Egypt, where they sold Joseph to Potiphar, the chief officer of King Pharaoh. It was soon clear that Joseph was no ordinary slave. He was so clever and did everything so well, that his master Potiphar soon put him in charge of his entire household. G-d blessed Joseph with success in everything he did, and Potiphar was very happy.

Everyone was satisfied with Joseph except Potiphar's wife, who always sought to make trouble for him. She complained to Potiphar that Joseph was untrustworthy, and the indignant Potiphar angrily ordered that Joseph be thrown into prison.

JOSEPH IN PRISON

The Egyptian prison was the last place Joseph expected to find himself in, but there he was, and there was nothing to do about it. Living among the prisoners, however, did not change Joseph's character or behavior. He behaved so nicely, and bore his new trials with such dignity, that the keeper of the prison soon recognized that Joseph was not of the type of prisoners that usually lived in the dungeon. So the keeper made Joseph superintendent over all the prisoners, and treated him with especial consideration and kindness.

One day two new prisoners were thrown into the dungeon. They were no ordinary criminals. One of them was the chief of the king's butlers, and the other the chief of the king's bakers. Potiphar, the captain of the king's guard, Joseph's former master, appointed Joseph to attend the important prisoners until the king reviewed their cases and decided what to do with them. Joseph did his best to make them comfortable.

(To be Continued)

THE MEANING OF THE LULAV

"Get your coat, Joel, and I'll take you with me to town," said Uncle Dan.

Once they were settled in the car and on their way, he turned to his nephew. "The holiday of Succos begins in just two days, Joel. Can you guess our errand?"

"I'll bet we're going to town to buy a 'Lulav' and an 'Esrog'."

"Right the first time. Living as we do on the farm, it isn't always easy to get what we need for the Jewish holidays. But I asked the Rabbi in town to order a fine set of 'Esrog and Lulav' for me as he does every year."

"At home," said Joel, "Daddy shops and shops till he finds just the ones that he thinks are perfect."

"It is a great 'mitzvah' (commandment) to buy the very best you can find and afford. You know what—let's make the ride pass quickly by playing a game. A chocolate bar for every correct answer."

"What are we waiting for? Let's go!"

"First, what is an Esrog?"

"An Esrog is a fruit of the citrus family. It looks a lot like a lemon. For Succos we must obtain a purely bred Esrog, the nicest possible. The Esrog has a pleasant odor and is also a good useful fruit. It represents the best Jews: those who are learned in Torah and whose lives are filled with mitzvos—good deeds."

"That gets you one chocolate bar. Now, what is a Lulav?"

"Another easy question. A Lulav is a branch of a special palm tree. The Lulav we use on Succos should be a fresh green branch, as straight as possible. The fruit of the palm tree—dates, are good, but without odor. Thus the Lulav symbolizes those Jews who, although not well learned, still perform many good deeds."

"Good answer! Now, here's a hard one. What do we place on the sides of the Lulav?"

"On the sides we place three 'Hadassim,' myrtle branches. The myrtle has a wonderful aroma. It stands for those Jews who devote their lives to study of the Torah. We place also two 'Aravas,' willow branches— a symbol of those poor Jews who have neither Torah study nor good deeds to their credit. We are commanded by the Torah to use all four kinds—Esrog, Lulav, Hadass, Arava, together, to show that the congregation of the Jews stands together—good and bad. We don't leave anyone out, and the Almighty answers us more readily when we are united."

"Take a breath while you think about the most important question: Just what do we do with these four kinds on Succos?"

Joel grinned at his uncle. "I'll save my breath to eat those chocolate bars. Every morning during Succos"—

"Except Saturday," interrupted his uncle, "when we may not touch them."

"Well, every morning of Succos, except Shabbos,"

« 110 »

said Joel, "we take the lulav, with the myrtle and willow tied to it, in our right hand. In our left hand we take the esrog. We say the special blessing for this occasion in our prayer book, then holding them together, we shake the lulav carefully. Daddy also waves the lulav in all four directions and up and down in a special way. We do all this early in the morning before the regular morning prayers. We should do this in the Succah if possible."

"Is that the only thing we do with the 'four species'?"

"No. Every Jew that owns a set takes it to the synagogue. During the beautiful prayer of Hallel— Praise to the L-d, which is recited on holidays, the men march and wave their lulavim in a special pattern. It looks very beautiful, too."

"There doesn't seem to be anything you don't know about a lulav and esrog. I'll have to buy enough chocolate bars to last you a month."

The ride did pass quickly. "Here we are. Let's see how nice the set is that the Rabbi has for us this year."

THE SILVER RINGS (5)

(To be Continued)

Published & Copyright 1961 by
MERKOS L'INYONEI CHINUCH, Inc.
770 EASTERN PARKWAY
Brooklyn 13, N. Y.
HYacinth 3-9250

No. 39

THE OLD MAN

"I will not! I don't want to!" shouted David as he stamped his foot for emphasis. "After school and homework, this is my only chance to play. It's not fair to ask me to stay home and keep Grandpa company. That's so boring!"

"Let the boy go," said his grandfather to David's mother. "He's right. I don't want him to miss his fun on my account."

David ran over to his friend Jacob's house. Together they went to the playground. They had spent about five minutes on the swings when Jacob suddenly said: "Let's go over to that old man. He looks as if he's lost."

The elderly man standing near the gates of the playground looked up when the boys came over.

"Excuse me, sir. Can we be of any help to you?"

"Thank you very much, boys. Do you know where Sherman Avenue is? Near Cleveland Street?"

David answered: "Sherman Avenue is three blocks this way to your right. Then you have to turn left and—"

"Wait," interrupted Jacob. "Come, sir, we'll walk with you and show you the way."

"Please don't bother. Continue playing," said the old man, who had a grey beard and a friendly smile. "I'll manage to find it."

"We'll enjoy helping you," insisted Jacob as David glared at him and whispered behind his hand:

"Now you've spoiled the one hour we have to play. By the time we walk there and back it will be time to go home."

Jacob paid no attention to David's scowls. Instead, he smilingly offered his arm to the old man as they crossed a busy street.

Finally, they reached the corner of Sherman Avenue and Cleveland Street.

"What a pleasure to meet such polite, helpful children," said the old man as he thanked them. "Let me give you each a quarter."

"We feel it's wrong to accept payment for helping someone . We are glad we had the mitzvah," smiled Jacob as they waved good-by.

David turned to him. "He could have found his way by himself and we could have played! Now it's time to go home."

"David, David! Don't you know that our Torah commands us to give honor to older people? My father taught me to stand up in the presence of my elders to show respect. How could we refuse to help this old man? Play isn't that important. I really am glad to have this mitzvah."

"I refused to stay home to keep my grandfather company because I wanted to play. Thanks to you, I ended up helping a strange old man instead."

"I guess after this you'll be a lot nicer to your grandfather. He deserves double respect from you. First, because he's old, and besides he's your mother's father."

"Yes," answered David. "From now on I'll put aside special times to keep him company. I too want to do what's right!"

JOSEPH IN PRISON
(Continued)

One morning, when Joseph brought them their breakfast, he noticed that they were very gloomy and sad.

"What is bothering you, Sirs?" Joseph asked them.

"We dreamed strange dreams last night," they said,

"and there is no one here who could explain them."

"G-d alone can reveal the true meaning of dreams," Joseph said. "Pray tell me, perhaps He will favor me with wisdom to explain them."

The officers laughed at him. "You miserable slave," one of them said, "What do you know about wisdom?"

"Never judge people by their appearance," Joseph said. "You need not tell your dreams to me if you do not wish to do so."

The Chief Butler then related his dream: "In my dream, I saw a vine before me: and in the vine were three branches; and as it was budding, its blossoms shot forth, and the clusters thereof brought forth ripe grapes; and Pharaoh's cup was in my hand; and I took the grapes, and pressed them into Pharaoh's cup, and I gave the cup into his hand."

Joseph gave him the following explanation: "The three branches are three days; within three days Pharaoh will lift up your head, and restore you to office: and you will give Pharaoh's cup into his hand, after the former manner when you were his butler." Thinking of himself and his future, Joseph added a personal request that the Chief Butler, when back in the palace, should kindly remember him to the king, so that he, too, might be released from his undeserved imprisonment.

The Chief of the Bakers saw that Joseph had well interpreted the Chief Butler's dream, and he told his dream too. He said: "I also had a dream, and I found three baskets of wheat-bread were on my head; and in the uppermost basket there was all manner of baked foods for Pharaoh; and the birds ate them out of the basket upon my head."

Joseph explained this dream to mean that in three days Pharaoh would have the Chief Baker hanged on the gallows, and that the birds would pick off his flesh.

Joseph's explanations proved right. Three days later was King Pharaoh's birthday. He reviewed the cases of the Chief Butler and Chief Baker. The first was restored to his position, but the Chief Baker was hanged. Happy, but ungrateful to Joseph, the Chief Butler forgot Joseph in the dungeon.

(*To be Continued*)

 REJOICING WITH THE TORAH

David was ashamed to cry, but he couldn't help himself. Of all the inconvenient times to get sick! Here it was the middle of the Succos holidays—and he had to get temperature!

His father came into the room. "There now, David, don't feel so bad. The doctor will be here soon. Maybe all you need is a shot of penicillin to be all well again."

"I hope so," replied David. "It's bad enough to miss eating in the Succah. If I can't go to the synagogue on Simchas Torah, that will be the end! I've looked forward to it so much!"

"That's right. Did you finish the flag you were making?"

Fresh tears came to David's eyes. "Yes, I did, daddy. There it is on my dresser. Now, I may not even be able to use it!"

Mr. Gordon picked up the flag. It was really beautiful. On one side was a detailed picture of a 'Simchas Torah' scene: Jewish men in prayer shawls, each with a Torah scroll in his hands, dancing together in a synagogue. On the other side was carefully lettered in Hebrew: "In Honor of Simchas Torah"—"The Almighty, Israel and the Torah are one."

"This is really special, my boy. After Simchas Torah we must keep it and hang up the flag in your room. You have the whole idea of Simchas Torah on your banner."

"Yes, I was looking forward to taking it along with me to 'Hakofos'." "What are Hakofos for, daddy?"

"Simchas Torah is a one-day holiday that comes immediately after Succos. Simchas Torah means 'rejoicing with the Torah.' The Holy Torah, which the Almighty gave our leader Moses, is divided into five books. These are divided into sections. Every Shabbos a section is read in the synagogue. By the end of the year we complete reading the Five Books of Moses. On Simchas Torah we read the last section of the fifth book, and then we begin again immediately reading the first section of the first book.

"That teaches us something very important. Our Torah is eternal, everlasting. We are never finished studying it, nor are we ever finished with obeying its laws. We must always continue to learn more and observe it better.

"Now about the Hakofos. The doors of the Holy Ark, where the Torah scrolls are kept, are opened. Every man in the synagogue is given a turn to carry a Holy Scroll. All the Scrolls are distributed to members of the congregation, who circle the synagogue chanting prayers, while carrying the Scrolls. Hakofos means circling around. Everyone kisses the Torah, and how they dance and sing! Seven times they circle the synagogue."

"It's so much fun!"

"It's more than fun. It shows that we love the Torah because it is our greatest source of happiness, it connects us to G-d Himself."

"And I love Simchas Torah morning when they read the Torah—the last part and the first. Every man and boy is called up to say a blessing on the Torah. Oh, I won't be able to stand it if I can't go this year."

"There's the bell. It must be the doctor."

A few minutes later the doctor finished his examination. "It's not too bad. A mild sore throat that this prescription should cure in two days."

"Yippie," jumped David.

"Not if you yell like that. Take it easy and you'll get to the synagogue as you wish."

THE SILVER RINGS (6)

THUS, HAPPY JOSE AND AKIBA, CALLED JAQUES EVER SINCE THEY ENTERED FRENCH TERRITORY, JOINED THE OLD MR. SIMONE BOUVOIR, WHO TRAVELLED EAST FROM HIS HOMETOWN OF NANTES TWICE A YEAR, TO SELL CLOTHES ALONG THE LOIRE RIVER, AND TO BRING BACK ALL KINDS OF OTHER PRODUCTS AND WARES,

(To be Continued)

Published & Copyright 1961 by
MERKOS L'INYONEI CHINUCH, Inc.
770 EASTERN PARKWAY
Brooklyn 13, N. Y.
HYacinth 3-9250

No. 40

ALWAYS WELCOME

The silver candlestick gleamed on the snowy white tablecloth. The Rubin family glowed as they stood in their best Sabbath clothes. As Mr. Rubin began to pour the wine into his silver cup, a knock was heard at the door.

"Who could that be now?" Mrs. Rubin asked in a puzzled voice as she went to answer.

She came back a moment later and whispered something in Mr. Rubin's ear. He answered firmly: "We must let him in."

"Very well," said Mrs. Rubin.—"Leah, put another setting on the table." Then she went out of the room.

Mr. Rubin went to the front door. The children

gasped as he returned a few minutes later followed by —a tramp. A dirty, unpleasant person wearing ragged clothes.

"Children, this is our guest, Mr. Green."

"Good Sabbath," said the stranger. "I'm Jewish myself."

Just then Mrs. Rubin returned, carrying an old suit of Mr. Rubin's. It was still in good condition. She had a complete change of clothing for the poor man.

"I believe these clothes would fit you, sir," she said. "Joseph, show Mr. Green where he can change."

When they had gone out of the dining room, Leah whispered: "Mother, must he eat with us? Can't you give him a sandwich in the kitchen? He'll spoil our whole Shabbos!"

"Is that a daughter of our forefather Abraham speaking? You know how hospitable Abraham was to every person? We must show this poor man real Jewish hospitality."

When Mr. Green returned to the table, he certainly looked much better in Mr. Rubin's clothes. His hands and face were cleaned, too.

As Mr. Rubin stood up to recite the Kiddush over wine, tears swelled in Mr. Green's eyes. "It's many years," he explained, "since I've heard Kiddush. I used to say it every Friday night, too. But I've had a lot of trouble and a hard life, and I turned the wrong way."

"I would like to you recite Kiddush tonight too," said Mr. Rubin as he handed Mr. Green a cup of wine.

"Forget your troubles and enjoy the Shabbos. I'd like you to be our guest all day. Now, don't start crying again!"

When Shabbos was over, Mr. Green spoke from the bottom of his heart: "I'll never forget what you did for me. In all my troubles, no one has ever been so kind."

"It was our Jewish duty," said Mr. Rubin.

"Now I'm going to try and find work and a decent room to live in."

"You're always welcome here. Do come next Friday to spend Shabbos with us. We would like to hear about your work and home."

"Thank you for your invitation. I won't rest until I have good news to bring you."

PHARAOH'S DREAM

One night, King Pharaoh had a strange dream. He was standing on the banks of the Nile, when suddenly seven strong and fat cows, followed by seven lean cows, rose out of the water. As Pharaoh was admiring the seven beautiful cows, the seven lean cows turned upon them, and ate them up.

Pharaoh awoke with a start, but then fell asleep and dreamed again: He saw a field in which stood seven full stalks of wheat; then seven bare stalks of wheat sprung out from the ground. Again, curiously enough, the seven bare stalks swallowed the other seven. Stranger still was the sight, as both the seven lean cows and the seven bare stalks of wheat showed no sign of having swallowed the others, remaining lean and as bare as before!

This strange dream upset King Pharaoh and he could not rest until he knew what the dream meant. Pharaoh sent for all his advisers, magicians, and astrologers. But none of them could explain the dream to Pharaoh's satisfaction. Some said, "You will have seven daughters who will die in your life time." Others said, "Seven weak nations will conquer us." None of these explanations satisfied Pharaoh.

"I will search the entire kingdom for a man who will interpret my dream," Pharaoh said. He commanded his servants to issue this proclamation: "Let all the wise men of the Kingdom who can interpret my dream hasten to the palace: the order must be obeyed on the penalty of death."

From all corners of the kingdom, the scholars and the wise men of Egypt flocked to King Pharaoh's palace.

Once again, they presented the king with all sorts of strange ideas. Some said, that seven Egyptian generals would attack and overcome seven foreign kings. Still others said that the King's sons would quarrel amongst themselves, and kill one another.

Pharaoh listened to all these explanations with growing impatience. He could no longer eat, sleep, or laugh. All his feelings and thoughts were taken up with his dream. "I am tired of all these foolish explanations. Send these old men from my house!" he ordered.

For twelve long and bitter years, Joseph had been in prison. One day G-d said, "The time has come to reward Joseph. Now I will reward him for all the years of slavery and misery which he suffered. I will make Joseph very great and very wealthy!"

At the palace, Pharaoh grew paler and weaker from day to day. When the Chief Butler saw the King growing ill with worry, he thought to himself, "If King Pharaoh should die and a new King should take his place, how do I know that he will continue to let me be his Cup Bearer?"

This thought frightened the Chief Butler. Approaching the King's throne, he knelt down, and said: "Long live his Majesty the King! I know someone who can interpret your dream. One day, when I made your majesty angry, I was sent to prison. In the same prison was a poor young boy, a Hebrew, who had been sold into slavery. While I was in prison I had a dream, and the young man told me what it meant. Every single word of his came true. If you send for him, he will set your heart at rest."

(To be Continued)

THE SEVENTEENTH OF TAMMUZ

"How refreshing," said David as he dried himself after his swim. "We're lucky to be here in camp and not in the hot city."

"How true!" agreed his bunkmate Joseph. "Did you hear we're all supposed to meet in the playroom after supper? I wonder what for?"

When everyone in camp had gathered, the head counselor arose. All heads turned to attention.

"Any one who expects some fun and games will be disappointed," he began. "For the next three weeks we are going to limit our fun. Does anyone know why?"

Several hands went up.

"Dan, you tell us."

"Tomorrow is the 17th day in the month of Tammuz. It is a very sad day. Many sad things happened to the Jews on that day."

"That's right. The 17th of Tammuz starts a three-week period of mourning. Therefore we fast at this day, from morning till sundown. Those who are not allowed to fast will eat only what is necessary for their nourishment—not for pleasure.

"Does anyone know why we mourn and fast? David?"

David answered: "Long ago, when the Jews were living in the Holy Land, the Romans invaded the capital city of Jerusalem on the 17th day of Tammuz. This marked the beginning of the end. For after that the

Romans succeeded in entering and destroying the Beth Hamikdosh in Jerusalem. Many Jews lost their lives defending their land and their Holy places. The rest were exiled to other lands. They knew that we had earned these troubles for our sins. Since then we observe the 17th of Tammuz as a fast day."

"Good answer!" said the head counselor. "Jews do not get married during these three weeks. Neither do we don new clothing for the first time or eat new season fruits for the first time, except on Shabbos. And if you are wondering why we made everyone get a haircut this past week, it was because hair cutting is also forbidden."

"Joseph, why are you raising your hand?"

"What other bad things happened to the Jews on the 17th of Tammuz?"

"I'll tell you about the first of these. You all know how the Jews received the Torah on Mt. Sinai and heard G-d speak the Ten Commandments. You know that then Moses Our Teacher, went up the mountain where he stayed forty days and forty nights learning all the details of the Torah. Then G-d gave Moses two tablets on which He had written the Ten Commandments. Moses went down to give this miraculous gift to the Jews. Imagine his grief when he found them dancing around a golden calf. They thought Moses would never return, and then the evil-doers among the Jews led them to calf worship. Heartbroken, Moses broke the tablets. That terrible day was the 17th Tammuz. This is one more reason why we mourn. and fast."

THE SILVER RINGS (7)

THE TWO BOYS JOINED MONSIEUR DUTOIT ON HIS TRIP NORTH FROM ORLEANS. HE TOO FOUND OUT THAT JOSE WAS A CAPABLE ASSISTANT WITH A SPECIAL KNACK FOR BUSINESS.

I DON'T KNOW WHAT YOUR TRUE STORY IS, AND I DON'T CARE. STAY WITH ME, AND YOU ARE BOUND TO BECOME A BIG BUSINESSMAN SOME DAY, AND AS WEALTHY AS THE FAMOUS MENDEZ BROTHERS

MENDEZ?!! THEY ARE MY UNCLES. I AM GOING TO JACOB DEL MENDEZ IN AMSTERDAM.

PLEASE, TAKE ME TO HIM AND MY UNCLE WILL SURELY REWARD YOU FOR YOUR KINDNESS TO US.

JACOB DEL MENDEZ WAS INDEED THRILLED TO WELCOME HIS NEPHEW AND HIS COMPANION, AND BOUGHT ALL THE MERCHANDISE FROM THE FRENCHMAN, IN GRATITUDE.

HE WAS EVEN MORE HAPPY TO HEAR HOW HIS YOUNG NEPHEW HAD SHOWN HIS GIFT FOR BUSINESS AT SUCH TENDER AGE. BUT THE BOY WAS NOT HAPPY.

DO YOU KNOW ANY THING ABOUT MY FATHER?

NO, WE KNOW NOTHING YET.

WHEN DEL MENDEZ DECIDED TO JOIN A GROUP OF JEWISH MERCHANTS TO CROSS THE SEAS TO THE NEWLY DISCOVERED COLONIES IN THE NEW WORLD.

WILL YOU COME ALONG WITH US?

NO, I WOULD RATHER REMAIN HERE AND SEE WHAT I CAN DO TO FIND MY FATHER.

(To be Continued)

SHALOH

Published & Copyright 1961 by
MERKOS L'INYONEI CHINUCH, Inc.
770 EASTERN PARKWAY
Brooklyn 13, N. Y.
HYacinth 3-9250

No. 41

OPEN HOUSE

"Hello, Mrs. Greenberg. I promised Jacob I'd come over to play with him."

"Fine, David. Come right in. Jacob is waiting for you."

As David passed the living room, he noticed Jacob's father sitting with a group of men around the table. They were studying large volumes of the Talmud.

Jacob greeted him happily. "Hi, David. I'm glad to see you. What shall we play? Checkers, monopoly, or shall we study social studies?"

"I'd like checkers. Speaking of studying, I noticed your father studying with some men in the living room."

"They meet three times a week here. Every Jewish

« 129 »

man is supposed to set aside time to study Torah. You're not finished learning when you finish school."

"I know that. My father learns Torah too. But doesn't your mother mind having them meet in your house all the time? It must be a lot of work for her."

"My mother doesn't mind at all. She thinks it's a great honor to have our house used for studying. In fact, there's a meeting here every Thursday night of the Synagogue Board, not to mention the graduate Yeshiva students who come to learn with Dad Shabbos afternoons."

"Well, if your mother doesn't mind all that extra cleaning and serving, she's different from all the ladies I know."

"My mother is always telling us stories about her home when she was a girl. Her father was a very learned man. Their home was always full of scholars and students and rabbis discussing and learning with my grandfather. Now, my mother says, she wouldn't feel natural if our home weren't the same."

"What about your grandmother?"

"Whenever she visits us, she tells me, 'Jacob, our sages say: Let your home be a meeting place for wise men.' She's always anxious to serve the men tea and ask if they need anything. It's her greatest pleasure."

"I think I'd like my home to be like that when I grow up."

"So would I—but right now, I'd like to start the checker game!"

FROM PRISON TO PALACE

When the Chief Butler told Pharaoh of the Hebrew slave in prison who could explain strange dreams, the king quickly commanded his servants: "Go and fetch the lad at once. But be gentle with him and do not frighten him!" The servants hastened to do the king's bidding. Taking Joseph out of his dark dungeon in which he had been imprisoned for so many years, they told him of the king's command.

"But how can I appear before the king in these dirty rags? Let me wash and change and make myself presentable."

"The king won't pay any attention to your clothing. He's interested in what you have to say."

But Joseph insisted, and so they allowed him to have his way. In his new clothing, Joseph, looking like a prince, was brought before the king.

The doors of the throneroom were thrown open, and a burst of dazzling light greeted Joseph's eyes, which had been so long used to the gloomy darkness of the dungeon. Seated upon a magnificent throne was King Pharaoh, clothed in purple and ermine robes, which were studded with precious gems. Upon his brow he wore a sparkling crown made of thousands of rubies, sapphires, emeralds and diamonds. The sunlight played upon this wonderful crown, creating a halo of golden light about the king.

But the throne upon which the king sat was by far

the most magnificent thing in the whole room! Surrounded by huge marble pillars was a throne of pure gleaming gold. Leading up to the throne were seventy wide marble steps. Each step represented one of the seventy languages that were spoken then.

Wide-eyed with awe and amazement at so much splendor, Joseph greeted Pharaoh. Pharaoh acknowledged Joseph's greeting, and the interview began.

"Tell me, what is your name?"

"My name is Joseph, Your Majesty."

"Joseph, you are probably wondering why you have been brought here before me. I sent for you because my servants told me that you can interpret dreams."

"O, King," said Joseph, "I am no dream-teller by profession. It is only when the good G-d opens my eyes and reveals to me things that are hidden from most men, that then, and only then, can I explain dreams."

"Well, listen to my dream, and perhaps G-d will help you once again." And Pharaoh went on to relate, as he had done so many times before, his strange dreams of the cows and the wheat.

Joseph listened carefully to Pharaoh's words. As Pharaoh spoke, the whole meaning of the dream became clearer and clearer to him. He knew that G-d was with him!

"Your dreams are but one, and they mean one and the same thing. The seven fat cows and the seven fat ears of corn are seven years of plenty, and the seven lean cows and lean ears of wheat are seven years of a terrible famine that will follow close upon their heels. The years of hunger will swallow up all that will have been saved during the years of plenty and leave no sign of the former prosperity.

"Now, therefore, I would advise you, great King, to prepare yourself for the years of famine during the years of plenty. Appoint a governor to go about the country and teach the people how to prepare for the coming hunger. Let him appoint officers in each town and village to collect one fifth of every farmer's crop. All the grain should be stored in the great cities, and when famine will sweep over the whole earth, you and your servants and all of Egypt, will not starve."

(To be Continued)

 TISHA B'AV

It was a hot, dreary July day.

"I'm boiling," said David. "I wish it weren't the 'nine days' so I could go swimming."

"Don't feel so sorry for yourself," answered Joseph. "The 'nine days' mean something, don't they? It's a time for deep mourning for the destruction of our Bet Hamikdosh. It's a time when we remember the great suffer-ingse of the Jews who lived at the time that Jerusalem was under siege. When you remember the terrible hunger and thirst those Jews suffered, you should be ashamed to feel sorry just because we don't go swimming for the last nine days of the 'Three Weeks.'

"Hunger and thirst were not the only troubles either. They were in the midst of a terrible war with a cruel enemy. Many were captured, tortured, killed. As the Jews saw their position, the end was too horrible to realize. The end was the destruction of their beautiful Holy Sanctuary—G-d's House, and exile from their beloved land."

"I'm ashamed to have mentioned swimming," said David. "It's time to wash up for lunch. Let's join the rest of the bunk."

The boys were in camp. When lunch was finished, the head counselor stood up. It was the signal for instant silence.

"Boys," he said, "you all know that tomorrow is Tisha B'Av, the ninth day of the month of Av. It is the last day of the three-week period in which we mourn the destruction of the Beth Hamikdosh in Jerusalem. Two times the Jews built a beautiful House in which to serve the Almighty and come closer to Him. But after many years the generations turned away from G-d and His commandments. Then G-d allowed His House to be destroyel. Both Houses were destroyed on the same day, Tisha B'Av, after terrible wars. A sad and evil day in our history.

"For the Beth Hamikdosh was a sign that G-d was in our midst. It was so beautiful that it dazzled all beholders. Many, many miracles occurred there. It was a constant reminder of our bond with the Almighty. Oh, what a terrible loss we have suffered!

"Since the first day of Av we have intensified our mourning. No swimming, no boating. Now I will instruct you in the observance of Tisha B'Av.

"First, this evening we will eat an early supper, for on Tisha B'Av we fast for a full day, from sunset to nightfall. Before sundown, we will eat a hard-boiled egg dipped in ashes, another sign of mourning. We will all change into sneakers, for leather shoes are not worn on Tisha B'Av. All chairs will be turned over, for we sit till afternoon on low chairs like mourners. No one will eat or drink tonight. Tomorrow, any boy under thirteen will skip breakfast if he is able. All healthy boys over 13 will fast all day. Girls over 12 fast too.

"This evening we will gather in the synagogue to read 'Eichah,' the Book of Lamentations written by the prophet Jeremiah, who lived at the time of the destruction of the first Beth Hamikdosh.

"Tomorrow morning we will pray and read 'Kinnoth,' Lamentations. We learn Torah, only such parts that refer to the destruction of the Sanctuary. We do not put on Tefillin until the afternoon, when we pray Minchah. We only wash the tips of our fingers all day Tisha B'Av.

"I think I've covered everything. Let us hope that by next Tisha B'Av we will have returned with Messiah to our Holy Land to rebuild the third and last Beth Hamikdosh."

THE SILVER RINGS (8)

AT THIS TIME IZCHAK LUMBROZO WAS WASTING AWAY IN A JAIL OF THE MARQUIS OF VICHY BECAUSE HE WOULD NOT DISCLOSE THE WHEREABOUTS OF HIS COMPANIONS WHO WERE HIDING IN A CAVE OUTSIDE THE CITY, AND FOR WHOM HE HAD GONE TO PURCHASE FOOD

TELL US WHERE YOUR FRIENDS ARE, OR ELSE YOU WILL NEVER GET OUT ALIVE FROM THIS STONE CELL.

I TRUST IN MY G-D. IF IT IS HIS WILL, I AM PREPARED TO DIE HERE

NOW TELL US WHERE YOUR FRIENDS ARE,

NO.

AT THIS TIME AT THE CAVE

DON IZCHAK HASN'T RETURNED, WHO KNOWS WHAT HAPPENED TO HIM.

WE MUST GET OUT OF HERE AS FAST AS WE CAN.

ABRAHAM, THE YOUNGER OF THE THREE SONS, HAD STOLEN AWAY. HE WOULD NOT LEAVE WITHOUT HIS FATHER, DESPITE THE STRICT ORDERS OF THE HEAD OF THE GROUP AND THE REASONING OF HIS BROTHER LEON THAT HE WOULD ONLY ENDANGER THE LIFE OF HIS FATHER, HIS OWN LIFE AND THAT OF THE REST OF THE GROUP

(To be Continued)

Published & Copyright 1961 by
MERKOS L'INYONEI CHINUCH, Inc.
770 EASTERN PARKWAY
Brooklyn 13, N. Y.
HYacinth 3-9250

No. 42

LABOR OF LOVE

"Come, David," Mrs. Gordon called cheerfully. "Help me carry out this trash. I've been cleaning closets all day."

"Every day you do another job for Passover, mother."

"Yes, because Pesach is only a week away! Isn't that wonderful? I can't wait."

"I think it's terrible," said David. "I wish it would never come. I like to eat bread and rolls much better than hard matzoh. And I don't like the hard work—scrub and clean and work for weeks before."

"I'm really sorry to hear you say that. I love Pesach as I love all the holidays," said Mrs. Gordon.

"I can't understand why, mother. You work the

hardest of all. For a month before Pesach you clean closets and scrub corners and wash dishes all day long. When Pesach finally comes, you have so much cooking to do. And yet you're so happy about it. I just can't understand."

"Tell me, David, do you remember the time you built a model city as a school project? Do you remember how hard you worked making the houses and roads? Didn't you mind the hard work, cleaning the mess of glue and paper and cardboard?"

"Mother, you know I enjoyed every minute of it. I even got a prize—it was so nice."

"You see, David, when you're working for something you love, you don't mind the hardships. I enjoy doing anything connected with a mitzvah. When I know that something I do is the will of G-d, then it is my greatest pleasure."

"I think it is an honor to celebrate Pesach. How can I mind eating matzoh for a week when I know G-d commanded us to do so in memory of the Jews being freed from Egypt. Why should I mind scrubbing every corner in the house when I know that by doing so I avoid the sin of having leaven in my home during Passover. Every commandment, every mitzvah I love because it is a gift from G-d, and I appreciate the gift and am very happy to obey it."

"It is better to enjoy the holidays than grumble," said David. "Just watch me this Pesach, I'll be the happiest boy in town."

FROM PRISON TO PALACE

(Continued)

Spellbound, the king listened to Joseph's words. Joseph spoke with a conviction born of truth, and with the wisdom of a true prophet. But Pharaoh was still not content.

"How can I know that your words are really true and will come to pass?"

"I have proof for you that is both joyous and very sad. Today, your oldest son will die, but you will find comfort in your youngest son who will be born to you this very day."

No sooner did Joseph finish his words than the royal trumpets sounded a sad message to the people. However, the very next moment the same trumpets heralded the birth of a new son to the king!

Pharaoh was overwhelmed! Never before had he seen so much wisdom in one so young!

King Pharaoh was very impressed with Joseph's wisdom.

"Did you ever hear of anything so wonderful before?" he asked his servants. "Surely this young man is favored by G-d. I will appoint him Prime Minister and Viceroy of Egypt, second only to the king. If anyone can save Egypt in the terrible time to come, it is surely this young man!"

The servants were shocked when they heard Pharaoh's

words. "What? A Hebrew slave boy to be the king's chief minister! Such an idea is absurd and, besides," they exclaimed, "Joseph does not know all the seventy languages of the world required of royalty by Egyptian law."

But King Pharaoh quieted their protests. "You did not hear him speak, as I did," he said. "You did not hear the wisdom that flows from the lips of this young man. He is no common slave, but the son of noble parents. I will prove to you that he is worthy of being Viceroy by testing him myself."

That night, Joseph lay thinking about all the strange events that had happened to him, when suddenly, his chamber was filled with a bright light. He looked about, but he could see no one. He looked again, and he could scarcely believe his own eyes. A vision was coming from the light!

"Do not be frightened, my boy," said the angel Gabriel to Joseph, "I have come here to help you. To-morrow, the king will call you to a test of the seventy languages of the world. I have come to teach them to you."

"But how can I learn so many languages in one night?" Joseph asked in surprise.

"Nothing is impossible, if it is the will of G-d," said the angel Gabriel, and when he left Joseph's chamber that night, Joseph knew, as well as he knew his mother tongue, all the languages of the seventy peoples of the world.

The next morning, Pharaoh sent for Joseph. This time Joseph ascended one step after the other, addressing words of greeting to the king in all seventy languages. He stopped on the very last step and addressed the king in Hebrew. Pharaoh grew pale. "In what tongue do you address me?" he asked in a frightened whisper, in a language known only to the two of them.

"Hebrew," answered Joseph, "my mother tongue."

Pharaoh trembled, and his knees shook. What if the people should hear of this? Their own king, supposedly all-knowing, not to know a foreign tongue. Why, thought King Pharaoh, I will become the laughing stock of Egypt if anyone should hear of this!

In a pleading voice, the King turned to Joseph and said, "Promise me that you will tell no one of my failure to understand your tongue. The people will no longer have any faith in their king if they hear of this."

"Set your heart at ease, O King," said Joseph. "I will not breathe a word of this to anyone." And King Pharaoh knew that he could trust Joseph to keep his word. Turning to his servants, Pharaoh said, "This is the man who has interpreted my dream. In wisdom and learning, he has no equal in all of Egypt. He will be my Viceroy. Nothing, however great or small, may be done without his consent and agreement. He is the man who will save Egypt from the famine!"

Pharaoh's servants heard their master's words, and bowed low in response. "Your command will be done, O King."

And to Joseph, King Pharaoh said, "You are no longer a Hebrew slave. From this moment on, you are Tsophenath Paneach, Revealer of Secrets. Viceroy of Egypt. Forget that your name was ever Joseph, forget that you ever lived in Canaan. Your home is here in Egypt."

Foolish Pharaoh! Little did he know that Joseph would always be Joseph, no matter what Pharaoh called him. Joseph would never break the ties that united him with his father's home.

(To be Continued)

 ## SHABBOS NACHAMU

"I still can't understand it," said Jacob to his friend David as they shined their shoes. They were in their bunk in camp, getting ready for Shabbos.

"Just yesterday was Tisha B'Av, a fast day, the saddest day of the year. Three weeks before, we began to mourn the loss of our Beth Hamikdosh. Now we're told that this coming Shabbos is a special, happy one."

"Maybe Sam, the head Counsellor, will explain it tonight at his regular weekly talk."

How wonderful the boys looked, at their line-up. They were hushed as Uncle Sam (which was what they called the head counsellor) rose to speak.

"This Shabbos is called 'Shabbos Nachamu,' the Sabbath in which Jews are comforted. I am going to teach you a song that best expresses the meaning of this day. It is called 'Ani Maamin,' I believe."

Uncle Sam had the boys repeat the Hebrew words of the song several times. Then he explained, "These words mean: I believe with complete faith in the coming of the Messiah. Even though he lingers, I still believe!"

"You see, boys, our prophets warned the Jews that if they did not stop sinning and return to G-d and His Torah, the Holy Sanctuary would be destroyed, their land lost in a terrible war, and the Jews scattered over the whole world. This awful prediction came true, and we mourned the sad events for three weeks which ended yesterday.

"But the Sages predicted and taught the Jews more than that. They promised—'Do not give up hope! G-d has given His word that some day He will send us a holy, royal man, a descendant of King David who will lead Jews back to their homeland, back to a life of peace and service to G-d. This Redeemer is called Moshiach— the anointed and chosen of the L-d.'

"We know G-d always keeps His promises. We look forward to the day when Moshiach will come as G-d has promised. The Jews will live happily and securely in their Holy Land and be a light unto all the nations of the world.

"This is the Sabbath on which the Jews comfort themselves with this hope and promise. Come boys, let us sing Ani Maamin—I believe!"

THE SILVER RINGS (9)

AT FIRST HE HAD TO BE TIED DOWN, IN ORDER TO PREVENT HIM FROM CONSTANTLY ATTEMPTING TO ESCAPE.

(To be Continued)

Published & Copyright 1961 by
MERKOS L'INYONEI CHINUCH, Inc.
770 EASTERN PARKWAY
Brooklyn 13, N. Y.
HYacinth 3-9250

No. **43**

JUST A STAMP

David ran breathlessly into the classroom. It was still early, and the teacher wasn't in yet.

"Anyone here able to give me a stamp? I must have a stamp right now!"

"What's the big rush?" asked Jacob.

"I'm entering the composition contest, and today is the last day to mail in the composition. I've worked hard on mine. I've spent the last two weeks writing and rewriting. This morning I could have cried when I saw we had no stamps at home. If no one can help me with a stamp now, all my work was for nothing."

Jacob sat smiling. His classmates couldn't know there was a debate going on inside his mind. He did have a stamp in his pocket. He was planning to write to his big brother in the navy during recess. He knew how much his brother loved to receive mail from him.

"My brother is more important than any old contest. David will never win anyway," ran Jacob's thoughts. "But then I suppose I could write the letter and mail it tomorrow. I think mother has more stamps."

He heard the boys saying: "Tough luck, Dave. Sorry—no one has a stamp."

"Wait, David," Jacob suddenly made up his mind. "You're lucky I happen to have a stamp with me."

"Thanks a million! I still have time to run and mail it before classes begin. Pray that I win, boys."

It was about a month later that David again ran breathlessly into the classroom. This time he was waving a letter in his hand and yelling: "I did it, fellows, I did it!"

"You did what?"

"I won a prize! I tied for second place! You remember the contest I told you about? Yippie!!"

"Hooray! Yea for David!" The classroom was in a joyous turmoil.

When everyone finally quieted down, David turned to Jacob and said: "If you hadn't lent me your stamp, I couldn't have mailed my entry on time. You have a big share in my winning."

"I'm proud that you won, and I'm proud that I was able to do you a favor," answered Jacob. "That's what friends are for, to help each other."

FROM PRISON TO PALACE

(*Continued*)

And then, in honor of his new Viceroy, the king ordered a great procession. He placed kingly robes about Joseph's shoulders, and gave him the golden signet ring that belonged to royalty alone.

In one of the king's golden chariots, drawn by his choicest steeds, sat Joseph. As the chariot rode through the court, 50,000 soldiers, their swords gleaming in the sunshine, paraded before the chariot. On both sides of the chariot, twenty thousand of the noblest and finest youth in Egypt, in gold and silver robes, stood at attention in honor of Joseph. And behind his chariot came the musicians and singers to gladden Joseph's heart. And above all the merrymaking and noise rose the voices of Pharaoh's heralds: "Long live the king. Long live Tzophenath Paneach! This is the man the king has chosen to rule Egypt. Let no man scorn his word, or dare to disobey his command, on penalty of death! To disobey him is to disobey the King!"

Piles and piles of precious gifts were heaped up before Joseph. Rubies, diamonds, pearls, emeralds, gold and silver, and beautiful clothing were presented to him. And from the king came a special gift of one hundred slaves. When Joseph beheld all the gifts, the great cheering crowds, the thousands of noble and important men who had come to pay honor to him, who only a little while ago, was a humble slave, he was overcome with gratitude to G-d, and cried, "Blessed is G-d who raises the beggar from the dust, unto a place among the noble!"

JOSEPH MEETS HIS BROTHERS

It was a great day for Joseph when Pharaoh appointed him Viceroy of Egypt. It was not the honor and glory that made him happy, but the thought that his dreams which he had dreamt thirteen years earlier, had come true. His own brothers and his beloved father had interpreted his dreams then: He, Joseph, would become like a king, and they would all come and greet him with royal honors! Well, the first part of his dreams had come true, though it took thirteen long years. Joseph knew that it would not be long before the other part of his dream would come true, too.

Joseph had now been Viceroy of Egypt for nine years. Seven of them were the years of plenty, when he was busy storing all the food for the seven lean years that were to follow. The years of famine began, and for two years he had been providing food for all of Egypt, and for many hungry people who came from faraway lands. Joseph was now waiting every day for the arrival of his brothers to buy food. He made sure that he would not miss them when they came. He placed agents at all gates leading into Egypt, ordering them to write down the name of every man coming into Egypt, as well as his father's name, and to bring the names to him every night. Joseph went through all the names himself.

Night after night he checked the names, until one night he jumped with excitement. For, out of a batch of names that one agent had brought him, he picked out, "Reuben, the son of Israel," out of another, "Simeon, the son of Israel"; in a third batch he picked out "Levi, the son of Israel," and so on, until there were ten names, the ten precious names of his brothers, in his hand. Benjamin, his youngest brother and most beloved of all, the son of his own mother Rachel, was not among them. But that was not hard to understand: Benjamin must have remained with his aged father. But why did they all come through separate gates? Could it be that they had scattered through Egypt in order to look for their lost brother? No doubt they were even now looking for him in all the slave markets of Egypt! Little did they dream that their brother was the mighty Viceroy Tzophenath Paneach! A happy smile covered Joseph's face. "We'll soon find out how my brothers feel about me. Are they really sorry they treated me so badly? How much would they give to free their brother if they found him slaving away?"

There was no time to lose. Joseph ordered all the store-houses closed, all but one. To the officer in charge of that store-house he handed in the ten names, and gave him strict orders that when the ten men arrived to buy food, he should have them arrested and brought before the Viceroy.

Three days passed, but the ten brothers did not turn

up. Joseph became worried. He sent out seventy of his strongest warriors and told them to bring in the ten men. "You cannot fail to recognize them; they are tall and majestic looking, tanned from the sun: they are shepherds from the Land of Canaan. Bring them in unharmed!"

(To be Continued)

 ## CHAMPION RUNNER

Mr. Jacobs addressed his restless class:

"I would like to ask a favor of you before you are dismissed. David Rubin has an infected foot, and I'm afraid it will take a while before he can return to school. It's lonesome for David, confined to bed or chair. He would appreciate some visits from his classmates. His parents have also asked for volunteers to help him keep up with his schoolwork. Since tomorrow is a legal holiday, it would be a good day to go."

"I'm going on a picnic."

"I'm going to visit my married sister."

"I'm going to the ball game."

"I think my mother would permit me to go," said Jacob Green.

"You can't go," said Jackie. "You know you have tickets to the ball game tomorrow. You got them for your birthday."

"I can exchange them for another game."

"I see," said Mr. Jacobs, "that Jacob 'runs like a deer' to do a good deed, just as our rabbis have taught us. Our feet should always run swiftly to help us serve G-d and man."

"You're crazy to give up your good time," said Jackie to Jacob.

Two days later Jackie met Jacob on the way to school.

"You missed a swell game. I told you you'd be sorry."

"I think I had an even better time."

"A better time studying with David in his stuffy bedroom than watching an exciting game? Who are you fooling?"

"Listen! I spent the day at David's house. In the morning we studied for over an hour. Then his father carried David out to a cot in the back yard where we played games and then ate lunch.

"After lunch we studied arithmetic. David's cousins came over and I played ball with them. Then his mother made a big roast—frankfurters, roast corn, watermelon. Then we studied Bible—and Mr. Rubin took me home. I wouldn't mind spending a day like that again!"

"And I felt sorry for you because you volunteered to help David! I see now that when you run like a deer to do a good deed, you end up doing yourself a favor. Watch me run after mitzvos from now on."

THE SILVER RINGS (10)

LEON LUMBROZO WITH DON ALFONSO A PHYSICIAN AND A HEBREW SCHOLAR, HIS DAUGHTER AND A FEW OTHER MEN SPENT WEEKS AND MONTHS MOVING NORTHWARD, IN CONSTANT DANGER. FINALLY THEY REACHED THE OUTSKIRTS OF PARIS.

WE'LL BE ABLE TO REST HERE A LITTLE, AS A PHYSICIAN I WILL BE ABLE TO EARN SOME THING HERE. IN ORDER NOT TO AROUSE ANY SUSPICION WE WILL MEET TOGETHER ONLY AT NIGHT AT A SMALL HOTEL, WHERE WE'LL BE STAYING.

ONE EVENING AN OLD MERCHANT WHO HAD JUST ARRIVED KEPT ON STARING AT LEON.

HE KEEPS STARING AT ME, I BETTER LEAVE THIS PLACE

DON'T BE AFRAID, YOUNG FELLOW, PARDON ME FOR STARING AT YOU

YOU REMIND ME SO VERY MUCH OF ANOTHER YOUNG BOY WHO LOOKS LIKE YOU, DON'T YOU HAVE A BROTHER BY THE NAME OF JOSE?

YES!

I WILL TAKE YOU ALL TO AMSTERDAM WITH ME, BECAUSE I ALSO LONG TO SEE JOSE

THUS, IN A FEW MINUTES LEON FOUND OUT THROUGH MR. DUTUIT THAT HIS BROTHER WAS ALIVE AND SAFE

(To be Continued)

Published & Copyright 1961 by
MERKOS L'INYONEI CHINUCH, Inc.
770 EASTERN PARKWAY
Brooklyn 13, N. Y.
HYacinth 3-9250

No. 44

A WATCHFUL EYE

Simon stood before the candy counter, trying to make up his mind. Should it be all chocolate—or filled with nuts—perhaps fruit? Oh! he'd like to have that candy in the red wrapper, it looked good! But hadn't his brother Joseph once mentioned that it might not be kosher? Why take a chance? He had better buy something else. He looked again, but nothing appealed to him. Simeon's eyes kept returning to the red wrapper.

"What difference would it make?" something within him asked: "Just this once won't harm. No one will ever know." No one else was in sight. The candy-store owner wasn't Jewish and didn't know the difference. This candy was probably better than anything else.

"I'll take that," Simeon pointed.

He automatically began to say the blessing for candy as he tore off the wrapper, but he stopped. It didn't seem right. The candy was good, but somehow Simeon didn't enjoy it as much as he thought he would.

That night in bed Simeon just couldn't fall asleep. He turned and tossed and thought:

"But after all, what harm did I do? No one will ever know—I wish I could fall asleep—I'm so tired— I may as well forget that candy—that light in the hall is bothering me—reminds me of the red wrapper—it's shining straight at me—that ray of light is like a finger— like—like— — —an accusing finger!" The tears came to Simeon's eyes.

Just then Simeon's mother came into the room to make sure he was sleeping comfortably. Instead, she found a dishevelled boy trying to hide his tears.

"Simeon, dear. Whatever happened?"

"Oh, mother, I may as well tell you. Today I took my candy money and I bought candy that wasn't kosher. I'm really sorry I did it, but no one saw me and no one will ever know."

"My child, don't say that. Of course Someone knows. There is Someone Who sees and knows about everything we do, Who hears everything we say, and even knows our most secret thoughts."

"Really, mother?"

"Yes, dear. Our Father in Heaven, The Almighty —we can have no secrets from Him. You made a bad mistake, Simeon. I hope you'll correct it by resolving that in the future you'll make doubly sure that whatever you eat is kosher."

"Believe me, mother, I've learned my lesson."

"And more than that—if you remember that G-d sees all you do and knows what you think, how can you do wrong?"

"If I ever begin to think no one knows what I'm doing, I'll think of that candy and remember that G-d is looking over my shoulder."

JOSEPH MEETS HIS BROTHERS

(Continued)

It was almost twenty-two years since Joseph last saw his brothers. He recognized them immediately, for they had not changed much. But they did not recognize him, for when they last saw him he was a young boy of seventeen, with not a sign of a beard on his chin. They had no idea that the mighty Viceroy before whom they fell on their faces, and to whom they gave royal honors, was none other than their own brother Joseph. But Joseph was in no hurry to reveal himself to his brothers: He had to find out more about them: he had to play a little game with them, to test their love for him and for each other.

Joseph addressed his brothers harshly: "You are not really here to buy food! You each entered the city from a different gate; you are really spies!"

"Oh, no," they replied. "Your servants are simple shepherds from Canaan who came here to buy food. We have one younger brother who stayed at home, and one of our brothers disappeared many years ago. We entered through different gates to search for him, but we were not successful."

"I don't believe you. Go and bring your younger brother!"

"We cannot! Our old father cannot bear to part with him!"

"That proves you are spies. You probably don't even have a brother and an old father. Into prison with you!"

After three days Joseph visited the brothers in prison.

"I have decided to let you prove your honesty. I will keep this brother here," Joseph pointed to Simon, "and the rest of you go back home. If you want this brother back, come back with your youngest brother."

Since Joseph spoke to his brothers through an interpreter, they thought he did not understand their language. So they spoke to each other freely.

"We deserve this. It is G-d's way of punishing us for what we did to Joseph."

Joseph, when he saw how sorry they were, left the prison to weep.

Leaving their brother Simon in prison, the brothers took the sacks of grain and food for their hungry families and returned home. They were very frightened when they **found the** money they had paid for the grain, back in their sacks. They never dreamed Joseph had ordered it returned. They only knew that something very strange was happening.

The food was finally all gone. The brothers had to return to Egypt to buy more. But the Viceroy had warned them not to return without their younger brother.

Their father Jacob begged them, "How can I let Benjamin go? If anything happens to him, now that Joseph is gone and Simon too, I will surely go to my grave!"

Then Judah spoke: "Father, if we do not go to Egypt soon, we and all our children will starve to death. I promise you with my life, to bring Benjamin safely back."

"Very well, go with Benjamin, take the money for the first food, plenty of extra money for the grain you will buy now, bring some fine present for that Viceroy, and may G-d be with you."

On this trip Joseph treated the brothers well, so well that they became suspicious again. This Viceroy behaved very oddly, indeed.

He even had them as guests at a feast. His supervisor refused the money the brothers offered for their first sacks of grain, assuring them it had been paid for the first time.

Meanwhile, Joseph seated them according to age, pretending to know so much about them from his "magic cup." He gave them presents, and to Benjamin he was exceptionally generous. Not that Joseph didn't have trouble holding back his tears when he saw his younger brother!

Finally, they loaded their donkeys with fresh sacks of grain, and happily departed for home. They did not suspect that Joseph had hidden his own silver cup in Benjamin's sack.

 WHAT IS SHEHECHIANU?

"Shovuos is such a nice holiday," said Sarah to her mother.

"Yes, it certainly is. I'm happy that we have such nice weather, too. It usually is on Shovuos."

"Come, Sarah, I've prepared some special treats for this afternoon. Help me set the table. I've bought new season fruits in honor of the holiday—peaches and grapes and cherries."

"Yummy—we haven't had those since last summer."

"That's right. These are the first ones I've seen in the stores. I always like to buy them for the first time each year for Shevuos."

Sarah washed and dried the fruit and set it out attractively in a bowl on the table.

"Ah," said Mr. Rubin, "I see you've prepared the usual 'shehechianus' for this Shovuos."

"What kind of fruit is 'shehechianu'?" asked little Ruth.

The rest of the family began to laugh. Ruth pouted: "Don't make fun of me "

"We are not making fun of you. That is a very good question. 'Shehechianu' is not the name of a fruit, but of a special blessing we say."

"But I know the blessing for fruit!" protested Ruth. "Blessed are you O L-d our G-d, King of the Universe, who creates the fruit of the tree."

"That's correct. You know that different fruits grow and ripen at different seasons of the year. When we eat any kind of fruit for the first time every year, we say an extra blessing before we eat it."

"Is that blessing Shehechianu?"

"Yes, Ruth, that blessing is called Shehechianu. It means: We thank the Almighty for keeping us alive and enabling us to reach this happy moment."

"Here, take this peach. I'll take one, too. Say together with me, and don't interrupt or speak out till after you swallow the first bite: 'Boruch Atoh Hashem Elokeinu Melech Haolom Shehechianu vKiymanu vHigianu Lizman Hazeh. Boruch Atoh Hashem Elokeinu Melech Haolom Boreh Pri Hoetz!' "

After she had swallowed the first bite, Ruth smiled: "Delicious, mother."

"I'm glad you enjoyed it. I hope you'll remember the new blessing and say it whenever you eat a fruit for the first time each season."

"I can't wait to say the blessing again!"

THE SILVER RINGS (11)

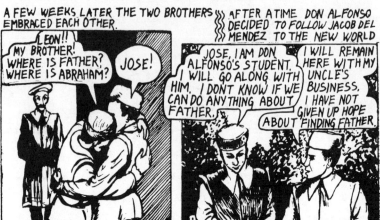

(To be Continued)

Published & Copyright 1961 by
MERKOS L'INYONEI CH!NUCH, Inc.
770 EASTERN PARKWAY
Brooklyn 13, N. Y.
HYacinth 3-9250

No. 45

THE PEACEMAKER

"Let's study at my house for the test," Rebecca said to her friend Miriam. "I'll ask Leah and Sarah to join us."

"I'll be glad to come. But Sarah and Leah aren't speaking to each other, so I don't think they'll come."

"What a shame! What happened?"

"Oh, they had a fight about a game of potsy. Leah won and Sarah said she cheated. Now they're mad."

"I don't like to see people angry at each other," declared Rebecca. "It's so much nicer to be friendly and happy together. Let's get them to make up and be friends again."

"How can we do that?" asked Miriam.

"I have an idea," exclaimed Rebecca. "Come with me to Leah's house first."

When they got there, Rebecca said in her friendliest voice, "Leah, we'd love to have you join us to study in my house."

"I'll come if Sarah doesn't. I'm mad at her," answered Leah.

"Mad at Sarah!" exclaimed Rebecca. "Why, she's your best friend! She even lent you her nylon party dress! You would never have passed in spelling if she hadn't studied with you! You were always staying over at each other's houses! I can't believe you won't talk to her any more!"

"Well, she called me a cheat."

"You shouldn't pay attention to what she said when she was angry and upset. I'm sure she's sorry and wants to be friends again."

"If Sarah is really sorry, I'll talk to her."

"Then I'll see you in my house in an hour. Good-bye now."

As they walked away, Rebecca said: "Let's go to Sarah's house now."

When they arrived, she went straight to the point.

"Listen, Sarah, don't be mad at Leah. She's your best friend, after all. Forget the argument and the mean things you said to each other. I know Leah is ready to forget if you are."

Sarah blushed. "I'm lonesome for Leah. I was waiting for a chance to be friends again."

"Then come to my house in about an hour. We'll all study together."

"I see, Rebecca," said Miriam as they walked to Rebecca's house, "you believe in bringing peace between people."

"Yes—the less quarreling, the more friendship—the better this world is."

IN DEFENSE OF A BROTHER

Eleven happy brothers were on their way to Canaan, returning to their father Jacob. Their sacks were full of food for their starving children, and they were all together at last. Here was also their brother Simon who had been held hostage by that "cruel" Egyptian Viceroy, Tzofnath Paneach. Here, also, was their youngest brother Benjamin, about whom their father had been so worried and anxious. Once again they felt united and strong. If only their brother Joseph were with them! O, how sorry they felt now! They had gone to no end of trouble trying to find their lost brother. They had searched all Egypt and brought upon themselves the suspicion of being spies. But thank G-d, they were on their way home now, and Benjamin was safe with them. They thanked G-d for all His mercies. . . .

Suddenly they heard a stern call from the distance: "Stop there, ho!"

The brothers stopped and turned their heads. Galloping fast toward them was the Viceroy's Chief Steward, leading a company of horsemen.

"How dare you steal my master's magic cup?" the Chief Steward exclaimed, as soon as he pulled up his horse in front of the astonished brothers. "Is this how you repay kindness and hospitality?"

The accusation came like a bolt from the sky, and the brothers grew pale and frightened. However, they recovered from the shock, and burst out all together:

"How can you accuse us of such a dreadful thing? Have we not proven to you our honesty by twice returning the money that we found in our sacks together with our food? We have never stolen anything from anybody, let alone from your noble master! With whomever the stolen thing be found, let him die, and we shall all be your master's slaves!"

Hastily they lowered their sacks from the backs of their asses, and opened them. Beginning at the eldest, the Chief Steward searched everybody's sack, while the brothers looked on confidently, as the search proved fruitless in one sack after another. It was Benjamin's turn now, and suddenly they froze with horror.

"Here it is!" the Chief Steward exclaimed triumphantly . . .

The brothers stood dazed and horrified, staring unbelievingly at the cup.

"I am afraid I'll have to take your youngest brother with me back to Egypt," the Chief Steward said.

The brothers did not doubt Benjamin's innocence. A thought flashed through Judah's mind: How easy it would be for him and his brothers to tackle the Chief Steward and his men, and free their innocent brother. But no, they would not take the law into their own hands; the last time two of them took the law into their own hands, their father was greatly displeased. They would all return to Egypt and clear themselves of the disgraceful accusation. Surely, there must be some mistake!

Silently, they packed their sacks again and followed the Chief Steward back to Egypt.

(To be Continued)

 ## WHAT IS A BROCHAH?

"Do I love a party!" exclaimed Miriam as she donned her ruffled pink frock.

"So do I," said her sister Leah. "I hear someone knocking on the door already. Let's rush."

It was a beautiful birthday party. After the games and the singing, Mrs. Rubin called the girls in to the dining room for refreshments.

Everybody "oh"d and "ah"d as they looked at the richly decorated table.

Leah, who was only four, reached out and popped a cooky in her mouth.

"Leah, that was wrong," said her mother. "You forgot something."

Leah hung her head. "I forgot to ask your permission. But it looked so good."

"Yes, you forgot to ask my permission to take a cooky," agreed Mrs. Rubin. "You also forgot something else that is even more important. There is Someone Else whose permission you must ask too."

"Whose?"

"I know," exclaimed Rose, one of the guests. "You have to ask G-d's permission."

"How do you do that?" Leah sounded puzzled.

"We are so used to having our good food served by our mothers that we forget where it all really comes from. Everything we eat is grown from the earth, or else comes from animals, who also depend on good crops for their food. The farmer never forgets that he has to depend on G-d to make the weather just right for his crops and pasture. If we have plenty of meat and vegetables, milk, eggs, fruit, and flour—it is the Almighty we must thank, for His kindness."

"So everything in the world really belongs to G-d," said Leah.

"Very smart," nodded Rose. "That is what your mother meant when she said you have to ask Someone Else's permission. One must ask G-d's permission before he eats something that G-d put on His earth."

"And if you take something that belongs to someone else without permission, that's stealing," said Miriam.

"You still haven't told me how to ask permission," said Leah.

"I'll tell you," said her mother. "For every different kind of food, there is a different short blessing. It is called a 'brochah.' In these 'brochas' we declare that we know that G-d made and gave this food to us and we thank Him for it. This is like asking His permission to use what is His."

"How can I learn these blessings?" asked Leah.

"I'll teach them to you," said Miriam to her little sister. "There is one brochah for bread and bread products, and one for cake, cookies and similar foods. There is one for fruits, another for vegetables. When we drink a beverage, there is another brochah. And for wine there is a special one. Just remember to say the proper brochah every time you eat or drink."

Here are several rules about these blessings:

1) When you eat a meal, you must say the brochah and eat some bread first. Then you need not make any other blessing during the rest of the meal, except on wine and fruit.

2) When we say a brochah, we should have the food before us, and not speak between the start of the brochah till we swallow the first bite.

3) When we eat two foods that require the same prayer during a short period of time, such as an apple and a pear, or a piece of cake and a cooky, we need say the appropriate brochah only once.

4) If we forgot to say the brochah, as long as part of the food is still uneaten, we may still make a brochah.

THE SILVER RINGS (12)

MONSIEUR DUTOIT AND JOSE CONTINUED THEIR WAY TO VICHY, WHERE ONE OF HIS UNCLE'S BUSINESS AGENTS HAD BEEN ORDERED LONG BEFORE TO ESTABLISH AN ACCOUNT FOR THEIR USE

THE MARQUIS'S MEN HAD FOUND OUT ABOUT THE ACCOUNT FOR THE BUSINESSMAN FROM AMSTERDAM. AS SOON AS JOSE AND MR. DUTOIT APPEARED

WE CAN THANK THE ALMIGHTY THAT THE ROBBERS ONLY TOOK OUR MONEY AND BELONGINGS. AND THEY DIDN'T EVEN TAKE ALL OUR THINGS, I STILL HAVE THE RING THAT FATHER GAVE ME. THIS GIVES ME HOPES THAT WE'LL FIND HIM YET.

YOU ARE UNDER ARREST YOUR MONEY IS CONFISCATED.

WHY? WE ARE HONEST MERCHANTS, MY CREDENTIALS WERE STOLEN.

JOSE HAD BEEN FORTUNATE TO BE CHOSEN TO HELP THE JAILER CARRY WATER AND CRUSTS OF BREAD TO THE PRISONERS.

DON IZCHAK LUMBROZO, NOW ONLY A SHADOW OF HIS OLD SELF NOTICED THE YOUNG BOY WHO HELPED THE JAILER

HE REMINDS ME SO MUCH OF MY SON.

(To be Continued)

שעורי למור הרת

SHALOH

Published & Copyright 1961 by
MERKOS L'INYONEI CHINUCH, Inc.
770 EASTERN PARKWAY
Brooklyn 13, N. Y.
HYacinth 3-9250

No. 46

PEN PALS

"I did not!"

"Don't lie. You did so!"

"What's the argument?" Jacob asked his friends who stood glaring at each other.

"Nathan gave me a push and my pencil case fell down. My new pen is broken. He had better get me another one," said Joel.

"I did not," protested Nathan. "I didn't push him on purpose. I just accidentally walked into him because I was carrying a big pile of books and couldn't see over them."

"You pushed me on purpose and you better make your mind up to buy me a pen."

« 169 »

"I think Joel is right," said Jacob. "Walking into him wouldn't have made him drop anything. Even so— it's your fault and you have to correct any damage."

"Thanks for taking my side," said Joel.

The boys began shouting and arguing, each trying to prove he was right. Just then David Gordon came along.

"Come here," called Jacob. "Listen to this:" He proceeded to tell David all that had happened. "Maybe Nathan will listen to you and get Joel a new pen."

"I wasn't there and I don't like to mix in quarrels, especially between friends of mine. Take my advice: I think both boys should go home and cool off their anger a bit. They're too upset to be reasonable. I'll see you later."

The others kept on arguing despite David's advice. But they could come to no conclusion. They went home angry as ever.

The next morning Jacob was astounded to see Nathan and Joel walking and laughing together. Their laughter turned to scowls when they saw him.

"What happened, boys? I thought you were mad at each other."

"My father fixed my pen. I thought the whole thing over and I decided it probably was an accident," answered Joel.

"We don't think you acted like a really good friend to butt in either," said Nathan as they walked away from Jacob.

Jacob turned to David: "What a good lesson I've learned. From now on I'll do as you did. I see, when you mix in quarrels you only make yourself trouble. No more fighting for me!"

IN DEFENSE OF A BROTHER

(Continued)

Joseph was in his state room when the brothers were brought in before him.

"What a disgraceful thing to do!" Joseph scolded them mercilessly. "Here, I invite you to my house, treat you like respectful guests, almost like my equals, and what do you do? You steal my magic cup! Any one else in my place would very well carry out your own verdict,—put the thief to death, and put you all in chains as slaves for the rest of your lives! But I will go easy with you! I will only keep the guilty one as my slave, and the rest of you go home to your father. . . ."

At Joseph's command, Benjamin was immediately seized by the guard and led away into the next room. Joseph followed him there and locked the door, leaving his brothers outside.

Thereupon Judah did a very daring thing. He broke through the guard and threw his weight against the door, forcing his way in. Joseph looked at him in amazement.

"Do you know what you deserve for breaking in like this?"

"I beg your pardon, my lord," Judah pleaded, "but I cannot let you take away my innocent brother. You know as well as I do the lad did not steal the cup. Now, if you want a slave, take me instead. Look at me. I am stronger and more capable than he. But let the boy go home to his father."

"The man in whose hand the cup was found shall be my slave!" Joseph replied sternly.

"I beg you, my lord, let him go in peace. We shall not leave him here even if we have to lay your whole country waste. . . . Don't you realize that we are capable of doing so? Haven't you heard of the mighty deeds Jacob's sons have done, with G-d's help? Give us our brother Benjamin, and you will spare yourself much trouble. . . ."

"Don't be foolish, my friend," Joseph replied calmly. "Do you imagine that you can frighten me with force? Me, next to Pharaoh the mightiest of all rulers? . . ."

"Do not make me angry, my lord, or I will draw my sword and kill you as well as Pharaoh."

"If you draw your sword, it will strike your own neck. . . ."

"Please, my lord, give us our brother and let us go home. Our aged father is waiting for us anxiously. What shall I tell him, if we come without Benjamin?"

"Tell him that the pail went after the rope into the well . . . that Benjamin went the way Joseph went. . ."

Judah became very angry, and barely controlled himself.

"I warn you for the last time, my lord," Judah roared, "give us back our brother before we paint the whole of Egypt red. . . ."

"Oh, I know you are a good painter . . ." Joseph said dryly, shaking his divining goblet and putting it to his ear. "Did you not paint Joseph's coat of many colors a good red, and send it back to your father saying: 'Joseph was surely torn to pieces . . . .'"

In a fit of rage Judah grabbed a big marble block and crushed it between his hands into small fragments and rubble.

Not to be outdone, Joseph winked to his son Manasseh. The latter came up to Judah, and angrily stamped his foot on the marble floor so that all the walls of the palace shook. As if Judah was not sufficinetly impressed, Joseph struck a huge marble block with his foot and shattered it into fragments.

Even Judah was amazed to see such a feat of strength, of which he thought only a member of his family capable. Turning to his brothers, Judah said: "Is it possible that the Viceroy of Egypt is related to us?"

(*To be Continued*)

 SELLING THE CHOMETZ

It was the week before Passover, and the whole family was busy with preparations for the holiday.

"How would you like to go with me to the Rabbi to sell our Chometz," Mr. Gordon asked David.

"Just wait till I get my jacket, please."

As they strolled to the Rabbi's house, David turned to his father: "Dad, I really don't understand this business of selling chometz."

"I'll be glad to explain, son. You remember learning that we Jews are not allowed to eat leavened bread during the eight days of the Passover holiday as well as the half day before?"

"Yes—we may neither eat nor even use leaven in any form. This reminds us also of the first Passover that the Jews ate unleavened bread in Egypt when they were freed from slavery. Our teacher said it is a very grave sin to eat leavened bread or even have leaven in one's house."

"That is right. That's why Mother is so busy scrubbing every corner of the house. That is why we turn out our trouser cuffs and pockets and clean out every drawer and closet. That is why we use an entirely different set of utensils on Passover—pots and pans, china and silver. You know how we cover every kitchen surface—stove, table, etc., before we use it on Passover. All this is just to make sure that not a crumb of leaven is used even accidentally."

"So if leaven is chometz, and we clean it out of the house, what are we going to sell to the Rabbi? And what does the Rabbi do with everyone's chometz?"

"Sometimes there is good food left before Passover that is all or partly leaven that one cannot just throw away. Like boxes of cereal, cookies, candy, certain medicines. We gather everything that has leaven, even a small part, into one place which we lock securely. We also lock up all the kitchen and dining utensils we use all year. We go to the Rabbi and give him permission to sell all chometz—leaven in our possession, to a non-Jew, the morning before Passover.

"The Rabbi sells the chometz of all the Jews who have given him the power, to a gentile. He makes a bill of sale containing all the addresses of these people. The gentile leaves some money with the Rabbi as a deposit. In this way, all the chometz becomes the property of the non-Jew. As soon as Pesach is over, the Rabbi goes to the gentile and buys the chometz back."

"What would happen if someone forgot to go to the Rabbi before Pesach?"

"Then he must burn all leaven he has in his possession during Passover. He may not eat it or use it or even sell it to a gentile after Passover—he can only burn it."

"Now I know why we sell the chometz to the Rabbi," said David. "That is how we make sure we do not have the sin of owning chometz on Pesach."

THE SILVER RINGS (13)

THE JAILER BEGAN TO TRUST JOSE MORE AND MORE, AND LET HIM TAKE CARE OF FEEDING THE PRISONERS BY HIMSELF.

THIS WAS THE FIRST TIME JOSE WAS ALONE IN THE CELL. QUICKLY HE REMOVED HIS SHOE, UNSCREWED THE HEEL, TOOK THE RING FROM IT AND PLACED IT ON HIS FINGER.

(To be Continued)

Published & Copyright 1961 by
MERKOS L'INYONEI CHINUCH, Inc.
770 EASTERN PARKWAY
Brooklyn 13, N. Y.
HYacinth 3-9250

No. 47

TO WHOM HONOR IS DUE

"Hey, David, come on out. Bring your mitt, I've got my ball and bat. Let's round up some of the boys for a game."

"I can't, Jacob. Guess who's coming to our house? The famous Rabbi Greenberg! I want to help my mother, and I surely don't want to miss his visit!"

"What? All that fuss about an old rabbi? Since when do you care about a rabbi's visit?"

"I can't understand *you*! Surely you've heard that Rabbi Greenberg is a famous Torah scholar. He has spent his whole life studying our Holy Laws. He has taught many others, many other rabbis even. It is a great honor to have him visit us!"

"Honor? Why?"

"Jacob, remember last Simchas Torah in the synagogue? Remember how we marched around with the Torah scrolls and rejoiced with the Torah? Remember how each man was called with the words, "Come give honor to the Torah?"

"Of course, I remember, Dave. But those were Holy Torah scrolls—the Torah that the Almighty gave us on Sinai. Naturally we love and honor it."

"I'm glad you understand that, Jacob. If you understand why we should honor our Holy scrolls, surely you can realize how much we should honor a man who has devoted all his life to studying these Scrolls! Rabbi Greenberg has spent his life learning Torah in order to know how to serve G-d better. He is able to teach us to be better Jews because of his studies. Don't you think that such a man is a living, breathing Book of the Torah? Imprinted in his mind is everything that we honor in the scrolls. Doesn't he deserve the same honor?"

"I never thought of it that way!"

"I'm helping my mother get the house ready. She feels as if a king were coming to us. She says Rabbi Greenberg wears the crown of Torah."

"I'd like to meet this Rabbi. May I?"

"Sure! He should be here in about an hour."

"I'll run home now to change into a nice suit. See you later, Dave!"

IN DEFENSE OF A BROTHER

(Continued)

Judah continued to plead in behalf of Benjamin; he pleaded and he threatened, but without avail. Losing his temper, Judah grasped his sword, but it stuck in its sheath and could not be pulled out.

"That man has special protection from Heaven!" Judah thought, "I might have surely killed him. . . ."

Still calm, Joseph said to Judah: "Isn't there a man of better manners and behavior among your brothers? Let him step forward and speak. I have had enough of you. . . ."

"I, alone, am responsible for Benjamin," Judah said, "for I have sworn to my father for his safety. . . ."

"Did you show such devotion to your brother Joseph, when you sold him for twenty shekels? . . ."

Judah's roar came like an earthquake: it shook the walls of the palace. . . . The guards were blown to the floor, and Joseph was shaken with fright. . . . King Pharaoh toppled down from his throne, and the whole of Egypt seemed to have been swept by a tornado. . . .

In the meantime Judah sent out Naphtali—the fast one—to count the fortresses of Egypt. Naphtali came back saying that there were twelve of them.

"You take one fortress each," Judah said, "and I will take on the remaining three! We will destroy the city! . . ."

"No!" the brothers pleaded with Judah. "Why should the innocent people suffer? There must be another way to move the cruel Viceroy. . . ."

But the "cruel" Viceory, Joseph, had already been moved to tears. He had tried his brothers and found them not lacking in devotion and self-sacrifice for one another. He was convinced that they regretted whole-heartedly their treatment of their brother Joseph, and would do anything to correct their terrible crime, which, after all, Joseph knew was a blessing in disguise. There was no need to pretend any longer and continue to play his difficult part. Besides, Joseph felt his tears bursting.

"Clear the guard," Joseph called, barely managing to hold his tears back. There must be no stranger present when he revealed himself to his brothers, so as not to shame them. Yes, he knew he was taking a chance, for the brothers might take advantage of the situation and seize him and kill him, before he would have a chance to tell them who he was. Nevertheless, he would not shame them in front of others. And when the room was cleared, Joseph's astonishing words came softly and affectionately, with tears streaming down his face:

"I am your brother Joseph! Do not worry about the past. It was G-d's will. . . ."

This time Joseph spoke directly to them in their mother tongue, in Hebrew, and not through an interpreter as before, for there was no need to pretend any longer.

THE REUNION

Twenty-two years had passed since Joseph was sold into slavery. For thirteen long years he had been a slave and a prisoner. But for the past nine years he was the Governor of Egypt, second only to Pharaoh himself.

Now the Governor of Egypt was busy harnessing the horses to the royal carriage. For this special occasion, he did it himself. Joseph was full of excitement, for the time had finally arrived when he would be seeing his beloved father Jacob again.

Joseph looked so handsome and regal as he rode forth, accompanied by princely courtiers, to meet his father Jacob. When Joseph saw his father approaching, he sprang down from his carriage and ran forward, flinging himself upon the neck of his aged father, embracing him and kissing him.

"Oh, father, dear father! I am the same son you knew and loved twenty-two years ago! I have not changed in my love for you or my love for my faith and people. Even though I have lived among evil people, I have not allowed myself to learn from them, but have remained true to you and everything you taught me, father."

Jacob embraced Joseph and held him close, kissing him tenderly. After a while, he spoke gently but feelingly: "Dear son, now I can die with an easy mind, knowing that you are alive and that you are living as a true Jew, as a true member of my family, as a true follower of Abraham and Isaac."

Accompanied with music and the blowing of trumpets, Jacob and all his family now made their triumphant entry into Egypt. And, ringing in Jacob's ears were the words of the Almighty:—

"I will go down with you into Egypt, and I will also surely bring you up again."

 ## THE SYNAGOGUE

"I'm so excited I can't stand still," exclaimed little Joseph.

"I was excited too, the first time I went to shul—to the synagogue," smiled his older brother David.

"Tell me what it's like," begged Joseph.

"I've told you so many times, but I'll describe it again. When you come to the synagogue, I'll call it the shul, you'll see many rows of seats for all the men who come to pray. At the back is a curtain. Behind that curtain are the seats for mommy and all the other ladies."

"But I'm going to sit in the men's section with you and daddy."

"Right. At the very front of the shul is the Aron Kodesh—the Holy Ark. Do you remember what that is?"

"That's like a little closet where they keep the Holy Torah scrolls."

"I'm glad you remember. In front of the Holy

Ark hangs a beautiful embroidered curtain which is drawn aside when the Scrolls are taken in and out.

"Near the middle of the shul is the Bimah—a little raised platform with a table in the middle. The table is also covered with a beautiful embroidered cloth. Here the Scrolls of the Torah are brought to be read."

"Are our seats near the Bimah?"

"Not too far away. We sit near the *mizrach* wall."

"What's that?"

"That's the east wall—the side which everyone must face when they pray. East is towards Jerusalem where once our Beth Hamikdosh stood."

Just then their father called: "Boys, come. Are you clean and neat?" Then, turning to Joseph:

"Joseph, today is the first time you are going to shul. Am I right in thinking you are old enough to behave properly?"

"Yes, daddy. I'll sit quietly near you and listen carefully. When all the men stand up, I will too."

"Good. For certain prayers we must stand. We also rise when the Holy Ark is open and the Torah Scroll raised."

"I will answer 'Amen' whenever everyone else does, and also 'Baruch Hoo u Baruch Schmo'—'Blessed is He, Blessed is His name.'"

"It looks like I'll be very proud of you, Joseph."

"Let's go already—I can't wait!"

THE SILVER RINGS (14)

ONE DAY EACH MONTH ONE OF THE BROTHERS OF THE MONASTERY CAME TO VISIT THE PRISONERS IN THE JAIL, ACCOMPANIED BY ONE OF THE YOUNG STUDENTS OF THE MONASTERY SCHOOL.

ABRAHAM LUMBROZO HAD LOOKED FOR THIS CHANCE FOR A LONG TIME

IF IN ANY PLACE, FATHER MIGHT BE FOUND IN JAIL, IF HE IS STILL ALIVE.

HE WAS WAITING OUTSIDE A CELL, WHEN A VOICE WHISPERED TO HIM

ABRAHAM, ABRAHAM, MAKE BELIEVE YOU DON'T KNOW ME OR FATHER, WHO IS HERE ALIVE, WE SHALL TRY TO ESCAPE TONIGHT. I HAVE THE KEYS TO THE DOORS.

MEET US AT MIDNIGHT IN THE WOODS BEHIND THE JAIL

THAT NIGHT HALF AN HOUR BEFORE MIDNIGHT...

FAST FATHER

(To be Continued)

SHALOH

Published & Copyright 1961 by
MERKOS L'INYONEI CHINUCH, Inc.
770 EASTERN PARKWAY
Brooklyn 13, N. Y.
HYacinth 3-9250

No. 48

FRIENDS IN NEED

"Turn the news on the radio," said Mr. Gordon to his wife. "I wonder if that hurricane is any closer to us."

The news announcer's voice came clearly into the room: "Hurricane Ida is definitely coming closer. It is expected to hit this area within 24 hours. All ships have been ordered back to port. Everyone is urged to protect his property against wind and water damage. We repeat: Hurricane Ida — — — —"

Mrs. Gordon turned to her husband. "What shall we do? I'm really worried."

"Don't be afraid! We must first remove all furniture and loose objects from outside. While we do that, the children will put wide tape across the windows to prevent them from shattering. I'll call the oil company and lay in a supply of fuel. Then I'll take you shopping for an extra supply of food. Let's get going."

Two hours later the Gordons were returning from their shopping trip.

"Children, have you finished your jobs yet?"

"Yes," answered David, "and I'm tired. I'm going to lie down and rest."

"Not yet. We haven't finished!"

"We even emptied the basement and took up the rugs! What else is there to do?"

"We have to prepare the Cohen's house across the street."

"The Cohens? They're not even home. They went to Chicago for a week."

"That's just it. Mr. Cohen left me his key in case of emergency. This is surely an emergency."

"You mean we have to do all that hard work in his house too? We're not responsible for any damage the storm might cause."

"No, David. Mr. Cohen would never demand any hard work from us. But our Torah teaches us that another person's property should be just as important to us as our own. Just as we are careful to protect our own possessions, so must we respect others'."

"I wouldn't feel right if I didn't do everything in my power to protect Mr. Cohen's home, even though I am not legally responsible."

"You're right, Dad. I'll help you and rest afterwards."

"Can we help too?" asked little Hannah and Joseph.

"You're never too young to help. Let's all go together."

JACOB IN EGYPT

When Jacob and his whole family, which numbered seventy people, came to Egypt, Joseph advised them to settle in the part of Egypt called Goshen. "It is good land for grazing sheep," he assured his father and brothers, who had many flocks of sheep. King Pharaoh was happy to agree, and gave them the land. And so they settled happily in their new home, reunited with their dear son and brother Joseph.

Jacob knew he was nearing the end of his days, so he sent for Joseph.

"First, my son, I want you to promise me that you will not bury me here, but take me back to the land of my birth, and bury me in the Cave of Machpelah, where my parents, my grandparents and my wife lie buried."

"I promise, father."

"Now, I want to bless your wonderful sons." Joseph brought his sons Menassah and Ephraim to his sick father's bedside. Jacob blessed them with many blessings. He also made them equal to his own sons, so that Menassah and Ephraim became members of the twelve tribes.

Jacob then called together all his sons. "Keep together, remain firm and true in your faith in our holy G-d, the G-d of Abraham, and Isaac," he begged them. Jacob lifted his hands and blessed all his sons, praying to G-d to bestow His gifts upon them.

JACOB'S LAST JOURNEY

At the very ripe old age of 147, our forefather Jacob died in Egypt, surrounded by all his children. His beloved son Joseph was at his bedside, as also Joseph's two sons Menasseh and Ephraim, together with the patriarch's other grandchildren.

In the last 17 years of his life, which Jacob spent in Egypt, he became known and beloved by all Egypt. And now that he died, he was sadly mourned by all. A period of grief and mourning throughout Egypt was proclaimed for seventy days, as though one day for each member of Jacob's family. When this period of mourning ended, the funeral procession began.

The hearse in which Jacob's body was laid, was borne shoulder high by the twelve tribes of Israel, in the order which Jacob had requested: Judah, Issachar and Zebulun on the east; Reuben, Simeon and Gad on the south; Ephraim, Manasseh and Benjamin on the west; and Dan, Asher and Naphtali on the north. In this order the tribes of Israel were also to march many years later on their way to the Promised Land. Behind the hearse followed Levi and Joseph, and Joseph's crown lay on top of the hearse. Behind them followed members of the royal family of Pharaoh, princes and nobles and common people, in a procession that seemed to have no end.

On the border of Canaan, 31 Canaanite kings were waiting to pay respects to the patriarch. Seeing Joseph's crown on the hearse, they placed theirs, too, alongside. A memorial service was held, in which great tribute was paid to Jacob. Esau, too, came from Mount Seir to attend the funeral of his brother.

Finally the procession reached Hebron, and halted at the Cave of Machpelah. But here a tragic incident happened which seemed for a time to spoil the seriousness of the moment. Esau refused to let Jacob be laid to rest in the Cave of Machpelah, claiming that it was his. Jacob's children claimed that the Cave of Machpelah was their inheritance when Esau had sold to Jacob his birthright and all claims to the land of Canaan, and that the deed was in Joseph's possession. But, in the ensuing fight between Esau's men and Jacob's mourners, forty of Esau's men fell. In the meantime, Jacob's hearse stood by the side, guarded by Jacob's grandsons, among them Chushim, Dan's only son. Chushim was a deaf mute and did not know what all the trouble was about. When it was finally explained to him, he grabbed a weapon and swung it across Esau's head. The mighty blow severed the head, which rolled into the Cave of Machpelah. Esau's men then took the headless body of their leader, and carried it back with them to Seir. Thus, their mother Rebecca's prophecy was fulfilled, for both Jacob and Esau were buried on the same day.

Jacob was laid to rest in the Cave of Machpelah, and after Shivah (seven days' mourning), Joseph and his brothers returned to Egypt where they had left their small children and all their possessions in the land of Goshen.

PLEASE, TEACHER

It was recess time. Moshe Stein spied his younger brother Abraham in the hall.

"I just got here, Abe. Go ask your teacher for permission to come with me."

Abraham walked over to the group of teachers who were standing and conversing.

"Hi, Mr. Green," said Abe as he tapped his teacher's shoulder to stop his conversation. "I want to ask you something."

"What is it, Abraham?"

"My brother's new Yeshivah High School has visitors' day today. He would like to show me around the place. They have a full Jewish and English high school program. He's here now waiting for me. Could you give me a pass?"

"Very well—but next time say please."

"Teach, you're a pal," said Abe as he slapped his teacher playfully on the back."

When they reached the building Moshe warned:

"Please behave yourself here. We treat our teachers differently in our school."

"What's wrong with the way we treat our teachers?"

"Just watch my classmates and you'll see what I mean."

They entered Moshe's large and beautiful classroom. Some of the students were talking, others reading or writing. Moshe showed Abraham to a seat in the back with the other visitors.

The teacher entered. Everyone stopped whatever he was doing and stood up. He motioned them to sit down, took the roll, and began the lesson.

After class Abraham watched each boy bow to Mr. Gordon as they left the room. In the hall he turned to Moshe: "I didn't realize how rude we are to our teachers till I saw how polite you are. I guess we'll know better when we get to high school."

"Why wait? Don't you know there is a mitzvah of honoring your teacher?"

"A mitzvah? A commandment?"

"Certainly. It is necessary to treat a teacher with great respect, to stand up when he enters or leaves a room, to address him properly, never to interrupt him or otherwise show disrespect. That isn't much to show our appreciation and respect for his learning, for his help to us. We should show such respect to anyone who teaches us anything. So don't wait to do this mitzvah in high school--go back to school and start now!"

AFTER MANY
RISKS AND
DANGERS
THEY REACHED
BORDEAUX,
THOUGH
CONSTANTLY
HUNTED FOR
BY THE
MARQUIS'
MEN

THAT VERY SAME DAY
THEY SET SAIL FOR
THE NEW WORLD, AFTER
A HEARTY FAREWELL
FROM THE KIND OLD
MR. DUTOIT.

A FEW MONTHS LATER THEY ALL SETTLED IN NEW AMSTERDAM
WHERE THEIR BROTHER LEON WAS WAITING ANXIOUSLY FOR THEM.

ONCE AGAIN THE
LUMBROZOS WERE
TOGETHER TO
START LIFE ANEW
AS RESPECTED
MEMBERS OF THE
SEPHARDIC
CONGREGATION,
UNTIL THEY MOVED
TO MARYLAND, WHERE
THE SON OF LEON,
JACOB, BECAME A FAMOUS PHYSICIAN.

THE END